BRAZIL

A Global Studies Handbook

GLOBAL STUDIES: LATIN AMERICA
& THE CARIBBEAN

BRAZIL

A Global Studies Handbook

Todd L. Edwards

A B C CLIO

Santa Barbara, California • Denver, Colorado • Oxford, England

2 -27- 9

Library of Congress Cataloging-in-Publication Data

Edwards, Todd L.
  Brazil : a global studies handbook / Todd L. Edwards
      p. cm. — (ABC-CLIO's global studies series)
  Includes bibliographical references and index.
  ISBN 978-1-85109-995-5 (hard copy : alk. paper)
  ISBN 978-1-85109-996-2 (ebook) 1. Brazil—Handbooks, manuals, etc. I. Title.

  F2509.5.E39 2008
  981--dc22

                                                    2007016500

        12   11   10   09   08   1   2   3   4   5   6   7   8   9   10

Production Editor: Anna A. Moore
Editorial Assistant: Sara Springer
Production Manager: Don Schmidt
Media Editor: Ellen Rasmussen
Media Resources Coordinator: Ellen Brenna Dougherty
Media Resources Manager: Caroline Price
File Manager: Paula Gerard

ABC-CLIO, Inc.
130 Cremona Drive, P.O. Box 1911
Santa Barbara, California 93116-1911

This book is also available on the World Wide Web as an ebook.
Visit http://www.abc-clio.com for details.

This book is printed on acid-free paper ∞

Manufactured in the United States of America

Contents

Series Editor's Foreword

In a world in which borders are blurring and cultures are blending at a dizzying pace, becoming more globally aware and knowledgeable is imperative. This is especially true regarding one's immediate neighbors, where the links are most intense and most profound. For this pragmatic reason, knowing more about Latin America is especially relevant to people living in the United States.

Beyond such a practical consideration, Latin America is a fascinating region of the world on its own terms, and it is worth the time and energy to get to know the region better simply as a matter of intellectual curiosity. By providing a readable and engaging introduction to a representative selection of the region's countries, this series hopes to engage readers and nurture their curiosity in the region and its peoples.

One point that this series will make abundantly clear is that Latin America is not a homogeneous region. For example, its population is remarkably diverse. Indigenous peoples are spread throughout the region, constituting the majority of the population in countries where the largest of the region's magnificent pre-Colombian civilizations were centered. Descendents of the Iberian European colonizers continue to dominate the region's political and economic landscape, though recently arrived immigrant populations from Europe and Asia have made significant inroads into the economic, political, and cultural aspects of these countries. The Atlantic slave trade network brought hundreds of thousands of Africans to the Latin America to labor in the plantation economy. The African cultural legacy is particularly relevant to modern Brazil and the Gulf-Caribbean countries. And the process of racial mixture, or miscegenation, that occurred freely and consistently over the past 500 years of the region's history has created a unique *mestizo* identity that many modern Latin Americans embrace as their own.

Obviously, therefore, one characteristic of the region that makes it so intriguing is that it is so vastly different from one country to the next and yet, at the same time, the countries of the region bear striking similarities. In addition to sharing a physical continent and space in the Western Hemisphere, the countries of Latin America also share a basic, common history that stretches from the colonial period through the present day. And the region is also bound together in many ways by language and culture.

In terms of its geography, Latin America is a vast region, encompassing more than one-half of the entire Western Hemisphere. Further, its natural environment is one of the more diverse in the world, from the deserts in northern Chile to the lush and ecologically diverse rainforests of the Amazon River basin. It is also a region rich in natural resources, providing the world with many of its foodstuffs, energy and mineral resources, and other commodities.

A few basic statistics can help to illuminate the importance of learning more about the region. Latin Americans constitute approximately 12 percent of the world's total population, and Latin American countries make up approximately 6.5 percent of the world's landmass. By some estimates, the Spanish language is the most spoken language in the Western world and is second only to Mandarin Chinese among all linguistic groups worldwide. The vast majority of Spanish speakers reside in Latin America. Portuguese, the native language of Brazil, is among the world's ten most spoken languages.

Among the developing world, Latin America ranks consistently at the top in terms of most economic and social indicators in aggregate terms, but the region still struggles with chronic poverty and suffers from highly skewed patterns of income distribution. A consequence of this income gap has been growing out-migration, with more and more Latin Americans each year making their way to better opportunities in wealthier and more economically developed countries. Recent efforts to promote greater economic integration through regional free trade agreements throughout the Western Hemisphere also illustrate the growing importance of a greater knowledge and awareness of Latin America.

In terms of politics and governments, Latin America finds itself squarely in the traditions of Western liberal democracy. Most Latin Americans embrace the values of individual freedom and liberty and expect their political systems to reflect these values. While this has not always been the reality for Latin American countries, as of late democracy has been the norm. In fact, all of the countries of Latin America today with the exception of Cuba have democratically elected governments, and all are actively engaged globally.

The specific volumes in this series introduce Mexico, Brazil, Chile, Costa Rica, Cuba, and Argentina. They represent all of the different subregions in Latin America and they range from the smallest countries to the largest in terms of population, landmass, and economic wealth. The countries included in the series vary in terms of their ethnic and class composition, with Cuba and Brazil containing large Afro–Latin American populations and with Mexico representing a society shaped by a rich and vibrant indigenous culture. The inclusion of Cuba, which remains the region's stalwart socialist experiment, offers ideological variation within the series. Argentina, Brazil, Chile, and Mexico represent the region's top four economic regional powerhouses, whose places in the global economy are well established. These four countries are also the region's most influential actors in the international arena, not only serving as leaders within the Latin American region itself but also exercising influence in the world's premier international bodies. On the other hand, Costa Rica and Cuba demonstrate the challenges and possibilities for the region's many less influential global actors and smaller economies.

Finally, it should be noted that Latin American culture is seeping much more into the mainstream of U.S. culture.

People in the United States enjoy the foods, music, and popular culture of Latin America because they are all more readily available in and appealing to the U.S. population. In fact, one might argue that the United States itself is becoming more Latin. Evidence indicates as much, as the numbers of those who identify themselves as Hispanic or Latino in the United States are growing rapidly and disproportionately to other ethnic or racial groups. According to the 2000 U.S. Census, the Hispanic population in the United States constitutes about 12.5 percent of the total U.S. population and is now the country's largest ethnic minority group. Even more striking is the incredible growth rate of the Hispanic population in the United States relative to the total population. In just twenty years, the Hispanic population more than doubled, and if this trend continues, Hispanics will constitute a majority of the U.S. population in about fifty years. The fact that Hispanics in the United States maintain strong ties to their countries of origin and maintain an affinity for the culture and lifestyles common to the region makes Latin America all the more relevant to understand.

The volumes in this series provide a basic introduction to some of the countries and peoples of Latin America. In addition to a survey of the countries' histories, politics, economies, and cultures, each volume includes an extensive reference section to help point readers to resources that will be useful in learning more about the countries and even in planning to visit them. But above all, the hope for this series is that readers will come to a better appreciation for Latin America as a region, will want to learn more about it, and will eventually experience the richness that is Latin America.

—*James D. Huck, Jr.*
Series Editor

Preface and Acknowledgments

On my first business trip to São Paulo, in 1997, I was struck not only by the enormity of the city and the vitality of its economy but also by the depth of Brazil's history and the complexity of its modern society. At the time, I worked for a large Spanish bank in New York, which owned an important bank in Brazil, as a Latin American investment strategist, advising international investors on politics, economics, and stock markets in the region. As Latin America's biggest economy, and with one of the region's most important stock markets, Brazil was logically on most investors' radar screens as a potential destination for their capital. My main job was to help guide these investors in their decision-making process— helping them to pick both countries and companies in which to invest. As a result, I spent a lot of time in Brazil, and a lot of time analyzing Brazil's most pressing contemporary issues. It is safe to say, in fact, that not a day went by in the ten years I worked on Wall Street that Brazil was not discussed in considerable detail.

One day during that first business trip in 1997, I was riding in a taxi, shuttling between seemingly endless meetings with government officials, economists, consultants, corporate executives, politicians, and the like. At some point, running late as always, we became stuck in traffic on one of São Paulo's major arteries. Amazingly, as far as I could see in all directions were skyscrapers—I seemed to be lost in a sea of traffic on the ground and of skyscrapers on the horizon. The impression was striking. It hit me hard that this city was absolutely huge, substantially larger than the city of New York, in which I spent the bulk of my working hours. It was also abundantly clear that Brazil supported an enormous, vibrant, and industrialized economy.

As traffic resumed, we made our way through the various commercial and financial centers of São Paulo, stopping periodically for my appointed meetings. Winding through the streets of this enormous city, I was also struck by the repeated displays of the country's complex history and fascinating modern society. Interestingly, São Paulo has no fewer than three financial centers. In effect, it has simply created a new financial hub each time the old one has become outdated. In the taxi I traveled from my hotel, located near the Avenida Paulista financial center (and later our Brazilian affiliate), to both the somewhat antiquated financial center in the older heart of the city and the most modern one on its recently developed outskirts—these were paths that would become well worn in my subsequent, frequent visits to Brazil. The older center is the home of the country's main stock exchange, a few holdout brokerage firms that have not moved to more modern locations, and several banks, including a number of state-owned banks, vestiges of Brazil's days of state-directed development. In my journey back and forth between the city's business hubs I passed architecture representing nearly all the eras of Brazil's history, from beautiful buildings dating to colonial times to sleek modern skyscrapers housing multinational corporations. The fact that all these buildings are located so close together—colonial buildings, nineteenth-century mansions, shabby mid-twentieth-century government office buildings, and ultra-modern skyscrapers—fascinated me.

These drives between meetings, not to mention the meetings themselves, also revealed to me the enormity of Brazil's development challenges. For example, shortcuts to the city's airports often cut through the unbelievable poverty of its *favelas,* or shantytowns. In the business centers, I encountered countless people working, or simply begging, on the streets. It was disconcerting to be dressed in formal business attire and stopped at a traffic light and see dark-skinned Brazilian children begging for spare change, from time to time checking in with their adult "bosses" and perhaps dropping off their most recent earnings.

Just as visible as the problems of poverty were the issues of inadequate and uneven infrastructure development—it was often unclear whether it was better to travel on the city's traffic-choked highways or its countless secondary and residential streets. Also unavoidable were the manifestations of pollution, from contaminated streams to heavy smog, although these were often no worse than conditions encountered in a number of U.S. cities.

Another striking feature of Brazil, again impossible not to notice during a day's work, is the complex racial makeup of its population. One sees nearly every shade of human color imaginable—in effect a full range from black to white, but with indigenous characteristics visible as well. And while much is made in Brazil and elsewhere of Brazil's "racial democracy," the notion that Brazil is somehow free of the racial prejudice existing in countries like the United States, it is impossible to ignore the association in Brazil between race and poverty. Unfortunately, the darker the person, the lower that person is likely to be in socioeconomic status. In my experience, it was actually quite rare to find Afro-Brazilians working at higher levels of finance; it was much more common to find darker Brazilians serving the ubiquitous "*cafezinhos*" (small, strong coffees) that are such an important part of most business meetings. However, I did often encounter Japanese Brazilians, not to mention Brazilians of Jewish ancestry.

On another business trip, a visit that included a number of meetings in Rio de Janeiro and Brasília, I happened to stop for a few hours in the Brazilian Congress in Brasília. At the very time of my visit a political crisis was unfolding in what was called the "ruling coalition" of the Cardoso administration. Moments after entering the building, a large crowd of correspondents surged out of the Chamber of Deputies. In the excitement, the doors to part of the chamber were shattered, adding to the sense that something important was taking place. Some time later we learned that the commotion was related to the resignation of Luis Eduardo Magalhaes, an important player in President Cardoso's political coalition, from his post as the government's congressional whip in the Chamber of Deputies.

To the untrained observer, domestic and foreign alike, this seemed like very bad news, possibly a negative omen for the likelihood of further economic reforms (economic reform was a major reason foreign investors were attracted to Brazil). However, I was being shepherded through the halls of government by a well-connected Brazilian political insider, who promptly informed me that this was all part of a political game, in effect a strategic move by Magalhaes and his party to gain more power within the ruling coalition. At a minimum, it was nothing close to an end of the coalition itself, as some pessimists suggested.

I was fortunate to be able to relate this version of events back to New York and London almost immediately. Despite a panic in the financial markets reflecting fears of political crisis in Brasília we suggested that investors remain calm—or perhaps even increase their positions in Brazil at these more attractive prices. I made a much larger and more important discovery that day, however, regarding Brazil and its political system. Quickly I realized that the Brazilian political system is substantially more complicated than meets the eye, but at the same time it became clear that Brazil's democracy is strong, functioning relatively smoothly despite its apparent quirks. While there is an undeniable need for political reform in the country, a topic I will discuss at length in the chapter on government and politics, the country has been remarkably successful in building a strong, healthy democracy in the decades since military rule ended in the 1980s.

I hope these impressions of Brazil convey my personal fascination with this enormous and complex nation—not to mention my affinity toward its warm and generous people.

I have been a student of Brazil now for almost twenty years and plan to continue as such for the rest of my life. This book is designed to be an introduction to Brazil for readers who are, for whatever reason, likewise interested in this country. It is intended to serve as a "stand alone" introduction to the country—no prior knowledge of Brazil is expected of readers. It is also designed to serve a wide variety of audiences—from high school and college students interested in researching and writing about Brazil to businesspeople planning a work-related trip to the country to interested travelers planning to visit the country. The idea, then, is that this book can provide an important foundation of knowledge for those interested in learning more about Brazil, whether this is the sole book consulted or it serves as a gateway into further exploration.

The book is divided into two main parts—a narrative section and a reference section. The narrative section, which is interdisciplinary in nature, is divided into four chapters that reflect key subject areas: geography and history (chapter one), the economy (chapter two), politics and government (chapter three), and society and culture (chapter four). Chapter one introduces readers to the country's fascinating history as well as its immense and diverse landscape. The chapter is arranged chronologically, starting at the time of the "discovery" of Brazil in 1500 by Portuguese explorers and ending with the recent reelection of President Luiz Inácio Lula da Silva (Lula). This discussion of Brazil's history, including the unusual events surrounding its monarchy in the nineteenth century, underscores the country's unique nature.

Chapter two is an examination of the Brazilian economy. The first section provides events in chronological order; the second section deals with a number of important contemporary issues relating to the economy. As suggested above, the Brazilian economy is huge and in fact is one of the largest in the world (a little-known fact for much of the U.S. population). It is also a complex, highly industrialized economy. However, as a developing nation, Brazil also faces significant obstacles, most notably a large component of the population that lives in poverty. In this chapter I discuss these important issues and Brazil's efforts to overcome them.

Chapter three focuses on Brazil's government and politics. Again, I first cover the key issues in chronological order, starting with Brazil's colonial administration and finishing with the transition to democracy and the most recent democratically elected presidents. We then deal in some depth with a number of topical issues facing the country and its political system. While this book recognizes that Brazil has experienced considerable political instability in the past, including extended periods of authoritarian rule, it also attempts to stress the unprecedented nature of current political events. Most importantly, for the first time in Brazil's history the country will see two consecutive presidents, from two different parties, elected to two back-to-back terms of leadership. In effect, political stability, in the form of a vibrant democracy, has been achieved in Brazil.

Chapter four is an exploration of Brazilian society and culture. This chapter breaks from the chronological mold of the first three chapters and is roughly divided between topics that relate to society and those more specifically associated with Brazilian culture. For example, I spend a good deal of time looking at the various groups that have come together to form the Brazilian population, from Native Americans, Portuguese settlers, and African slaves to later waves of immigrant populations. Together these groups have formed Brazil's unique population and culture. I also cover issues like Brazilian customs, Brazil's unique "brand" of the Portuguese language, and Brazilian cuisine and music. Although constrained by space limitations, I have also attempted to introduce readers to the country's rich traditions in the arts—from literature to film to fine art.

The chapters of the narrative section are followed by a reference section. This section starts with a timeline of Brazilian history—again from the time of the discovery of Brazil in 1500 to the recent reelection of Lula. This is followed by a section on famous figures of Brazilian history, from rebellious slaves and famous writers and musicians to key political figures and internationally famous sports stars. This is followed by a short section on key words and phrases used in the narrative section of the book, a helpful aid to interested readers. Additional reference materials are then provided, including resources for further investigation and an annotated bibliography.

Many people have contributed in one way or another to the production of this book. I would like to first thank ABC-CLIO and its team of editors—especially Alex Mikaberidze—for all of the work that has gone into this project. I would also like to thank James Huck, the series editor, who invited me to be a part of this interesting project. I want to thank my former teachers and fellow students at Tulane University's Roger Thayer Stone Center for Latin American Studies. Specifically I want to thank Richard Greenleaf, Roderic A. Camp, and Andrew Morrison, who provided guidance and inspiration during my graduate studies at Tulane. I also want to thank all of my Wall Street colleagues and clients who likewise provided inspiration to my career as well as considerable insight into contemporary Brazil. Among these are John Purcell, Peter West, Amalia Estenssoro, Octavio de Barros, Aya Tanaka, Jeff Noble, Gustavo Teran, Gerard Watson, Olivier Lemaigre, Curtis Butler, and Luis Laboy. Last but not least I would like to thank my wife, Laura Edwards, both for all of the work that she has put into this book and for all of the patience she has shown as I have attempted to write it. It is to her that I dedicate this book.

—*Todd Edwards*

PART ONE
NARRATIVE SECTION

CHAPTER ONE

Geography and History

THE PHYSICAL SETTING

Like the United States, the Federative Republic of Brazil is a continent-size country. In fact, there are only four countries in the world that are larger than Brazil: Russia, Canada, China, and the United States (including Alaska). The largest country by far in South America, Brazil is also four times the size of Mexico. Present-day Brazil covers 3,286,426 square miles, extending roughly 2,700 miles from north to south and about the same distance from east to west. The coastline, which stretches 4,600 miles, is just as close to the west coast of Africa as it is to the United States. Brazil borders every country in South America except Ecuador and Chile and makes up nearly half of the South American continent. At the risk of belaboring the point, it is essential to recognize Brazil's enormous size in order to understand a wide variety of issues relating to the country's history and contemporary outlook.

Brazil's 2001 census counted a population of 174,468,575 inhabitants, making it the fifth most populous country in the world (after China, India, the United States, and Indonesia). The majority of Brazil's population is concentrated in its coastal cities, and as we will see, particularly in the industrialized South-East. São Paulo is Brazil's largest city, with almost 17 million people living in the metropolitan area; Rio de Janeiro is second with around 6 million.

Brazil has abundant natural resources, with nearly every mineral needed for an industrialized economy. Among the few exceptions are coal and petroleum, although by the 1990s the country managed to provide more than two-thirds of its

Comparative size of Brazil.

electricity from offshore petroleum wells and its huge hydro-electric plants.

There are five climates in Brazil: equatorial, tropical, semi-arid, highland tropical, and subtropical. Ninety percent of Brazil's territory lies in the tropical zone, but most of the population lives in areas where the temperature is moderated by ocean winds and altitude. (Over the years the climate has been highly criticized and blamed for everything from laziness to ill health. However, modern public health measures have for the most part taken care of these related issues.) Brazil does not experience the extreme cold seen in Europe and the United States, nor does it experience hurricanes or earthquakes. However, floods and droughts are common, and the effects of these have been exacerbated by poor land use from colonial days to the present. Brazil's Northeast is particularly vulnerable to droughts, and has been so throughout much of the country's history.

Brazil, like the United States, is divided into states and has a capital district, called the Federal District, which is similar to the District of Columbia. Brazil has twenty-six states in addition to the Federal District (which is typically known as greater Brasília). Brazil's huge size, not to mention the difficulties of travel within the country, especially before modern air travel, has supported a notable degree of variation among its regions. In fact, some have compared Brazil's five regions to islands in a huge archipelago. A quick look at the country's five main regions will help explain why.

The North

The North includes the modern states of Rondônia, Acre, Amazonas, Roraima, Pará, and Amapá. Brazil's North is the land of the Amazon basin and is by far the largest in terms of territory, comprising nearly half of the country (42 percent). There are more than 2.4 million square miles of tropical rain forest in the Amazon, although sadly more than 12 percent of the original forest has been cut down; more than 10,000 square miles are destroyed every year. There have been many discussions about the Amazon's tremendous potential (including Henry Ford's failed attempt to grow rubber in the 1930s), but the reality is that the gigantic rain forest is inhospitable to most "modern" economic pursuits. Overland travel is nearly impossible—rivers were really the only feasible means of transportation before airplanes. Deforestation (cutting down whole sections of the forest) is a significant

The five regions of Brazil.

problem, since rain leaches the soil if the forest canopy is cut down, making agriculture and ranching unsustainable over time. In effect, this region cannot support intense human settlement, although attempts to settle the area continue.

The Northeast

Brazil's Northeast is made up of the states of Maranhão, Piauí, Ceará, Rio Grande do Norte, Paraíba, Pernambuco, Alagoas,

Sergipe, and Bahia. Brazil's Northeast was the heart of the early Portuguese colonial settlement (although the region makes up just 18 percent of modern Brazil's landmass). In fact, Pernambuco was in early colonial times one of the most profitable colonies in the world. Unfortunately the region's prominence began to fade as early as the late seventeenth century; the region's downturn was worsened in the nineteenth century by a failure to modernize the sugar industry. The result of the region's failure to modernize is ongoing, pervasive poverty, and the Northeast is characterized by many as the single biggest pocket of misery in the Americas.

Much of the Northeast's coast (called the *zona de mata* or forest zone, for the original forests that once covered the area but were subsequently cut down) is a humid strip that has proved ideal for plantation agriculture; beyond lie two strips less suitable to human habitation. One is known as the *zona de agreste* and is a semiarid region. The second is called the *sertão,* a large arid region that has been plagued for centuries by periodic drought. The gap between rich and poor is probably more pronounced in this region than anywhere else in Brazil (or in the whole of Latin America, for that matter). Historically, the region has been dominated by a "landed oligarchy," a small group of wealthy individuals whose strong influence continues to this day. The Northeastern state of Bahia is the heart of the country's thriving Afro-Brazilian culture, a direct legacy of the country's long history of slavery.

The Center-West

The Center-West today includes the states of Mato Grosso, Mato Grosso do Sul, Goiás, and the Federal District of Brasília. The region has in modern times become one of the fastest growing regions in Brazil (in part due to the creation in the late 1950s of the new capital, Brasília; the capital previously had been located in Rio de Janeiro for centuries). However, the vast central plateau remains largely underpopulated. The region makes up 22 percent of Brazil's territory and has witnessed a boom in agricultural productivity in recent decades. The architecturally futuristic Brasília was created from scratch in the central plateau both to symbolize Brazil's confidence in its future and as a way to develop the interior and shift the country's focus away from dominant São Paulo and the South-East.

The South-East

The South-East is made up of the states of Minas Gerais, Espírito Santo, Rio de Janeiro, and São Paulo. While only representing 11 percent of the national territory, the region is densely populated when compared to the rest of Brazil and accounts for a tremendous percentage of the country's economic activity; it is the center of Brazil's industrial economy. Rio de Janeiro was Brazil's capital until the early 1960s; since then Rio has fallen in relative importance compared to neighboring states, not least due to its infamously high level of violent crime. São Paulo was a relative backwater until the mid-nineteenth century, but since that time it has become the locus of Brazilian growth and industrialization. Minas Gerais, considered important in colonial times as the hub of mining wealth, is now growing with a combination of agriculture and industry. Espírito Santo is primarily an agricultural state, with a focus on coffee and cacao.

The South

The South includes the states of Paraná, Santa Catarina, and Rio Grande do Sul. Comprising only 7 percent of the national territory, it is the smallest of Brazil's five regions. It is also the only region that is temperate in climate. The region has some light industrialization, but it is mostly dedicated to growing grain and raising cattle. Rio Grande do Sul, as we will see below, has played an important role in Brazilian history, having flirted with separatism twice in the nineteenth century. In turn, while the state experienced heavy inflow of immigrants, especially Germans, in the late nineteenth century, more recently it has been the source of much out-migration to other parts of Brazil, as people leave the state in search of cheaper land. Finally, the state of Paraná has experienced an agricultural boom as the locus of coffee production has shifted south from São Paulo.

PORTUGAL'S DISCOVERY OF BRAZIL

In March 1500, King Manuel of Portugal celebrated the launch of a new ocean fleet, just one year after Portuguese explorer Vasco de Gama had returned from his celebrated voyage around the African continent that opened up the sea passage to India. It was de Gama's success, in fact, and all that it signaled in terms of riches and new territories, that motivated the Portuguese Crown to support this new and more involved venture.

The new voyage, with thirteen ships and some 1,200 crew and passengers, would be headed by Pedro Álvares Cabral. The goal was the same as that of Vasco de Gama: to sail around Africa through the Indian Ocean. The reality would be quite different, as the lead ship commanded by Cabral veered off course, swinging out to the west and into the Atlantic Ocean, eventually reaching the coast of present-day Bahia on April 23, 1500. There is some speculation among historians that the move off course was not a mistake by Cabral, but rather a disguised attempt to beat the Spaniards in a sort of New World land grab based on prior knowledge of the New World. There is, however, very little historical evidence to support this notion—most evidence suggests Cabral was originally headed to India.

While a momentous event, the discovery of Brazil must be placed in its historical context. Brazil's discovery was just one component of a process of Portuguese overseas expansion

Pedro Cabral, sixteenth-century Portuguese explorer. (Library of Congress)

that started at the beginning of the fifteenth century, almost a hundred years before Columbus reached the Americas. Interestingly, in relative terms the discovery of Brazil generated much less enthusiasm than Vasco de Gama's arrival in India, since its geography was largely unknown and its profit potential as yet undiscovered (in fact for several years Brazil was even thought to be a large island). There are a number of reasons that Portugal, in reality a tiny country, was able to stand

---

Treaty of Tordesillas

The Treaty of Tordesillas, signed on June 4, 1494, divided the New World between Spain and Portugal. Interestingly, it was signed just two years after Christopher Columbus's initial voyage to the New World and before Portugal had even set foot in Brazil. The treaty settled an ongoing dispute between the two countries, which followed a series of papal bulls issued by Pope Alexander VI dividing the New World between them. The Portuguese argued against the pope's Line of Demarcation, in part because the pope was Spanish, and later reached an independent agreement with Spain, the Treaty of Tordesillas. In the new agreement the line between the two kingdoms' possessions was moved to the west, giving Portugal access to the New World through a strip of land along the east coast of modern-day Brazil. Even this shifting of the line gave Portugal much less territory than Brazil controls today, but of course at the time the territory was essentially unknown.

---

out in Europe as both independent and successful at moving beyond its borders. Historians generally focus on three critical factors.

Sustained political stability is perhaps the most important factor: Portugal, like Spain, fought a long war of reconquest against the North African Muslims who had occupied the Iberian Peninsula since the eighth century. However, the Portuguese were successful in liberating their kingdom some 200 years before the Spanish (i.e., by the thirteenth century). In turn, by the fifteenth century, Portugal was a united kingdom with considerably less internal conflict than was experienced in the other major European powers of the time. Portugal was able to forge a lasting alliance with England in 1386, and the marriage of Portugal's King João to the granddaughter of England's King Edward III led to a consolidation of the dynasty (the House of Avis, 1385–1578) and created the political stability that was the foundation of the movement to overseas exploration and trade. To this may be added the intense

Pope Alexander VI establishes the Line of Demarcation to define the spheres of Spanish and Portuguese possessions in the New World in May 1493. Portuguese dissatisfaction with this arrangement led to the Treaty of Tordesillas in 1494. (MPI/Getty Images)

interest in exploration of members of the Portuguese royal family, most notably Prince Henry, known as "Henry the Navigator."

A second important factor supporting the Portuguese exploratory efforts is that by the beginning of the fifteenth century, overseas expansion and trade served the interests of the most important groups involved, from the prospects for wealth it offered the merchant class, the possibilities of new sources of income for the Crown, and opportunities for the Catholic Church to spread Christianity to a way of keeping the Portuguese nobles busy (and able to find lands for their sons beyond the firstborn). Special mention must be made of the role of the merchant class, as it was critical to overseas trade and well respected by the Crown. Together with the royal family, the merchant class helped produce the major advances in technology that made Portugal the leader in overseas exploration (important examples in which the Portuguese excelled include shipbuilding, navigation—with the most advanced tools of the time—and map drawing).

A final important point concerns the overriding push to explore and trade. Given the country's small population at the time (1 million people, compared with 3 million in England, 7 million in Spain, and 15 million in France), it was simply impossible for Portugal to consider settling its colonies in a way similar to England or Spain. In other words, sending large groups of people to settle new territories was simply out of the question. Rather, the Portuguese model was to create a network of militarily fortified trading posts to conduct commerce with local populations. Thus, overseas expansion and trade became a sort of "national pastime." The process was all-encompassing and included the search for new lands, the search for new sources of wealth, and the search for souls to convert to the "true cross" of the Roman Catholic Church.

PORTUGUESE SETTLEMENT OF BRAZIL

To understand the patterns of Portuguese settlement of Brazil, it is important to remember that the country's increasingly bold sailings had brought it into contact with a variety of different places, from empty islands in the Atlantic (like Madeira and the Canaries) to the shores of Africa and ultimately to India. For the first decades after discovery, Portugal treated Brazil like the rest of its trading posts (or *feitorias*) that were set up in Africa and Asia. The Portuguese Crown leased Brazil to a group of Lisbon merchants, who were charged with exploiting the land's few tradable commodities, the most important being brazilwood but also including monkeys, slaves, and parrots. However, two developments caused the Portuguese Crown to sharpen its focus on Brazil: the Crown's need to make up for declining activity in the Indian Ocean and increasing incursions on Brazilian soil by the French and Spanish.

The new strategy, given the Crown's scarcity of resources, was to create a system of hereditary land grants, or "captaincies," which were given to wealthy nobles. The nobles were given possession of the land, not ownership. This possession gave the donataries a number of economic rights, like the collecting of fees. The hope, of course, was that these men would make use of their territories (by exploiting brazilwood, among other things). Fourteen captaincies were granted between 1534 and 1536, but they proved overall unsuccessful. In fact only two—São Vicente (south of present-day São Paulo) and Pernambuco (in the Northeast) were actually successful. In general terms, the failure reflected issues including a lack of experience and resources, internal rifts, and continuous attacks by indigenous groups. The two successful captaincies seemed to exhibit a combination of better relationships with Indian communities and more profitable economic activity, particularly as relates to sugar production and export. Over time the Portuguese Crown repurchased the captaincies, although the territories remained as administrative units.

Following a pattern of ever-increasing commitment to the new colony, the Portuguese Crown decided to send a royal governor to Brazil; this did not void the captaincies, but rather allowed the Crown to recapture some of the authority that had been granted at a time when royal resources were scarce. The new governor, Tomé de Souza, arrived in 1549 and founded the city of Salvador (which would then become the capital of the colony for more than two centuries, until it was moved to Rio de Janeiro). Tomé da Sousa arrived with a group of more than 1,000 people and moved to fulfill the Crown's goals of occupying, colonizing, and administering the new lands.

One interesting historical event affecting Brazil's early development was Portugal's "union" with Spain, which was to last sixty years, from 1580 to 1640. The union was created in response to the lack of a legitimate royal heir to the Portuguese throne; Spain formally took over the Portuguese throne, and thus controlled Brazil, during these years. The Spanish did not, however, move to take full control of the colony, busy as they were trying to consolidate control of their own lands elsewhere in the Americas. They did,

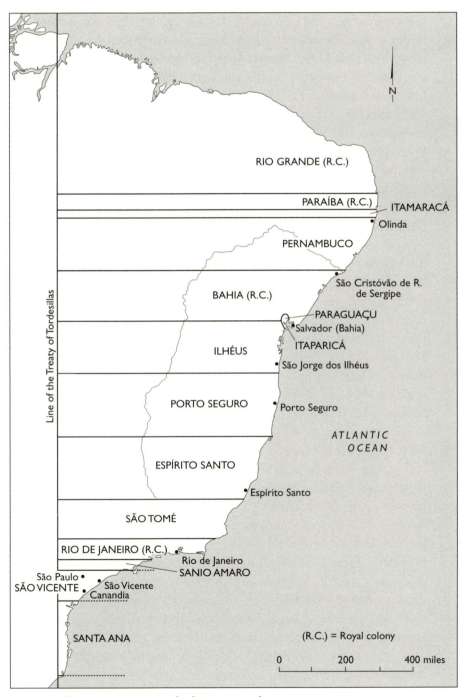

Brazilian captaincies in the late sixteenth century.

however, assist the colony by improving administrative and judicial procedures. Holland took the opportunity during these years to move against "Spanish imperialism" by invading Brazil's Northeast in 1624; the Dutch managed to control their outpost in Brazil (including Recife and the highly profitable sugar trade) for nearly thirty years before being run out of the colony by local residents. Upon returning to power, the Portuguese Crown would continue expanding its territorial control in Brazil.

Economic activity in early Brazil revolved around brazilwood, a valuable commodity in Europe due to its dye-making qualities. In fact, this early activity would give the country its name (the first name, Vera Cruz, or Land of the True Cross, died out fairly quickly). However, by the time the captaincies were created, the principal crop produced in Brazil was sugar cane, grown on immense plantations. For more than a century Brazil would be the world's leading producer of sugar (this total focus on a single plantation commodity would also set a pattern that existed throughout the colonial era and into the twentieth century). The sugar-producing regions in colonial Brazil were in Pernambuco and Bahia, and Recife and Salvador became important ports.

In a nutshell, this was Brazil's colonial economy: single-crop agriculture, based on slave labor, using enormous tracts of land in Brazil's Northeast. In the sixteenth century the slave labor force was largely Indian, but this would change by the seventeenth century, when imported African slaves would assume increasing importance. This shift from Indian to African labor was the result of a number of factors, but the most important was the drastic decline in indigenous populations as a result of European diseases. By the seventeenth century Brazil's Northeast was one of the richest regions in the Americas. Brazil's role was supplying foodstuffs and minerals for European trade—a limited group of products were exported in large quantities based on a landholding system that encouraged massive holdings.

This illustration depicts activity at a Brazilian sugar mill. The labor-intensive cultivation of sugar for export fueled the importation of African slaves to Brazil beginning in the mid-sixteenth century. (Library of Congress)

While sugar was the dominant crop, other pursuits were important as well. Cattle ranching, with its range of by-products offered to sugar-producing regions, is a good example. International sugar prices began to fall in the latter part of the seventeenth century, but disaster was avoided by the discovery of gold in the 1690s, located in the present-day states of Minas Gerais, Mato Grosso, Goiás, and Bahia. While the sugar economy would never return to its "good old days," it continued to represent the most important source of export income—even at the height of the gold boom the value of sugar exports exceeded those of gold exports (at least in legal trade).

The discovery of mineral wealth led to a tremendous gold rush in colonial Brazil, with migrants from all parts of the colony (but especially the Northeast) and even from Portugal itself heading to the mining regions. While diamonds were also being mined by the 1720s, Brazil became the top gold producer in the world. The tremendous wealth led Minas

Gerais to become the fastest-growing region in Brazil in the eighteenth century, supporting a number of cultural developments, such as the construction of ornate Brazilian baroque churches in the region. As sugar defined seventeenth-century Brazil, the rise, and then decline, of mining would define the eighteenth.

The tremendous growth in mining in the eighteenth century required labor, and Brazil's answer was slave labor. This era witnessed both the movement of African slaves from other parts of Brazil to the mining regions and an increase in slave imports from Africa. While the boom did help Portugal cover its debts, particularly with England, it did nothing to help the mother country join the industrial revolution that was starting in England and western Europe; the mining boom also did nothing to change Brazil's pattern of economic development. The shifting population in the eighteenth century, resulting from the gold rush, led to the creation of a new captaincy for São Paulo and Minas de Ouro (in 1709), then a separate captaincy for Minas (1721), and finally, separate captaincies for Mato Grosso and Goiás (1748). In fact the final reflection of this general change in Brazil's colonial activity was the move of the colony's capital from Salvador in the Northeast to Rio de Janeiro (1763) in the South-East. The move was designed to better control the highly profitable mining area.

THE INDIGENOUS POPULATION

The Portuguese discovered lands that were, of course, already populated; Brazil held a wide range of indigenous people that spoke all sorts of languages and displayed numerous systems of social organization. These groups differed from the well-known Incas of Peru and Aztecs of Mexico in that they were typically hunter-gatherers and far more dispersed in settlement patterns than the dense populations in Peru and Mexico. For the most part Brazil's Indians lived at subsistence level, with groups typically being highly mobile. In general, the forests of Brazil have been unsuitable for farming, except for slash-and-burn patches of crops planted for a few seasons. It is often argued that Brazil's difficult environment was in fact a leading cause (if not the leading cause) of the lack of permanent settlements, except for the few tribes occupying the coast or large riverbanks. There is considerable debate regarding the number of people living in Brazil in 1500; while most estimates fit in a range between 500,000 and 2 million, some estimates put the number much higher.

There is very little known about the Indian reaction to the Portuguese arrival, not least because these groups were preliterate. The Portuguese reaction, on the other hand, was documented by the voyage's scribe; these views tended to focus on the exotic, with the Indians seen as physically perfect and living in a terrestrial paradise. However, there is no doubt that the arrival of the Portuguese was a disaster for the Indians, as their way of life was disrupted, their people were enslaved, and their populations dwindled.

The indigenous population experienced nothing short of a demographic catastrophe, dying by the thousands and experiencing a complete disruption in their patterns of settlement. While harsh treatment and enslavement contributed to the catastrophe, the main cause of the Indian population's decimation was disease. With no immunities to European diseases like smallpox, measles, or influenza, the native groups died in staggering proportions. Two particular waves of disease had a devastating effect on the colony: some estimates suggest that in 1562 and 1563, as many as one-third to one-half of Brazil's Indians succumbed to disease. As the indigenous population declined near the coast, the Portuguese pushed into the interior on slave raids to maintain the labor force. By the eighteenth century Indians had essentially disappeared in the Northeast, a development that led directly to an increased focus on African slavery.

There were four main indigenous language families in Brazil at the time of discovery: Tupi (or Tupi-Guarani), Ge,

---

The *Bandeirantes*

As the Indian populations of the coast began to die out, the Portuguese increasingly moved to capture Indians from the interior for slave labor. The most famous Indian slavers were the *bandeirantes,* who were named for their flags, or *bandeiras,* which were carried at the front of the expeditions. The bandeirantes also searched for precious metals. Most of their activity took place in what is now the state of São Paulo. These were large companies of warriors, often of mixed-race origin (Indian/Portuguese) drafted by colonists to search the interior for Indian slaves as well as gold. Often the number of Indians and mixed-blood bandeirantes outnumbered whites. Jesuit missions, with numerous Guarani Indians, were a favorite target. One of the most notorious bandeirantes was Antônio Rapôso Tavares, who in 1628 led a force of 3,000 men against a small group of Jesuit missions. The missions were burned, and the captured Guarani were marched back to São Vicente in chains. In general, while the relationship between the Crown and the bandeirantes was complex, the search for Indian slaves and precious metals and the expansion of territory were goals that were compatible with Lisbon's agenda. Given the role of the bandeirantes as the principal early explorers of Brazil's interior, they have become heroes in the country's folklore and imagination.

Carib, and Arawak. Other language groups existed but for the most part were found in the peripheries of Brazil. The Tupi-Guarani were found along much of Brazil's coast, while the Ge occupied the vast, open plateau of central Brazil. Tupi-Guarani was standardized by the Jesuits in Brazil and became widely spoken, often more prevalently than Portuguese. The Amazon basin was occupied (and contested) by the three main language groups—the Tupi, Arawak, and Carib. Nearly all of the eastern tribes in Brazil have disappeared. And while numerous tribes remain in Brazil (some of which were isolated until recently, even living in Stone Age conditions), today's indigenous population is but a fraction of its original total and Brazil's overall population. We will discuss in detail the issues facing modern indigenous populations in Brazil in the chapter four on Brazil's culture and society.

COLONIAL BRAZIL

Slavery and Social Structure in Colonial Brazil

The Portuguese relied on the institution of slavery from the very beginning in Brazil. In the early colonial days (i.e., the sixteenth century), slaves were primarily taken from the Indian population. However, the rapid decline in the indigenous population, not to mention its resistance to Portuguese control and enslavement, led the Portuguese to turn to Africa to meet their need for labor. By the seventeenth century the majority of slaves had shifted from Indian to African origin. In fact, by 1580 the Portuguese were importing more than 2,000 African slaves a year to toil on Brazil's Northeastern sugar plantations. Despite the horrendous loss of human life on the voyage from Africa, Brazil imported more African slaves than any other region of the Americas (credible estimates put the total at some 3.5 million or more). This fact explains why Brazil has the largest population of African descent of any country outside of Africa, a critical factor in understanding the contemporary culture and society of Brazil, which will be discussed more fully in chapter four.

The master–slave relationship was perhaps the most critical relationship in the colony's social structure. It formed the foundation of Brazil's hierarchical social structure—Brazil's colonial elite could not imagine a Brazil without slavery. The social structure was dominated by white males of Portuguese descent, who were typically large landholders. Women—wives and daughters—were clearly dominated by the patriarch. Given the fact that white women were very few in number, there was a considerable degree of racial mixing, first between white men and Indian women, and over time more

The arrival and sale of new slaves in the city of Pernambuco around 1822. In the sugar-growing region of northeastern Brazil, harsh plantation slavery produced high mortality rates among laborers and required that newly enslaved Africans be imported on a regular basis. (Library of Congress)

so between white men and black women. Below the large landholders in the social hierarchy were lesser landholders, and below these were a small group of landless individuals who were occupied as tradesmen, artisans, soldiers, and so forth. Below this category was a group of white free men, typically banished by the Crown from Portugal for a variety of crimes. At the very bottom of the ladder were slaves.

The Harsh Realities of Brazilian Slavery

The following are direct quotes, one from an African slave describing the terrible voyage to Brazil from Africa, the other from the French wife of a Brazilian following her visit to a Brazilian plantation.

Mahommah Gardo Baquaqua was captured near the end of the slave trade in 1840 and sold in Brazil. According to Baquaqua,   *(cont.)*

(cont. from previous page)

The only food we had during the voyage was corn soaked and boiled . . .. We suffered very much for want of water, but was denied all we needed. A pint a day was all that was allowed, and no more; and a great many slaves died upon the passage. There was one poor fellow so very desperate for want of water, that he attempted to snatch a knife from the white man who brought in the water, when he was taken up on deck and I never knew what became of him. I supposed he was thrown overboard . . ..When any of us became refractory, his flesh was cut with a knife, and pepper or vinegar was rubbed in to make him peaceable. I suffered, and so did the rest of us, very much from sea sickness at first, but that did not cause our brutal owners any trouble . . .. Some were thrown overboard before breath was out of their bodies; when it was thought any would not live, they were got rid of in that way (Conrad 1994, p. 27).

Describing her visit to a Brazilian plantation in the late nineteenth century, the French wife of a Brazilian man remarked that

Here it was that the miseries of slavery appeared to me in all their horror and hideousness. Negresses covered in rags, others half naked, having as covering only a handkerchief fastened behind their back, and over their bosoms, which scarcely veiled their throats, and a calico skirt, through whose rents could be seen their poor, scraggy bodies; some negroes, with tawny and besotted looks, came and kneeled down on the marble slabs of the veranda. The majority carried on their shoulders the marks of scars that the lash had inflicted; several were affected with horrible maladies, such as elephantiasis, or leprosy. All this was dirty, repulsive, hideous. Fear or hate, that is what could be read on all these faces, which I have never seen smile (Conrad 1994, p. 83).

The emergence of people of mixed blood was a significant development for the colony, and one we will discuss at length in later chapters. Mixed-bloods (*mamelucos* or *caboclos* when between whites and Indians; *mulattoes* when between whites and blacks) were one rung above blacks in the colonial social ladder. However, there is clear evidence that opportunities for the mixed-race (free) population were historically much greater than in the United States, where mixed-race people were almost always designated nonwhite—that is, black. While cultural factors are undoubtedly important, one basic reason for this was a persistent labor shortage in the colony's nonslave, labor force; free people of color were also far more prevalent than in the colonial United States. For now, suffice to say that race relations were far more fluid in colonial Brazil, with a somewhat hazy continuum between white and black and a tendency to "bend the rules" when it came to race relations.

The Church in Colonial Brazil

As mentioned, one of the original goals of the Portuguese explorers was to convert the "heathen" masses to Christianity. This was clearly the case with the discovery of Brazil. Along with the state, the Catholic Church was one of the main institutions involved in the colonization of Brazil. Catholicism, not surprisingly, was recognized as the state religion. In very general terms the church was subordinate to the state in Brazil—it was in charge of people's everyday lives and behavior, and it also aided in ensuring obedience to the state.

In the very early days of settlement there were a number of Franciscan and secular priests meeting the needs of the settlers. One of early Brazil's most significant developments was the arrival of the Jesuits in 1549. Early Jesuits became the dominant Roman Catholic influence by controlling education and creating their famous Indian missions. They were often criticized by the colonists, who accused them of stealing their

Ruins of the Mission of San Miguel, located outside of São Miguel das Missões in northwestern Rio Grande do Sul state in southern Brazil. Jesuit missionaries built the mission between about 1735 and 1745 to catechize the Guaraní Indian population and also to protect them from Spanish and Portuguese slave traders. (Bojan Brecelj/Corbis)

scarce labor supply. The Jesuits also antagonized the Crown, which resented their secretiveness, not to mention their visible and growing wealth. The Jesuits, as well as other religious orders, played a central role in helping impose the Portuguese culture and language on the colony.

There was constant friction between the colonists and the missionaries throughout much of the colonial period, at least until the late eighteenth century. The missionaries, of course, were acting to win converts to Christianity, even if their methods were at times harsh. The settlers, on the other hand, were interested in Indians for slave labor. A law was passed in 1570 stating that Indian slavery was permissible if the Indians rejected Christianity (and then were captured in a "just war"). The missionaries argued that Christianization would take time; as the controversy ensued, thousands of natives were enslaved.

Colonial Political and Economic Institutions

Portugal went through a series of steps that over time increased its commitment to Brazil, from the "factory" period to the captaincies and finally to building a royal government. It was only with the onset of the great sugar cycle in the 1570s and 1580s that Brazil—and primarily Bahia and Pernambuco —became a centerpiece in the Portuguese Empire, as the colony became the largest producer and exporter of sugar in the world. As we will see below, Brazil would ultimately become more important economically than the mother country, a primary factor in its eventual independence.

The sugar cycle reversed course in the late 1600s, causing severe economic problems in Portugal. Recovery would set in before the turn of that century however, as the discovery of gold drove the beginning of a new era in the Luso-Brazilian economy (the prefix "Luso" is often used to refer to Portugal; it comes from Lusitania, the Roman name for the territory that is now Portugal). One major problem associated with the newly discovered and abundant gold was that Portugal abandoned any early attempts to industrialize its economy (not to mention modernize and/or diversify its agricultural economy). Rather, the mother country was content to strengthen its relationship with England, providing wine and olive oil in exchange for England's textiles, manufactured goods, and wheat. Imbalances favoring England (in other words when Portugal bought more goods from England than it sold to her) were simply covered by Brazil's large supply of gold and diamonds.

The eighteenth-century gold cycle led to a number of important changes in the colony. First, the gold rush brought the first large wave of immigration from Portugal to Brazil (as many as 600,000 people from Portugal may have arrived in Brazil in the first sixty years of the eighteenth century). Second, the demand for slaves grew dramatically in the mining areas. The depression in the Northeast's sugar industry led to an internal movement of slaves to the South-East, but importation of African slaves also continued to grow. Third, the gold cycle set in motion the expansion of Brazil's frontier—Brazil's western frontier was explored and settled during this time. Finally, a number of important changes were made to the colonial administration, such as the move of the colonial capital from Salvador to Rio de Janeiro.

The eighteenth century saw the most important treaty regarding Portugal's overseas possessions since the Treaty of Tordesillas in 1494. The Treaty of Madrid, signed by Portugal and Spain in 1750, was an attempt to solve a number of frontier disputes, including the disputed territory in southern Brazil called Colonia Sacramento (which would eventually become Spanish-speaking Uruguay rather than a Brazilian province). This "boundaries treaty," as the Treaty of Madrid is often called, was based largely on the idea that occupation of territory equated to ownership (*uti possidetis*). The treaty gave Portugal possession of vast territories to the west of the Line of Tordesillas in South America. While disputes over boundaries did not end, the Treaty of Madrid would largely give shape to the Brazil that exists today.

Importantly, by 1750, the Portuguese Empire, which started in Africa and the Orient, had come to be based on Brazil and the Atlantic. First sugar and then gold had driven this dramatic advance in Brazil's status. However, by the end of the eighteenth century gold income began to decline sharply, leading to yet another era in the Luso-Brazilian world. But it must be noted that by the middle of the eighteenth century, Brazil had become richer than its mother country. Ironically, the tables had turned, and the fate of Portugal now depended on the fortunes of Brazil. This state of affairs was increasingly obvious to the colonists, and colonial elites began to have increasing doubts about their continued subordination to Lisbon.

Imperial Reorganization (1750–1808)

By the second half of the eighteenth century Brazil had become by far Portugal's most important overseas territory; in fact many historians have pointed out that at this point Portugal could no longer have survived on its European territory alone. Brazil had become the central element in the wealth of the mother country, not to mention one of the government's main sources of income.

There were three Portuguese rulers at the time: Dom José I (who reigned from 1750 to 1777), Dona Maria I (ruling from 1777 to 1792), and the Prince Regent Dom João (ruling from 1792 to 1816). These leaders turned to three influential people—in effect "prime ministers"—to design Crown policies, the most famous of which was the Marquês de Pombal. In general these men, all of noble birth, hoped to raise Portugal's intellectual and economic status to match the more advanced countries of Europe. They also held a firm belief in the absolute power of the king but felt that "enlightened" government could drive more rapid progress. Given Brazil's vital importance to Portugal, these men sought to enlarge Brazil's territory and strengthen its administrative, judicial, and military institutions. They also worked to ensure that the colonial economy developed strictly for the benefit of Portugal.

The Marquês de Pombal had his work cut out for him, as he had to lead the Crown's efforts to rebuild Lisbon after a massive earthquake and fire in 1755. He also had to lead efforts to recover from the severe financial drain of wars with Spain in the 1760s through 1770s over the borderlands in southern Brazil and to compensate for the depletion of Brazil's gold mines.

In addition to undertaking a major overhaul of the colony's administrative structure, Pombal also pushed to increase the profit coming from Brazil, in part by reducing smuggling. One way was the creation of three monopoly trading companies designed to exploit commodities from Amazônia and

Marquês de Pombal, Portuguese statesman who became de facto prime minister of Portugal from 1750 to 1777. (The Art Archive/Museu Historico Nacional Rio de Janeiro Brazil/Dagli Orti)

Pernambuco and to energize the coastal whaling industry. Pombal's policies in particular were aided by two events taking place at the time: the United States' independence from England and the French Revolution, with the subsequent rise of Napoleon Bonaparte. The first caused England to look for new sources of raw materials, while the latter—and the resulting revolution in Saint-Domingue, or modern-day Haiti—

destroyed the world's largest sugar producer; together they led to important new markets for Portugal's colonial products.

By the late eighteenth century, Brazil's position was becoming increasingly powerful relative to Portugal's. In fact, the mother country owed its positive international trade balance almost entirely to Brazil. This development would help pave the way for Brazil's eventual independence, as colonial elites began to see that their interests were increasingly different from the interests of their mother country.

Anti-Portuguese sentiment grew, fueled both by enlightenment thinking and more material differences (for example, increasing taxes on colonists). However, open displays of opposition to the Crown were dangerous, so most of these ideas were expressed behind closed doors. There were, however, a number of plots against the Crown. These were for the most part regional developments—they did not yet reflect a national consciousness or political movement. In one of the most famous conspiracies, called the "Inconfidência Mineira," a conspirator nicknamed Tiradentes (or tooth-puller) was hanged, decapitated, and quartered and the various pieces of his body displayed around the town of Ouro Preto in Minas Gerais to serve as a message to any would-be conspirators. While the conspiracy was a failure, it gained symbolic force over time—Tiradentes would eventually become a national hero, particularly after the fall of the empire and the proclamation of the republic.

In an interesting twist of fate, before these resentments and the plots they spawned could grow into anything resembling a nationwide independence movement, it was decided that the Portuguese monarchy, along with its large court, would be moved to Brazil following Napoleon's invasion of Portugal. On November 28, 1807, under English protection, the entire Portuguese royal family and part of its court left for Brazil.

Ironically, the reorganization of the Portuguese Empire, underway since 1750, reached its culmination as a function of unpredictable external forces. Brazil, which had become the empire's most important economic power, would then also become its political center from 1808 to 1821, at which time Dom João VI, king of united Portugal and Brazil since 1816, would return to Portugal. Events would then turn in an unexpected direction in 1822, when Dom João's son, Pedro, would proclaim Brazil's independence.

Upon his arrival in Brazil the prince regent (later Dom João) made a number of significant changes, most of which benefited Brazil at the expense of the mother country. Probably most important, and most damaging to Portugal, was the opening of Brazil's ports to all nations, thus ending three centuries of royal monopoly. The prince also founded a number of institutions, including medical faculties, the national library, and a botanical garden. The first printing press in the colony was set up at the time as well, although with significant limits on what could be printed. In response to pressures from Portugal for the prince to return (especially when Napoleon was defeated in 1814), the prince in 1815 raised the *Estado do Brasil* to be an equal partner with Portugal, thus legitimizing his continued residence in Rio de Janeiro. A year later his mother, who was still the formal monarch, died, and the prince regent was then crowned King of Portugal, Brazil, and the Algarves Dom João VI.

Independence

Importantly, Brazil's independence from Portugal did not arise from a revolutionary break with the mother country, and the country's unique path to independence meant it would experience considerable continuity with the colonial period. The starting point of independence was the transfer of the Portuguese royal family from Lisbon to Brazil. The process then continued with the opening of Brazilian ports and the effective end of the colonial system. Events taking place largely in Portugal also had a direct impact; in fact it can be argued that efforts to defend Brazil's newly won autonomy were transformed into a movement for independence.

While Dom João was firmly ensconced in Brazil, the cries for him to return to Portugal grew as politics there became increasingly complicated. Fearing the inevitable loss of his throne if he remained in Brazil, Dom João decided to return to Lisbon in 1821, leaving his son Pedro, named the prince regent, to govern Brazil. Upon his departure, Dom João warned his son to stay in Brazil if there were ever an irrevocable break between the two kingdoms.

Portugal, inspired by ideas from the Enlightenment and caught up in a growing movement to create a more limited monarchy, had called for a representative body to be formed to write a new constitution. Brazil would be entitled to some representation within this body. The assembly, called the Cortes, took an aggressive stance toward Brazil and its status in the kingdom. It was clear the assembly meant to return the colony to its previous subservient status. The process infuriated Brazilian elite, and the conflict in general reflected the difficulties of ruling two kingdoms whose interests were now clearly contradictory.

The Cortes adopted a number of measures that ended up strengthening the move for independence, such as bringing back to Lisbon several important government offices that Dom João had set up in Brazil. Most importantly, the Cortes also demanded that Pedro return to Portugal. However, Pedro refused. On September 7, 1822 Pedro, following his father's prescient advice, declared "*Fico,*" or "I shall stay," thus declaring Brazil's independence. A number of dispatches were sent from Lisbon, revoking Pedro's decrees, renewing the order to return to Portugal, and accusing various Brazilian ministers of treason. This strengthened the cause for a definitive break with Portugal. The prince, on a trip to São Paulo, delivered on September 7, 1822, the so-called cry of Ipiranga, "Independência ou morte" (Independence or death). This declaration formalized Brazil's independence, and on December 1, 1822, Pedro was crowned Emperor Pedro I (formal independence was declared the following September).

Brazil's path to independence was unprecedented in the history of the Western Hemisphere. It was the only case in which a colonial power moved its royal family to the New World. In fact, no other European king had ever even set foot in the New World, let alone ruled a kingdom from there. Likewise it was the only country to move from its colonial status to a monarchical form of government.

Brazil's independence did not come without a fight, as a number of battles ensued with remaining Portuguese troops. However, there was nothing of the kind of bloodshed and destruction witnessed in Spanish American wars of independence, nor the splintering of territories. It is indeed remarkable that Brazil did not break up into smaller countries. In turn, Brazil's unique path to independence meant that there was a stable, legitimate, and powerful political structure already in place, something sorely missing in the postindependence Spanish American republics. Finally, while ties were cut with Portugal, there was no significant change in the socioeconomic order; Brazil would continue to be dominated by its landholding elite, and slavery would remain the principal economic institution for years to come.

THE BRAZILIAN EMPIRE

At the time of its independence, Brazil was still an agricultural economy and a largely rural society; sugar remained the country's most important crop. The country contained some 4 million people, approximately one-half of whom were slaves from Africa or people of African descent. The social hierarchy remained the same as in colonial times: the land-owning elites dominated society, and slaves did the bulk of the work. As mentioned, there was some growth in other sectors, with lawyers, merchants, and other workers becoming increasingly visible in the larger cities. However, Brazil remained without question a rural society.

In many respects the Brazilian Empire can be judged a successful political experiment (or accident, for that matter), not least because it allowed Brazil to avoid the large-scale death, destruction, and dislocation seen in Spanish America during its Wars of Independence. It also provided sixty-seven years of relatively stable government and allowed for the development of generally effective government institutions. At least for members of the elite (who were outnumbered by blacks and mulattoes by a very wide margin), life under the monarchy was a relatively comfortable one. Nonetheless, given the absence of any significant change in the country's hierarchical social structure, the change in the form of government did not represent any meaningful improvement in living conditions for the majority of Brazilians.

Dom Pedro I (1822–1831)

In the early days of the empire, Pedro called for a constituent assembly, and the resulting 1823 elections illustrated the country's political divisions. The main split, reflecting tensions that existed before independence, was between the Brazilian party and the Portuguese party. The latter opposed independence and wanted to return to the "good old days" as a Portuguese colony. The Brazilian party was led by one of Brazil's most famous historical figures, José Bonifácio de Andrada e Silva, a leading member of Dom Pedro's government.

While the assembly met and drafted a constitution in 1824, Dom Pedro responded to fighting between the two parties by dissolving the assembly and issuing by decree his own constitution. Pedro's constitution included features from the assembly's draft but also included far greater powers for the monarch, called the *Poder Moderador* (moderating power). These powers allowed the monarch to dissolve the Chamber of Deputies at will, hire and fire government ministers, and veto legislation. Thus Brazil, while nominally "liberal" in its constitutional separation of power, was also dominated by an emperor who was able to control nearly all political outcomes.

The 1824 constitution defined a political system that was monarchical, hereditary, and constitutional. Interestingly, the empire would have nobility, but no aristocracy. This meant that the emperor could confer titles upon people (strong supporters, of course), but these titles could not be passed on to heirs. The country was divided into provinces, which would be led by presidents appointed by the emperor. One interesting feature of the new governmental structure was the Conselho de Estado, or Council of State. The council was made up of counselors who were appointed for life by the emperor. The council's role was to weigh in on grave matters and on general measures pertaining to public administration. These matters included declarations of war, pay adjustments, or issues in which the emperor intended to use his "moderating power."

The role of the United Kingdom was at this time essential to the survival, and development, of the newly independent Brazil. England helped finance Brazil's move to independence, and it also played a critical role in convincing world powers— particularly Portugal—to recognize Brazil's new independent status. In this process, England would become the most important foreign nation in Brazil's economic and foreign affairs. As historians point out, Brazil simply passed from the Portuguese Crown to the British sphere of influence.

Dom Pedro was ultimately seen in Brazil as too closely tied to Portugal and was increasingly criticized from all angles. One major setback occurred in the south: what is today Uruguay had been annexed to Brazil in 1821 as the Cisplatine Province. Locals there seized power in 1825, allying themselves with today's Argentina. In effect the struggle became a war for Uruguayan independence—and with the Portuguese gone, it became a war against the Brazilians. The final outcome, largely brokered by England, was the creation of Uruguay as a buffer between Brazil and Argentina. The conflict—a military and

financial disaster for Brazil—and its outcome—Brazil's loss of
the Cisplatine Province—represented a significant setback for
Brazil and its royal leader. It was also a major reason the military began to distance itself from the emperor

In addition to criticisms at home, Pedro became increasingly tied to succession issues in Portugal, especially when his
father, Dom João, died in 1826. Some Brazilians feared that
Pedro would try to reinstate the united kingdoms, since as the
oldest son of João he could have succeeded to the Portuguese
throne. In the midst of the turmoil, on April 7, 1831, Dom
Pedro I abdicated, leaving his son, age five, to claim the Brazilian throne. Dom Pedro I died soon after in Portugal in 1834.

For nine years a regency would exercise power, until the
young Pedro was crowned emperor on July 18, 1841, at the
age of fifteen. During those nine years Brazil was governed by
politicians acting in the emperor's name. The regency was
notable for the number of separatist movements that
occurred; in a number of cases the country's territorial unity
was at risk, and Brazil became subject to the same forces of
fragmentation that split Spanish America into several separate countries. The revolts were against both the government
in Rio de Janeiro and the principle of monarchy. At the heart
of this conflict were divisions among the Brazilian elite about
the way Brazil should be governed.

So the regency was marked by the greatest political unrest
in the country's history to this point. As a sort of appeasement
to the provinces, legislation was drafted during the period to
give the provinces more power, as well as to reduce the power
of the monarchical government. An attempt was also made to
reduce the power of the army. The most violent separatist
movement was known as the Cabanagem War, in which some
30,000 were left dead in Brazil's northeastern state of Pará, or
as much as 20 percent of the state's population. Another well-
known conflict was the War of the Farrapos or Farroupilhas,
which occurred in Rio Grande do Sul (the terms *farrapos* and
farroupilhas refer to poorly dressed or ragged people). This

conflict, which began in 1835, was not resolved until 1845. Other conflicts include the *Sabinada* and the *Balaiada.*

Dom Pedro II (1840–1889)

Dom Pedro II's accession to the throne in July 1840 helped to unify what had become a divided elite in Brazil. The emperor was a pragmatic and successful ruler, leading many to call the decades around mid-century the "golden years" of the empire, as the emperor and his ministers ruled in a relatively harmonious environment (although this harmony was seriously damaged by the outbreak of war with Paraguay in 1864). After the chaos of the regency, a process of recentralization occurred, as did moves to strengthen the power of the emperor through a process known as the *regresso.* Still, there were challenges to the monarchy, such as the 1848 Praieira revolution in Pernambuco, which was the last of the notable provincial uprisings (it was also the last of a series of revolts in Pernambuco, which had begun with the war with the Dutch many years earlier).

Two political parties had developed—the Conservatives and the Liberals—and they dominated Brazilian politics for three decades after Pedro II's succession. The emperor exercised his "moderating power" quite liberally at the time, including frequent moves to dissolve the chamber and calling for new elections when the chamber did not support the cabinet he preferred. Using this technique the emperor was able to shape the chamber to support a cabinet more to his liking. The "second empire" saw a succession of thirty-six cabinets, each lasting an average of fifteen months. The near-constant turnover permitted the two political parties to alternate in power, meaning the opposition always faced the possibility of returning to power. This institutionalized alternation of power reduced the incentive to resort to armed conflict. Probably the most important issue dividing the elite of the time was the centralization or decentralization of power, a debate that over

Pedro II became the second emperor of Brazil after his father, Emperor Pedro I, abdicated, having established Brazil as an independent nation from Portugal. A moderate man with a modern outlook, Pedro II helped stabilize the new nation. (Library of Congress)

time led to the rise of the republican movement. The issue of slavery was another important one.

Aside from domestic political issues among Brazil's elite, a big challenge to Brazil—and the emperor—at the time would come from the south, sparked in part by Juan Manuel de Rosas, Argentina's dictator, who was seen as a threat to Brazil's border region. In addition to long-simmering disputes with Argentina, tensions had been rising throughout the 1860s in the La Plata region, as Brazilians, Argentines, and Paraguayans attempted to manipulate politics in Uruguay, which was embroiled in political turmoil. Likewise, tensions existed between Paraguay and Buenos Aires, which controlled the Plate River, Paraguay's only access to the sea. In fact, for a good time Paraguay's access was effectively blocked, leaving the country increasingly isolated.

Two factions were struggling for power in Uruguay, and Brazil sent troops to fight with the country's *colorados,* who were linked to business and European powers. The colorados were fighting against the *blancos,* who represented largely rural and authoritarian landowners. Alleging hostile intervention by Argentina and Brazil, the blancos turned to the dictator of Paraguay, Francisco Solano López, for support, setting off a chain reaction that led to war. Argentina joined with Brazil in supporting the colorados, while Solano teamed up with the blancos, hoping in the process to conquer Brazil's Rio Grande do Sul in the process. Solano invaded both Argentina and Brazil, forcing the two and Uruguay's colorados into a "triple alliance." The war is known as the Paraguayan War in Brazil, though it is also often called the War of the Triple Alliance. The war would last five long years. While Brazil ultimately triumphed, it suffered significant casualties and a number of humiliating defeats in battle. Worse yet, Paraguay would lose as much as half its population.

The Paraguayan War would have significant long-term implications for Brazil's politics. To begin with, it caused Brazilians to take another look at slavery, as the slaves drafted into service performed quite well in battle and were given their freedom in return (as mentioned, the issue of slavery was already a divisive one). Second, Pedro II was forced to assert his authority, dismissing a liberal cabinet that disagreed with him over negotiations with Paraguay. This contributed to a decline in his personal reputation and authority. In fact he was accused at the time of abusing his "moderating power."

The Paraguayan cavalry attacks the enemy during the Paraguayan War, which began in 1865. During the five-year conflict, one of the bloodiest wars in Latin American history, Paraguay faced the combined forces of Brazil, Argentina, and Uruguay. (Library of Congress)

Third, the war pushed Brazil to expand its army. Brazil did not really have a national army when the conflict began, and despite a wave of volunteers, as well as help from the slave population, the officer corps was sobered by the army's numerous defeats. Army officers would come to play an important role in future Brazilian politics. Importantly, when the war was finally over, Brazil's military commander, the Duke of Caxias, Luís Alves de Lima e Silva, would become the nation's popular hero, not the emperor. Finally, the war forced Brazilians to take a closer look at themselves and their country. While they won the war, the costs associated with their victory over a tiny, isolated, and destitute country begged the question of whether Brazil was at all ready to join the more advanced countries of the world.

In many ways, there is a direct link between the Paraguayan War and the fall of the Brazilian Empire, as the war upset the domestic political balance. Two fundamental Brazilian institutions were increasingly questioned—slavery and the monarchy itself. Brazil's slave trade had ended in 1850, but slavery itself was still going strong some twenty years later. With the rapid expansion of coffee production, planters increasingly relied on slaves from the economically waning Northeast, but this would not be sufficient. Brazil was then forced to turn to immigration. However, as a slave country it had a hard time attracting free workers. This difficulty would be a driving force in the push for abolition, in effect a pragmatic effort to make Brazil more attractive to immigrants.

Brazil's path to emancipation of slaves was unique in the Americas; unlike the United States, which achieved abolition only with a bloody civil war, Brazil's path to abolition was a gradual one. The Rio Branco Law of 1871 freed children born to slave mothers, but the law was widely ignored. However, by the 1880s abolition had become a nationwide movement and a second national law, in 1885, freed slaves over sixty years old. Of course, slaves rarely survived to reach sixty. Still, by 1887 slavery was disintegrating, with the Army formally refusing to catch and return fugitive slaves. In good part this reflected the role slaves played in the Paraguayan War and officers' realization that the war would probably not have been won without slaves' noteworthy contribution. The final blow to slavery came on May 13, 1888. Princess Regent Isabel, acting on her father's behalf, signed the Golden Law, which emancipated the remainder of Brazil's slaves without compensation to their previous owners. Importantly, although emancipation was lauded by the 5 percent of the population still in bondage, legislation and common social practices severely limited real opportunities for blacks and mulattoes.

Many of the same people who had cast a critical eye on the institution of slavery also turned their attentions to the monarchy, which was increasingly seen as an outdated institution. Pressures for a more democratic, "republican" form of government grew in the latter half of the nineteenth century. The aftermath of the Paraguayan War saw a general increase in the questioning of the status quo, and the monarchy would not escape this trend. In 1866 a dissident wing of the Liberal Party split and formed a third national party, the Republican Party, in 1870. Also, a rift developed between the Catholic Church and the monarchy, in part due to a power struggle over who controlled ecclesiastical appointments; Pedro would win the battle but lose the war when in 1874 the church withdrew its support of the monarchy.

A final element contributing to the end of the empire was linked to the military, another institution fundamentally affected by the Paraguayan War. Army officers began to focus on education as a main instrument to bring progress to Brazil. However, the officer corps felt that neither the Conservatives nor the Liberals were helping advance this cause. Many officers turned to positivism, or scientific sociology, as developed by the French philosopher Auguste Comte. Brazilian positivists actually adhered to a wide range of beliefs, and in general it did not prescribe specific doctrines. Rather, the positivists supported a scientific approach to understanding history and society and in general were skeptical of Brazil's increasingly archaic institutions. One faction of officers was highly critical of the empire, which they saw as placing excessive importance on planters and lawyers, and the country's complete failure to modernize.

This confluence of events—the Paraguayan War, increasing criticism of the empire and the emperor from Army officers, the rapid rise of republicanism, the rift with the Catholic Church, and the end of slavery—combined to bring down the monarchy. Likewise, the prospect of succession added to the mix. The idea of Pedro II's daughter as monarch was highly unpopular in Brazil's male-dominated society, while the same group of men was against her husband, the Conde d'Eu, who was a French-born nobleman. In this case nationality was the key problem. Thus, Brazilian elites had growing doubts about the monarchy, its out-of-touch emperor, and the prospects for a woman as next in line to the throne. More radical voices took the argument even further, identifying the monarchy as *the* main obstacle to Brazil's progress. As such, just a little over a year after emancipation, on November 15, 1889, a virtually bloodless civilian-military coup forced Pedro to abdicate. The emperor sailed to exile in Portugal, while Brazil was left in the hands of an Army general, Deodoro da Fonseca.

While it was the military that moved to fill the void left by the departing emperor and control government, real power was in the hands of the planter elite concentrated in the coffee regions of São Paulo and commercial and banking interests in the cities of the South-East. In other words, like independence, the fall of the empire and the abolition of slavery brought little in the way of structural or social change to Brazil; traditional elites would continue to dominate the country both politically and economically.

THE REPUBLIC (1889–1930)

The structure of Brazil's government changed significantly with the republican constitution of February 24, 1891, since it was based on a more decentralized federalist structure that ended the empire's centralized authority. This shift between centralization and decentralization is a major theme in the history of Brazilian government. The new constitution guaranteed autonomy for the provinces, which were renamed states. The country itself was renamed the United States of Brazil, and the positivist motto, "Order and Progress," was added as an emblem on the new national flag.

The military's role in the coup led to its active role in politics. In fact, from 1889 to 1930 the military would overthrow two constitutional governments and intervene at the state level on numerous occasions. Civilian rule was eventually regained, in part due to disagreements among various branches of the military. An alliance was formed between major *paulista* (i.e., from São Paulo) landowners and dairy-producing elites in the nearby state of Minas Gerais, an arrangement in which power would be alternated between the

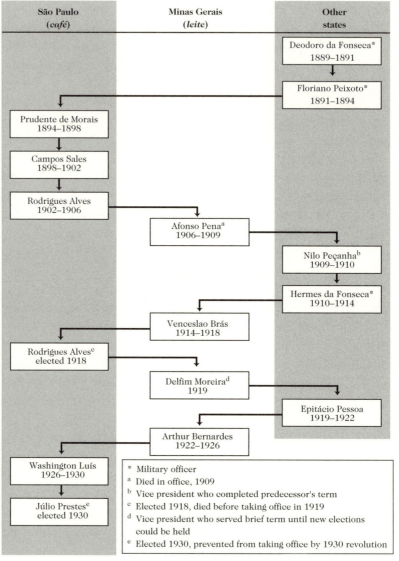

Presidencies during the "Café com Leite" period.

Men, women, and children pick coffee berries at a São Paulo planta-tion around 1900. (Library of Congress)

two groups. Known as the *Café com Leite* (coffee with milk) alliance, the agreement would form the political backbone of what is often referred to as the "Old Republic."

Importantly, while this era was characterized by wide-spread optimism as well as by efforts to bring "civilization" to Brazil's urban settings, political crises would vex the republic from its very beginning. In fact, the years following 1889 would be notable for the significant degree of political uncertainty, a reflection of an underlying struggle for power among elite groups. After two successive military leaders, civilians took control in November 1894; the arrival of paulista President Prudente José de Morais Barros signaled the ascendancy of São Paulo, its growth being driven by expanding coffee exports, increasing industry, and major population growth driven by immigrants from Europe and from within Brazil itself.

Canudos

The early years of the republic produced a somewhat strange but severe conflict called the Canudos War. The war centered on a millenarian movement by a group, the Canudenses, who believed that the impending millennium (1900) would see divine judgment and the destruction of the corrupt, modern world. The movement was founded by a lay Catholic mystic, Antônio Vicente Mendes Maciel, known to his followers as Antônio Conselheleiro (or the "Counselor"). Canudos was a religious settlement built on an abandoned cattle ranch in the drought-plagued backlands of the state of Bahia.

The Counselor's followers at Canudos adhered closely to their leader's plan, in which people were assigned specific types of work and life followed a set routine. Many of the group's members also openly questioned the new Brazilian republic and its secular nature. The record does not suggest that this was a group of religious fanatics. Instead, a number of factors, including the end of the monarchy, depressed economic conditions, and persistent drought combined to make the Counselor's community attractive to its members.

Those who held power at the national level and were committed to the new secular republic worried that the independent mind-set of the Canudenses might spread. It was feared that such an event could potentially spark another regional insurrection, potentially dangerous for the new republic. While this did not happen, the movement of thousands of northeasterners to the Counselor's "holy city" of New

Jerusalem begged for intervention by the state. The movement also occurred at the very time the Vatican was pushing its ultramontane campaign to restore orthodox practice around the world; in essence this movement was a direct attack on the practice of folk Catholicism, led by European-trained clergy. Ironically, the fact that the Counselor was deemed a dangerous heretic helped encourage people in Brazil's backlands to join his movement.

The so-called New Jerusalem grew quickly, reaching a population of potentially 35,000 people at its height in 1895, making it the second largest city in the state of Bahia at that time. The drain of workers, in addition to tales of fanaticism, drove elites to demand federal intervention. The Counselor's apparent unwillingness to cooperate in turn drove a decision to disarm residents and destroy the city. The first two government expeditions were soundly routed by the backlands fighters, leading the government to call in Colonel Moreira César (a veteran of another infamous regional uprising in the South) to squash the settlement. The third attack was again a total failure. Not only were the federal troops ambushed and largely destroyed, but the famous Moreira César was also killed in battle. News of the defeat spread throughout the country. As can be imagined, the disturbing developments were seen as a real threat to the new republican order.

A fourth expedition was then organized, massive in size and made up of all different types of troops, from state and federal troops to ex-slaves along with modern, heavy artillery purchased from Germany. The end came in 1897 as Canudos was pounded into oblivion. Male prisoners had their throats cut, and the body of the Counselor, who had died before the end of the battle, was exhumed. In old-fashioned style his head was cut off and displayed in a number of coastal cities. The very few survivors, essentially women and children, were taken to coastal cities, the former made servants or prostitutes, the latter often "adopted" into questionable circumstances.

Economy of the Republic

After the turn of the century, Brazil, like the rest of South America, was increasingly drawn into the global economy. While Brazil had always been tied to international markets—from sugar prices to the eighteenth-century gold rush to global demand for coffee—integration continued and even increased in pace. However, the war meant that trade (mainly imports) was cut, and after the war foreign investments in Brazil were at least partially withdrawn. This led to a sort of spontaneous process called "import substitution," in which local products had to make up for the sharp decline in previously imported goods—typically capital goods (the tools and machines used in the production of other goods).

Economic growth at the time was strong, not only in Brazil but in the neighboring countries in South America, as demand and prices for mineral and agricultural exports remained high. Coffee in particular continued to boom, and coffee exporters began to diversify into other industrial pursuits, such as processed foods and textiles. A large number of industrial workers were immigrants, and Brazilian employers continued to prefer immigrant laborers to native blacks and mulattoes.

By the 1920s, immigrants made up more than half the labor force in manufacturing, and an even larger percentage in transportation. These workers, typically from southern Europe, also brought with them anarchist and anarcho-syndicalist ideas from Spain and Italy. Working conditions in Brazil were typically terrible, and the dream of better wages, better housing, and the like appealed to such workers. Advances were made, but it is clear that the vast majority of workers continued to live in poverty in Brazil. Labor activity continued to increase in the war years, especially in São Paulo and other large cities, but employers won out, as strikes were met with brutal repression. In fact leaders were often imprisoned or deported back to Europe. The large supply of willing laborers also gave employers a strong advantage, and politicians, the military, and the church saw repression as necessary to keeping the peace and advancing the country.

A major shift took place in Brazil during the years of the republic. The country had been an overwhelmingly rural nation during the empire. In the Old Republic Brazil witnessed major urbanization, with thousands of rural residents migrating to cities by the 1930s. This era also saw major industrialization, city beautification projects, and major construction projects, but there was always a negative side to urbanization, as families typically lived in squalor and at significant distances from their places of work. Slum eradication programs, mandatory vaccination programs, and other state initiatives caused antigovernment sentiment and riots. One riot in Rio in November 1904 was nearly enough to topple the national government, although stability was restored fairly rapidly.

The republic brought with it universal male suffrage, although fewer than 3 percent of the population would vote as late as 1930; elections were still staged and often manipulated, and fraud by local political machines was common. Elites were pleased by the system, which was nominally democratic but allowed state machines to govern, typically in alliance with rural bosses, or *coroneis*. National-level politics were controlled by a few key states: São Paulo, Minas Gerais, and Rio Grande do Sul (as well as the city of Rio de Janeiro).

Typically elites were members of old, established families and often longtime owners of property. At the time, political disputes typically reflected disagreements over patronage or the use of government revenues, but there was little disagreement at the social level. As one president noted, labor issues were best considered matters for the police. There were no ministries for health, labor, education, or social welfare. And while nominally following positivist principles, Brazilian positivism emphasized order and progress and not the public education fostered in other Latin American countries like Mexico and Argentina.

By the 1920s there were clear signs of growing discontent, particularly from groups excluded from the existing political system. Labor militants were increasingly organizing workers, causing police crackdowns and often deportations, and the Communist Party was founded in Brazil in the early 1920s. Discontent was also visible in Brazil's regions, which were not benefiting from the country's economic progress (the federalist system meant that wealthy states grew richer, while poor states grew poorer). Signs of frustration were also visible within the military; a spontaneous barracks revolt at Copacabana Fort in Rio in 1922 was the beginning of the *tenente* movement, which by 1930 would help bring down the republic.

On July 24, 1924, the anniversary of the Rio revolt, another group of young officers and cadets in São Paulo and Rio Grande do Sul rose in revolt. Unlike the previous group, who were mostly gunned down, this group headed for Brazil's interior to regroup as a guerilla force. The group became known as the Prestes Column, after the group's leader and highest ranking officer, Luis Carlos Prestes. The group crisscrossed Brazil, traveling some 25,000 kilometers and passing through fifteen states between October 1924 and February 1927, when the group slipped into Bolivia and then disbanded. Prestes eventually resurfaced in Uruguay and became head of the Brazilian Communist Party. This revolt, among others on Brazil's periphery, would significantly weaken the regime. The republic ultimately could not withstand the impact of the Great Depression and succumbed to a military coup.

The Wall Street stock market crash of 1929 was felt throughout the world. In Brazil the most immediate effect of the global crash was a plunge in coffee prices. São Paulo producers reacted by breaking the unwritten "coffee with cream" agreement with Minas Gerais to alternate the presidency. São Paulo would try to retain control of the government as a hedge against further economic downturn. The 1930 election therefore saw a split within the Brazilian elite, with an opposition coalition against São Paulo made up of the states of Minas

Gerais, Rio Grande do Sul, and Paraíba. The opposition's efforts, including a move to recruit the exiled tenentes, were successful. Political peace dissolved in 1930, as President Washington Luís insisted on imposing another paulista rather than returning power to Minas Gerais. The opposition, dubbed the Liberal Alliance, picked Getúlio Vargas from the state of Rio Grande do Sul. The Conservatives narrowly won the election. With widespread allegations of fraud, Vargas and Liberal Alliance supporters, including many of the tenentes from the failed uprisings of the 1920s, toppled the republic and installed a new government. Thus the republic and the rule of the "coffee with cream" oligarchy came to an end. The 1930 revolution would mark the entrance of important new groups into national politics.

Brazil's Old Republic (1889–1930), then, was controlled by oligarchies, which in turn were able to control the various state machines. There was no attempt to enlarge the electorate; women were not allowed to vote, and requirements of property ownership severely limited the number of men who were allowed. The most dynamic provinces dominated national government—specifically São Paulo, Minas Gerais, the city of Rio de Janeiro, and to a lesser extent Rio Grande do Sul. Coffee planters in particular dominated the era; industrialists had yet to gain power. One of the most significant changes of the era involved immigration—landowners and factory owners increasingly turned to European laborers as a source of cheap labor. As we move to the Vargas era, we will see both a dramatic change in the political landscape and the growing importance of the working classes.

THE VARGAS ERA (1930–1954)

As in 1889 at the end of the empire, the end of the Old Republic came at the hands of the military. An opposition group formed around Getúlio Vargas, who ran for president in 1930 but was defeated (although amidst abundant charges of

President Getúlio Vargas (center, facing camera) with General João Gomes, minister of war, and other cabinet officers at a funeral ceremony for officers and soldiers killed in quelling the recent Brazilian revolt in Rio de Janeiro, December 4, 1935. The fighting in Rio de Janeiro lasted only a few hours; loyal troops quickly gained command of the situation. In the northern states of Grande do Norte and Pernambuco, however, rebels were in control for several days. (Bettmann/Corbis)

electoral fraud). The winning candidate was Júlio Prestes, the governor of São Paulo, from the same state as incumbent Washington Luíz. In an ensuing coup in 1930, top military leaders deposed Luíz, who still remained in office, and gave the presidency to Vargas instead of Prestes, invoking revolutionary powers in the process. Washington Luíz headed off into exile. The 1930 revolution was supported by the majority of the population; even the educated population resented the paulistas' blatant attempt to keep themselves in power. In addition to the political leaders of Minas Gerais and Rio Grande do Sul, key supporters of the coup included São Paulo opponents of the official Republican Party, tenentes, and coffee growers. The fact that elections had lost much of their legitimacy due to widespread fraud was also important.

"Racial Democracy" and Gilberto Freyre

Brazil received more African slaves than any other country in the Americas. Despite the brutality of slavery, which relied on force wherever it existed in the Americas, some have argued that Brazil's experience with slavery was somehow a gentler one. In fact many have argued that modern Brazil represents a sort of "racial democracy."

One of the most well-known proponents of this view was Gilberto Freyre, who became perhaps the most influential twentieth-century interpreter of the Brazilian character. Freyre, who lived from 1900 to 1987, was born to a distinguished family in Recife in Brazil's Northeast. He argued that the Portuguese colonizers of Brazil were inherently less prejudiced against Africans than other Europeans. This, he said, was at least partially the result of the centuries-long exposure of the Portuguese to the darker-skinned Moors of North Africa, who for so long had actually represented a higher culture in the Iberian Peninsula. In his writing he often idealized the paternalistic relationship that existed between masters and their slaves.

Freyre authored a number of influential works, including *Casa Grande e Senzala* (*The Masters and the Slaves,* 1933) and *Sobrados e Mucambos* (*The Mansions and the Shanties,* 1936). He proposed that Brazilians represented a new race in the tropics, a new people of mixed origin, and that Portuguese tolerance was a central driver in Brazil's unique racial "paradise." The key for Brazil was prevalent racial mixture and the opportunities the country provided for people of mixed blood. Freyre's work has been widely criticized by modern scholars, who argue that his theories simply make white Brazilians feel better about their country's foundation on the institution of slavery. However, while the criticisms are certainly valid, the historical context must also be taken into account. Freyre was responding to the so-called scientific racism that preceded him, which held that Africans were biologically inferior to white Europeans. At a minimum, Freyre helped to debunk these racist theories as well as to assist Brazilians in coming to grips with their unique position in the New World.

Getúlio Vargas's call for nationalistic reform and social legislation was welcomed. With no legislature in place, Vargas had the freedom to rule by decree; in the process he was solidly supported by a new generation of army generals. The events of 1930 turned out to be a major turning point in Brazilian history. Getúlio Vargas would hold power, in two separate periods, for about twenty years. The first and longest period lasted from 1930 until 1945. The second period lasted from 1950 until Vargas committed suicide in 1954, on the day the military was prepared to oust him from power. Vargas was a consummate politician and strategist and was popular throughout much of the time he retained power. As we will discuss below, Vargas built a corporatist state that managed to arbitrate between the competing groups of Brazilian society. The ability to successfully represent employees and workers provided an important component of the support Vargas needed to remain in power.

The immediate success of the new Vargas government would depend on its ability to restore economic stability in the face of global economic crisis (as well as quickly address Brazil's weakened economic conditions, which included a lack of foreign reserves, a devalued currency, and chronic inflation). One angle of Vargas's response was to focus on improving the quality of urban life and addressing the needs of urban workers. While historians continue to debate the extent to which Vargas succeeded on this front, the change in discourse alone, with its focus on common Brazilians and issues that affected them like housing and education, was unprecedented in the country's history. This is one key reason why the Vargas years represent a turning point in Brazilian history.

President Vargas, widely known by Brazilians as Getúlio, moved quickly to change the old political system. He replaced all state governors, except for the governor of Minas Gerais, with "interventors" who would report directly to him. This would diminish the power of the state political machines and mean that state conflicts would be settled in the nation's capital, Rio de Janeiro, instead of locally. This assertion of federal authority, yet another example of the country's swings between centralization and decentralization of power, threatened state political elites.

The most dramatic reaction to Getúlio Vargas's rise to power, and the threat it represented to state power, occurred in São Paulo, which was still bitter about its recent political defeat as well as angered by what many called its "occupation." The situation was made worse by the drastic decline in international demand for coffee. Vargas's interventor in the state, João Alberto, would prove unable to deal effectively with the disgruntled and demanding paulistas. They brought together their fury at João Alberto and a strong sense of state loyalty to oppose Vargas, demanding a return to constitutional rule and even Vargas's departure.

The tensions escalated into an armed rebellion, with the state's militia managing to hold off federal troops for four months. The paulista political elite mistakenly thought leaders from Rio Grande do Sul and Minas Gerais would join them, but they ended up fighting the federal army on their own. This armed conflict is called the Constitutionalist Revolution. The rebels ultimately surrendered in October 1932. Vargas responded with restraint. Not only were the peace terms fairly soft but Vargas ordered the federal government to pay half of the debt incurred by the rebel forces. The paulistas' move ended up playing into Vargas's hands by seriously discrediting calls for decentralized government. It also significantly reduced the paulistas' strength in national politics—it would take nearly thirty years for a paulista to return to the presidency.

Vargas continued his move to centralize power at the Constituent Assembly of 1933–1934, which produced the Constitution of 1934, Brazil's third constitution. State autonomy was significantly reduced in the new constitution—for example states could no longer tax interstate commerce. The constitution also saw the beginnings of nationalist and social policy, such as restrictions on foreign ownership of land and a declaration of government responsibility for economic development and social welfare. Still, changes were on the whole moderate, as both houses of the legislature were kept and elections for both the Congress and the presidency were to be direct. Vargas was elected to a four-year presidential term by the assembly, and at this point it still looked like Brazil would return to democracy; the country, however, was to turn in a very different direction.

By 1934 Brazil entered a period marked by agitation and significant political conflict. Significantly, ideological radicalization was on the rise. Two groups, both national in scale and highly ideological in nature, had developed in Brazil. The Ação Integralista Brasileira, or "Integralist Party," was founded by Plínio Salgado in 1932. The Integralists were Christian, nationalist, and traditionalist and were similar in a number of ways to the fascist parties growing in Europe, with uniformed, paramilitary groups that took part in aggressive and orchestrated street demonstrations. Despite the group's clear affinity for street brawls with opponents, however, they lacked the racist and militaristic characteristics of European fascists—especially the Germans.

On the opposite end of the spectrum was the "Popular Front Movement," called the Aliança Libertadora Nacional. This movement was started as a coalition between communists, socialists, and other leftist radical groups, but it was run by the Partido Comunista Brasileiro (PCB) or Brazilian Communist Party. The PCB, in turn, was controlled by Luis Carlos Prestes, the old tenente leader turned communist boss. Prestes's ties to Moscow, as well as general efforts to organize workers, set off alarms among the elite, who tried to respond with repressive laws.

By 1935 the two groups had become openly hostile and confrontational, with street brawls and increasing use of terrorist tactics. That year the communists would launch three barracks attacks aimed at overthrowing the Brazilian government. After brief fighting, which led to some casualties among officers and enlisted men, the pro-government forces crushed each of the revolts. The attacks were entirely unsuccessful and gave Vargas the justification he needed to crack down on the left and the supposed "Bolshevik threat"; the crackdown came in the form of arrests, torture, and declaration of a state of emergency. The Integralists assumed they would be the beneficiaries of the communists' missteps, but Vargas had very different plans in store. These tumultuous events provided him with the perfect excuse for further centralization of power, as well as a dramatic increase in presidential power.

For two years, Congress cooperated with Vargas, agreeing consistently to renew the ninety-day state of siege declared after the 1935 revolts. National attention began to focus on impending elections in 1938, which had been scheduled by the Constituent Assembly that also elected Vargas president. Vargas was ineligible to run for this term (he could have run again after the four-year term). While preparations were being made, Vargas was conspiring with his top generals, setting up a coup that could preempt the election.

On November 10, 1937, Getúlio Vargas read aloud on national radio a new constitution, following yet another military intervention. That same morning the legislature had been dissolved and occupied by soldiers—congressmen were refused access. This would mark the beginning of what Vargas called the *Estado Novo* (New State). Democracy had disappeared in Brazil; it was replaced by an authoritarian government that resembled Mussolini's Italy and Salazar's Portugal.

There would be a final showdown between the government and the Integralists. Ironically, the Integralists expected to benefit by the new dictatorship, assuming their leader, Plínio Salgado, would be given a cabinet position. However, Vargas responded by banning all paramilitary organizations, adding extra restrictions on the Intregralists. In response, some of its members attempted an armed attack on the presidential palace in March 1938. A shoot-out ensued, including Vargas and his daughter returning fire from their window, but the attack ended with the arrest of Integralist participants and exile for Salgado; at least four of the attackers were killed.

Just as the failed communist uprising gave Vargas the opportunity to repress the left, the coup gave Vargas the opportunity to repress the Integralists. This meant that there was no longer any organized opposition to Getúlio Vargas. Not only did he appoint himself president for another term but also when the time came for the next elections he cancelled them due to "wartime emergency." Vargas would remain president until 1945, through World War II. While some in the country were sympathetic to Nazi Germany (including members of the military), Brazil would ultimately side with the Allies, adroitly securing significant benefits from the United States in the process. Brazil would supply air and naval bases, as well as vital commodities; the United States in return would give Brazil the modernized bases and major financial aid. Importantly, U.S. aid in the construction of a large-scale steel project, Volta Redonda, represented the first time the United States committed funds to foster industrialization in a developing country.

One significant aspect of the Estado Novo was an increasing role of the state in the economy. A whole host of new initiatives, such as new state-owned corporations, marketing cartels, and a new labor code, gave the federal executive unprecedented control of the economy. Vargas also built a propaganda machine, called the Departamento da Impresa e do Propaganda, and used it to build a sense of national pride and to teach Brazilians about the "national family" to which they belonged. Vargas used schools and the press to build patriotism among Brazilians. Getúlio Vargas thus became the "father of the country." Not surprisingly, Vargas's authoritarian regime also used a repressive apparatus to keep the people in line—detention, torture, and even summary executions of political enemies were key components of the Estado Novo (the head of the police in Rio de Janeiro was the well-known Filinto Muller, whose staff had a secret working arrangement with Nazi Germany's Gestapo).

There was considerable public support for Vargas and the Estado Novo. While many were moved by the pageantry, banners, and flags, others were motivated by the concepts of improving efficiency and moral and national pride; still others felt Brazil could industrialize more easily without the constant threats coming from the left. Getúlio was particularly popular with the working classes, as social legislation brought benefits to these Brazilians. And while many of Vargas's promised social policies did not pan out in practice, large numbers of Brazilians attained protected government jobs and benefited from improved infrastructure. For these reasons Vargas was also widely known as the "father of the poor."

After World War II the authoritarian Estado Novo became something of an embarrassment for the Brazilians, given that the war—in which Brazil actively participated—had been dedicated to the defeat of fascism; in the postwar environment Brazil's dictatorship looked like an anachronism. The United States also had issues with South America's largest dictatorship and put Getúlio on a short list of Latin American leaders and regimes that it felt needed to be replaced. In this environment, there was a sharp increase in political polarization in Brazil. Vargas became the target of criticism from all sides: the left, state political bosses, liberal constitutionalists, parts of the military, and so forth. Vargas, in response, attempted to shift his authoritarian regime to the left and promised elections for October 1945. His rhetoric focused increasingly on workers, the family, and the middle classes. However, Vargas's own intentions remained vague, and he refused to define his own role in the upcoming elections. The armed forces became particularly agitated by Vargas's ambiguous political intentions and growing populist rhetoric.

The generals' concerns were shared by the United States. In fact, the U.S. ambassador to Brazil, Adolph Berle, suggested publicly that Vargas resign from office, while the U.S. secretary of state advocated a return to democracy. Vargas, ever the political opportunist, tried to use the perception of U.S. intervention to spark a nationalist reaction, but this time it was simply too late. In October 1945, the army gave Vargas an ultimatum: either resign or be deposed. Getúlio Vargas opted to cooperate, leaving Rio de Janeiro for his ranch in his home state of Rio Grande do Sul. Vargas managed to stay busy, dabbling in local politics, receiving visitors, and waiting for his chance to return to power. Ironically, the dictator of the Estado Novo would eventually return to power as Brazil's elected president.

THE SECOND REPUBLIC (1946–1964)

Presidential elections were held as scheduled in December 1945; the contest was held between two generals and was won by Eurico Dutra (approximately six million votes were cast, nearly three times as many as had voted in 1930 in the last presidential election). Dutra ran for the Partido Social Democrático (PSD), beating Eduardo Gomes, who ran for the União Democrática Nacional. The Communist Party also put in a strong showing.

A constitutional convention was also held in an attempt to restore many of the features of representative government that were abandoned during the Estado Novo. Notably, decentralization of power was a major theme, as strong central government was equated with the dictatorship of the Estado Novo. Still, Vargas's second shot at power came in 1950, when he was elected to the presidency democratically. The term would be marked by financial instability and increased confrontation among interest groups. For example, Vargas announced in 1954 that the minimum wage would be doubled, something he had previously promised not to do. The move, coupled with his appeals to workers for votes, angered employers. Attacks on Vargas escalated, and financial instability continued unabated, leading President Vargas to despondency.

One of Vargas's main adversaries was Carlos Lacerda, a well-known newspaper publisher. On August 5, 1954, an attempt was made to assassinate Lacerda at an anti-Vargas rally. While Lacerda escaped serious harm, his bodyguard was killed. To make matters worse, Vargas's own security guard was implicated in the crime. This gave Vargas's enemies tremendous leverage in their attempt to discredit the president. While Vargas almost certainly did not know of the plot, the event contributed to his political isolation, and his psychological despair continued to mount. The movement calling for Vargas's removal also continued to grow, culminating in a manifesto to the nation signed by twenty-seven generals demanding his resignation.

As opposition rose, Vargas responded one last time: on August 24, after a lengthy cabinet meeting in the presidential palace, Vargas retreated to his bedroom and committed suicide with a bullet to the heart hours before a military coup would have ousted him from the presidency. He left behind an inflammatory suicide letter in which he portrayed himself as a victim, pointing his finger at his enemies, both domestic and international. The public responded with tremendous grief, stunned by his suicide. The animosity that had been targeted at the president suddenly shifted to his attackers (Carlos Lacerda was even forced to leave Brazil in exile). As a result, Vargas's suicide led to a period of political caution, as both his enemies and supporters feared political and labor instability and the possibility of military intervention. As a result the volatile political environment calmed and the country enjoyed a few years of relative quiet. Vargas was succeeded by his vice president, João Café Filho, who governed cautiously and paved the way for peaceful elections in 1955.

Juscelino Kubitschek, a former governor of Minas Gerais, was elected to a full presidential term in 1955 and inaugurated in 1956. Kubitschek wisely initiated large weapons purchases to garner support from the military; he also managed to build an effective coalition in Congress, despite only gaining 36 percent of the vote in the election. Kubitschek unrolled a plan for economic development, called the Programa de Metas (Program of Goals). The program set a series of ambitious targets for increased output by economic sector, bringing the state and the private sector together to accelerate industrialization and development. At the same time Kubitschek initiated a bold plan to build a new capital, Brasília, in the country's interior (a long-standing dream in Brazil since the mid-eighteenth century). Together the plans helped reduce the prevailing political tensions. Kubitschek's motto was "Fifty years of progress in five," and the degree of success was nothing short of impressive. Still, economic imbalances, like chronic balance-of-payments deficits and growing inflation, were direct results of Kubitschek's ambitious plans. In fact, his critics, in a play on words with his slogan "Fifty years' progress in five," suggested Kubitschek's program resulted in "Fifty years' inflation in five."

Thus, while Juscelino Kubitschek's achievements were impressive (not the least was completing his presidential term, despite constant predictions that he would fall), he retired from office leaving significant economic challenges facing Brazil. These problems were then inherited by Jânio Quadros, Kubitschek's successor after the 1960 elections. Quadros started his term by implementing a politically difficult and economically painful stabilization program in the midst of economic crisis. However, for reasons never adequately explained, Quadros suddenly resigned after spending only seven months in office. One commonly accepted explanation for his move is that he assumed, incorrectly, that Congress would reject his resignation and offer him emergency powers. However, Congress did not play into Quadros's plans and simply accepted the president's resignation. Brazil's economic crisis was then overwhelmed by political crisis, as the country was left without a president.

Power passed to the elected vice president, Getúlio's former labor minister, João Goulart, a populist and a political enemy of the armed forces (who felt Goulart was prepared to accommodate the communists and help them gain power). Goulart was actually the running mate of Quadros's opponent in the election of 1960—Brazil's electoral laws allowed him to be elected vice president since he outpolled Quadro's own vice presidential running mate. Ironically, Goulart was returning from government business in the People's Republic of China when he assumed power, hardly an auspicious start for those fearing a radical move to the left. While many in the military did not want to let Goulart become president, a compromise was reached; he would become president but with significantly reduced powers. Specifically a parliamentary system was devised, in which executive power would be given to a prime minister and Goulart's cabinet would be accountable to Congress. It was an unwieldy and ultimately unworkable arrangement. However, Goulart worked to reverse the situation, succeeding when the full presidential powers were restored in early 1963. Goulart would last less than three years as Brazil's president.

Economic difficulties continued to plague Brazil in the early 1960s, and Goulart's top economic team was forced to work out a stabilization agreement with the International Monetary Fund (IMF). Under the agreement, the government was forced to reduce its budget deficit, put tough controls on wages, and significantly reduce available credit, standard fare for stabilization programs. Unfortunately for Goulart, not only did he have to worry about economic woes but he also had to face growing political problems. In particular, members of the military, not happy with Goulart from the beginning, were plotting to overthrow his government. The left was also stirring up politics, even managing to secure government financing and organizational support. Things were also heating up in the countryside, with rural unionization legalized in 1963. By early 1964, Brazil was embroiled in both political and economic crisis, and it seemed that Goulart had run out of options. As has happened so frequently in Brazilian history, the problem would be settled by the military, in a coup d'etat that ended civilian rule.

On March 31, 1964, a military revolt spread rapidly across Brazil as military units seized important government offices in both Rio de Janeiro and Brasília. In effect, there was no resistance, and violence was limited. Within twenty-four hours João Goulart was forced to flee to Uruguay in exile. The military moved to fill important government positions, turning to fellow conspirators and their civilian allies to do the job. Once again, Brazil had opted for an authoritarian solution to its political problems.

Many historians argue that behind the scenes the real issue this time was the rising threat of class conflict. Vargas had opened the door to organizing the urban working class, but this was seen as more or less acceptable to the upper and middle classes. However, Goulart seemed to pose a bigger threat, accompanying radical rhetoric with active mobilization of both peasants in the countryside and the urban working classes. In other words, the threat of an organized lower-class alliance, combining both urban workers and rural peasants, against the elite establishment was growing. As in the past, the military used its power to veto civilian politics, this time to create a military-led "bureaucratic-authoritarian" regime.

BRAZIL'S MILITARY DICTATORSHIP (1964–1985)

The coup to oust Goulart would mark the beginning of two decades of military rule in Brazil. At least initially, the military intervention was greeted enthusiastically by the media, the church, and elites in business and politics. The coup, called the "revolution" by its military engineers, was seen as necessary to counteract the upheavals and social instability that were the feared results of Goulart's reforms—in this sense it was seen as a preemptive strike to stop the lower sectors of Brazilian society from increasing mobilization and growing power. The initial enthusiasm, however, would begin to wane as the military's repressive tactics, including torture, became more widely known by the public.

Importantly, unlike other dictatorships in Latin America dominated by a single "strongman," the new military government would be run by the full military bureaucracy, with Brazil's generals actively seeking to transform the state and Brazilian society. This was the first of a number of "national security regimes" to be seen in Latin America—others followed in Argentina, Chile, and Uruguay. These regimes focused on creating economic growth in a "controlled" political environment; repression of human rights was a key ingredient.

There were a number of distinct phases of military rule in Brazil, but each of the regimes was headed by a four-star general, and all witnessed coalitions of military officers, technocratic administrators, and civilian politicians (from this coalition comes the label "bureaucratic-authoritarian"). In the early years the military ruled without dramatically changing the structure of the government. However, in 1967 a new constitution was passed by Congress; by this time all opposition politicians had been removed. At this point the president would be elected by an electoral college, but only military officers could be candidates. The constitution also allowed the president to rule by decree, even if the legislature were in session. So what had started as a relatively moderate dictatorship in 1964 turned into a markedly more repressive regime.

The year 1968 was critical in the evolution of military rule. As in other parts of the world, Brazil witnessed huge protests and demonstrations, typically staged by student organizations. The military, fearful of growing opposition and equating democracy with subversion, began cracking down on "the communist threat." Through a number of institutional acts in late 1968 the military allowed for indirect elections, eliminated all existing political parties and replaced them with two government-controlled parties, suspended the legislature, and suspended habeus corpus (a person's right to challenge detention or imprisonment) for crimes against "national security." The year 1969 would bring yet another constitution, further strengthening the executive's power and weakening individuals' rights.

It is generally agreed that the years between 1968 and 1975 witnessed the darkest hours of military rule in Brazil. Political parties and workers' unions were outlawed or limited to government-controlled groups. Censorship was ubiquitous. Congress was marginalized, and its actions were limited. The military-controlled universities and many of the country's top intellectuals, musicians, writers, and artists went into exile. Most startling, torture, executions, and disappearances became common occurrences. Opposition and resistance within Brazil had effectively vanished.

Brazil's Economic Miracle

Brazil's military rulers moved quickly to invigorate the economy. In essence, business—both domestic and foreign—had gone along with the coup because of fears surrounding Goulart's populist rhetoric, high and rising inflation, and the mobilization of workers and peasants. The military, then, had to prove that it could engineer economic growth and development. Brazil's so-called economic miracle took place in 1968 to 1974, under the rule of General Emílio Garrastazú Médici. The "miracle" referred both to high rates of growth and the enormous infusion of capital, often foreign, that was devoted to developing Brazil's infrastructure (the Transamazonian Highway is a good example) and basic industry, not to mention purchases of military hardware.

The economy returned to growth after 1967. From 1968 to 1974 the rate of economic growth averaged an amazing 10 percent, with exports more than quadrupling. Importantly, manufactured goods finally surpassed coffee as the country's leading export—these types of achievements generated the talk of the Brazilian miracle. However, the miracle would fade by the

Foz do Iguaçu waterfalls on the Paraná River in Brazil, a major tourist attraction. Construction of a massive hydroelectric dam on the river between Brazil and Paraguay was another of the projects of the "miracle" years (dubbed by some the "Pharaoh Projects"). The dam was not completed until 1991; it generates some 77,000 gigawatt-hours per year. (Corel)

end of the 1970s, and Brazil's generals would then face a number of economic problems, like high inflation, high and growing levels of government debt, and fading economic growth.

While the government attempted a return to growth in 1982, global events would dash its hopes. The world was hit by a major recession, caused in large part by high U.S. interest rates (which were designed to end its own inflationary problems). The recession drove down the prices of Brazil's exports, but the high interest rates meant the cost of servicing the foreign debt was increasing and reaching unsustainable levels. In fact, in 1982 Brazil had the single largest foreign debt in the world: $87 billion. Brazil, like Mexico and Argentina, had to suspend payments on principal and agree to a tough economic plan with the IMF to obtain emergency financing for short-term obligations.

FROM LIBERALIZATION TO REDEMOCRATIZATION

Brazil's political violence reached new peaks in 1969, as the country experienced guerilla warfare for the ensuing four years. The government responded with extensive repression. In 1969 the U.S. ambassador was kidnapped; he was then released without serious harm in exchange for fifteen political prisoners. By 1973 the military regime had all but wiped out the guerilla movement.

General Ernesto Geisel assumed the presidency in 1974 and signaled a desire to return to democracy. This period would be dubbed the *abertura,* or political opening. The more moderate leaders within the military government argued that a reduction in repression, amnesty for dissidents, and a stronger role for the opposition could actually prevent more radical opposition to the regime. The Brazilian Democratic Movement was the main vehicle for opponents of the regime and would become the Party of the Brazilian Democratic Movement (PMDB) when the government reinstated political parties in 1979.

The problem for the government, however, was its clear inability to win free elections; the new government learned this the hard way when it allowed relatively free congressional elections, which the opposition party won in a landslide. The harsh economic conditions would make efforts to return to democracy even more difficult as more and more people actively opposed the regime. The process was begun under Ernesto Geisel. President João Figueiredo (1979–1985) would then take the reins from Geisel, working to fulfill a campaign promise for direct elections in 1982. In a first since 1965, in November 1982, Brazil directly elected all state governors, with the PMDB winning the big races in São Paulo, Rio de Janeiro, and Minas Gerais. The government party lost control of the Chamber of Deputies but retained control of the electoral college, which was set to elect a new president in 1985.

The Constitution of 1988

The 1988 constitution was drafted by a constituent assembly that began on February 1, 1987, and ended on October 5, 1988, when the new constitution took effect. The constitution in general weakened the executive and strengthened the legislative and judicial branches of government (yet another example of the battle between the forces for centralization and decentralization of power; in this instance those promoting decentralization won). The constitution is extensive and progressive. However, it has been criticized for dealing with a number of subjects that have nothing to do with constitutions (critics point out, for example, that Brazil's deep social problems cannot be solved by constitutional fiat). With 245 articles and 70 transitory provisions lawmakers seemed to put everything they could conceive of in the constitution, perhaps believing this would ensure the laws would be obeyed. With such a broad purview, enforcement has been difficult, to say the least. The constitution has also created a number of new problems. One of these relates to excessive decentralization of power, which has created huge fiscal problems for the federal government. However, this decentralization of power must be understood in its historical context—this document represents the formal end of the repressive authoritarian dictatorship that had ruled Brazil for twenty years.

The 1985 presidential election was won by the PMDB candidate, Tancredo Neves, who had shrewdly won enough votes from the government's party, the PSD, to win over the electoral college. However, Neves fell ill and underwent emergency surgery on the night before his inauguration, and never recovered. A former senator and candidate for vice president with Neves, José Sarney, would become president upon Neves's death. Ironically, while Sarney would be Brazil's first civilian president in more than twenty years, he had for years been a PSD leader and for some time a key player in the military regime.

The Sarney presidency was largely centered on the process of redemocratization, but the weakened economy would severely limit its overall success. Likewise, Sarney had few strong allies; democratic forces distrusted him because of his previous involvement with the military government, while the military resented his desertion to the democratic opposition. The term would end badly, with rampant inflation and general policy drift.

FERNANDO COLLOR DE MELLO (1990–1992)

Sarney was followed by Fernando Collor de Mello, a relatively unknown politician who had been the governor of the poor northeastern state of Alagoas. The young Collor ran in 1989 against a former labor union leader named Luiz Inácio Lula da Silva, better known as "Lula" and Brazil's current president. Collor favored a relatively free-market program, while Lula called for a more left-leaning social democratic program. Fernando Collor de Mello won the election in a run-off ballot, but his presidency would prove to be a disaster; he was ultimately impeached.

During his presidential term Collor tried to implement economic stabilization, cooperating with the IMF, but this ultimately failed to reduce Brazil's rampant inflation. One of his policies, freezing financial assets, turned out to be wildly unpopular. In short, by 1991 annual inflation was running at a rate of 1,585 percent, and all hope of gaining fiscal control was lost. The president also began a series of reforms, dubbed "neo-liberal" for their emphasis on opening the economy to freer trade, privatizing state-owned companies, and deregulating the economy. Collor did not make it through his term, however, as he was involved in a huge corruption scandal. In September 1992 Brazil's Chamber of Deputies voted overwhelmingly to impeach the president, and Collor was forced to resign. Notably, after nearly twenty-five years without democracy, the impeachment process took place entirely within the democratic system, with no meddling or intervention by the military. To many, this was a strong signal that democracy had taken hold.

Itamar Franco, the vice president and a relatively unknown politician, succeeded Collor. Franco's government suffered however, as this former senator lacked a strong party base, was not a connected "player" in Brazilian politics, and had very little in the way of a plan to end Brazil's economic malaise. The country continued to suffer from rampant inflation and a huge government deficit. Franco simply did not have the ability to undertake the tough stabilization program Brazil needed. Many argue that the most important decision made by Itamar Franco was to appoint Fernando Henrique Cardoso to the cabinet post of finance minister in early 1994 (after a brief stint as minister of foreign relations).

FERNANDO HENRIQUE CARDOSO (1995–2003)

Unknowingly at the time, Itamar Franco changed the direction of the country, both politically and economically, when he appointed Fernando Henrique Cardoso at the end of 1993. Cardoso launched yet another stabilization program, called the Plano Real (Real Plan), with the help of a highly talented team of economists to fight Brazil's rampant inflation. This time the stabilization worked, so well in fact that the finance minister would take his newly won popularity to the 1994 presidential elections and win. Cardoso, a famous left wing intellectual and former senator from the PSDB, was able to trounce Lula with 54 percent of the vote. While Cardoso became a major factor in maintaining Brazil's new economic stability, the road forward for him would not be an entirely smooth one. Importantly, both Cardoso and Lula had been staunch opponents of the military regime; both also founded their own political parties, the PSDB and Brazil's Workers' Party (PT), respectively.

Initially, at least, things went fairly smoothly for Cardoso. The currency, the *real,* remained stable, and the president was able to kick-start the privatization process. One nagging economic problem remained—the large public sector deficit.

Cardoso focused largely on the stabilization and liberalization of the economy. Some critics argue that this left him little time or political capital to address Brazil's tremendous problems of poverty, illiteracy, and landlessness. Supporters respond that without stabilization, efforts to solve Brazil's deeper problems would simply have been wasted.

Fernando Henrique Cardoso managed in 1997 to push through an amendment to the constitution that allowed him to run for reelection. Difficulties would, however, begin to hit the next year, as financial crises, which started in Asia, made their way first to Russia and then to Brazil. Cardoso's economic team responded by raising interest rates and increasing taxes in a doomed attempt to save the currency. Capital flight surged, as Brazilians moved to protect their financial assets.

This climate of financial crisis permeated the elections that took place in October 1998, again pitting Cardoso against his foe Lula of the PT. Cardoso won the election with 53 percent of the vote. This time around, however, Cardoso was helped by voters' anxieties surrounding further financial crisis; many felt there was no alternative to Cardoso and his orthodox policies. After the election Cardoso and his team once again moved to cut public spending and hike interest rates and taxes, under strong pressure from the IMF. The country received $41.5 billion in credits from the U.S. government and international agencies, and at least for a time the capital flight slowed.

However, the crisis persisted into 1999, ironically significantly worsened by ex-president and then Minas Gerais governor, Itamar Franco, who announced that he would freeze his state's debt payments to the federal government. Capital flight again surged as investors worried about government insolvency. The government attempted a controlled devaluation of the currency of 8 percent; this failed, and the central bank had to let the currency float freely in the markets—after losing more than 40 percent of its value, the devaluation stabilized at a loss of around 25 percent.

Thankfully for Brazil, fears of a major recession and a return to high inflation proved unjustified. After a mild economic contraction, Brazil returned to growth, and inflation came well under control. Many consider Cardoso's second term to be somewhat disappointing, as no real headway was made in pushing through the much-needed economic reforms. He did, however, manage to pass an important fiscal responsibility law in May 2000 in attempts to avoid future government debt problems.

On the other hand, given Brazil's history of economic and political instability, the fact that Cardoso was able to tame Brazil's inflation, advance an important first round of reforms, survive a major devaluation, and pave the way for another round of democratic elections must be recognized as a very significant achievement. This is particularly the case since Cardoso handed the reigns of power over to the left, and specifically to Lula of the Workers' Party. Many supporters consider Fernando Henrique Cardoso to be the key player in Brazil's return to economic and political stability. In this sense his accomplishments should not be taken lightly.

LUÍZ INÁCIO LULA DA SILVA (2003–PRESENT)

The environment leading up to the 2002 elections was difficult, to say the least. Lula was running for the fourth time as the PT's presidential candidate, running against Cardoso's hand-picked successor, José Serra, Cardoso's minister of health and a personal friend.

Several issues complicated the elections and transition of power. First, the business community, both domestic and international, had severe reservations about Lula, but he maintained a consistent and comfortable lead in the preelection polls. Concerns included Lula's limited international experience and his lack of hands-on governing experience. There was also concern about the extent to which PT militants would influence a Lula presidency, pushing policy to the left. Furthermore, there was generalized anxiety about the future of economic liberalization, the environment for foreign direct investment, the potential for default on the huge government debt, and Brazil's role in hemispheric free trade. On top of this, Argentina's 2002 economic collapse spread to Brazil and Uruguay and necessitated the help of the IMF. The crisis played out both in Brazil's real economy (given Argentina's role as a major trading partner of Brazil's) and its financial markets, where interest rates spiked and the currency weakened.

While Lula pledged to play by the rules, few in the financial community believed a Lula presidency would be anything like Cardoso's. Most believed there would be a sharp lurch to the left, driven by party ideology rather than hands-on experience in government.

In the end, in a sign of strength for Brazil's democracy, Lula, rather than Cardoso's hand-picked candidate, won the election. In a clear mandate for change, Lula received 46.4 percent of the vote in the first round of the election versus 23.2 percent for José Serra. And in the second round, Lula received a whopping 61.4 percent of the vote, the largest percentage of any election in the country's history. Clearly, Lula received a strong mandate from the Brazilian people.

The early days of the Lula presidency proved the skeptics wrong, as Lula picked solid candidates to fill his cabinet as well as to run the central bank. For the business community, the two most important posts for government credibility were the head of the central bank and the minister of finance—and on these two Lula did not disappoint. The market reaction was quick and significant—the high rates of interest moderated and the currency strengthened. Both of these represented early signals of a growing trust that Lula would run the country based on pragmatism rather than ideology.

Unfortunately for Lula, his first term has turned out to be more difficult than probably expected. Lula was able to win a second presidential term in a second-round run-off in October 2006, but his administration has been hit by a number of corruption scandals. Revelations of corruption by the PT initially threw reelection prospects in doubt, caused gridlock in the Congress, and damaged Lula's reputation (not to mention forced Lula to fire his most important political aid). Importantly the scandals have damaged the PT, which was seen as the only clean party in Brazilian politics. This image helped to win over a substantial number of voters who had no taste for the PT's leftist policies. In turn, while Lula remains a strong and charismatic leader, many Brazilians no longer see Lula as the person who will be able to bring progress and reform— some even say that as a result of these scandals, Lula has lost a historic moment to transform Brazil. While such statements may be overly dramatic, there is no question that Lula has been weakened by the scandals.

In the immediate aftermath of the October 2006 elections it is too early to make any real judgments about Lula's two terms in office. However, at a minimum Lula can claim credit for low inflation and the maintenance of economic stability. Likewise, Brazil's current rate of economic growth is respectable, although it is one of the lowest of the world's developing nations, which are benefiting from global growth and strong commodity prices. The rate of job growth is also acceptable. Finally, Lula's use of cash transfers, among other targeted policies, is starting bring real benefits to the country's extreme poor. These achievements should not be underestimated.

However, the presidential elections have also underscored Brazil's tremendous diversity and its persistent inequalities, both between the rich and poor and between regions like the South-East and the Northeast. Lula is overwhelmingly popular in the country's poor Northeast, while he is significantly less popular in the relatively prosperous South and South-East. The division was illustrated during the run-up to the election by an anonymous e-mail circulating on the Internet entitled "The Solution is Separating."

The e-mail showed a map of Brazil in which the country was divided between the South and the North. The North showed a picture of Lula, with the caption, "They get him." The South showed a picture of Geraldo Alckmin, Lula's opponent from the PSDB, saying, "We get him." Lula's challenge in his second term will be a tough one—not only will he need to maintain economic stability and continue to deliver on his promises to the poor but he will also need to prove to the country's relatively prosperous groups that he can accelerate economic growth and modernization.

References and Further Readings

Alden, Dauril. "Late Colonial Brazil, 1750–1808," in Leslie Bethell (ed.), *The Cambridge History of Latin America, Vol. I.* Cambridge, U.K.: Cambridge University Press, 1984: 601–662.

Baer, Werner. *The Brazilian Economy: Growth and Development.* New York: Praeger Publishers, 1989.

Bethell, Leslie. "The Independence of Brazil," in Leslie Bethell (ed.), *The Cambridge History of Latin America, Vol. III.* Cambridge, U.K.: Cambridge University Press, 1985: 157–196.

Burns, Bradford E. *A History of Brazil,* 3rd ed. New York: Columbia University Press, 1971.

Conrad, Robert Edgar. *Children of God's Fire.* University Park: Pennsylvania State University Press, 1994.

Da Costa, Emilia Viotta. *The Brazilian Empire: Myths and Histories.* Chicago: University of Chicago Press, 1985.

Eakin, Marshall E. *Brazil: The Once and Future Country,* 2nd ed. New York: St. Martin's. Griffin, 1998.

Fausto, Boris. "Brazil: The Social and Political Structure of the First Republic, 1889–1930," in Leslie Bethell (ed.), *The Cambridge History of Latin America, Vol. V.* Cambridge, U.K.: Cambridge University Press, 1986: 779–830.

Fausto, Boris. *A Concise History of Brazil.* Cambridge, U.K.: Cambridge University Press, 1999.

Font, Mauricio. *Transforming Brazil: A Reform Era in Perspective.* Oxford, U.K.: Rowman and Littlefield, 2003.

Hemming, John. "The Indians of Brazil in 1500," in Leslie Bethell (ed.), *The Cambridge History of Latin America, Vol. I.* Cambridge, U.K.: Cambridge University Press, 1984: 119–144.

Johnson, H. B. "The Portuguese Settlement of Brazil, 1500–1580," in Leslie Bethell (ed.), *The Cambridge History of Latin America, Vol. I.* Cambridge, U.K.: Cambridge University Press, 1984: 249–286.

Levine, Robert M. *The History of Brazil.* Westport, CT: Greenwood Press, 1999.

MacLachlan, Colin M. *A History of Modern Brazil: The Past against the Future.* Wilmington, DE: Scholarly Resources, 2003.

Mauro, Frédéric. "Portugal and Brazil: Political and Economic Structures of Empire, 1580–1750," in Leslie Bethell (ed.), *The Cambridge History of Latin America, Vol. I.* Cambridge, U.K.: Cambridge University Press, 1984: 441–468.

Meade, Teresa A. *A Brief History of Brazil.* New York: Facts on File, 2003.

Moog, Vianna. *Bandeirantes and Pioneers.* New York: George Braziller, 1964.

Schneider, Ronald M. *"Order and Progress": A Political History of Brazil.* Boulder, CO: Westview Press, 1991.

Schwartz, Stuart B. "Colonial Brazil, c. 1580–1750: Plantations and Peripheries," in Leslie Bethell (ed.), *The Cambridge History of Latin America, Vol. II.* Cambridge, U.K.: Cambridge University Press, 1984: 423–500.

Silva, Andrée Mansuy-Diniz. "Portugal and Brazil: Imperial Re-Organization, 1750–1808," in Leslie Bethell (ed.), *The Cambridge History of Latin America, Vol. I.* Cambridge, U.K.: Cambridge University Press, 1984: 469–510.

Skidmore, Thomas E. *Politics in Brazil, 1930–1964.* New York: Oxford University Press, 1967.

Skidmore, Thomas E. *The Politics of Military Rule in Brazil: 1964–85.* New York: Oxford University Press, 1988.

Skidmore, Thomas E. *Brazil: Five Centuries of Change.* Oxford, U.K.: Oxford University Press, 1999.

Skidmore, Thomas E., and Peter H. Smith. *Modern Latin America.* New York: Oxford University Press, 2001.

CHAPTER TWO

The Brazilian Economy

INTRODUCTION

By most measures, today's Brazilian' economy is among the
ten largest economies in the world, with many pegging it at
number nine currently. Gross domestic product (GDP),
which adds up a country's final goods and services not directly
transformed into other goods and services, is likely to have
reached $605 billion in 2005, the largest economic output in
Latin America. Brazil is typically classified as a middle
income country, although given the degree of poverty and
income inequality, most also consider the country a developing nation. Brazil's modern economy is diversified, although
with dramatic variations in the level of development in different regions.

Most of the country's heavy industry is concentrated in the
South-East and South, while the Northeast has traditionally
been the poorest region, since the sugar boom went bust in
colonial times. It is estimated that the 2004 GDP per capita
was $8,100, but as suggested income distribution is highly
uneven; Brazil has been consistently cited as one of the most
unequal societies in the world. Some 37 percent of the population lives below the poverty line.

Dividing GDP by sector, roughly 10 percent of Brazil's output comes from agriculture, 39 percent from industry, and
51 percent from services. Of the labor force, 20 percent is
dedicated to agriculture, 14 percent to industry, and 66 percent to services such as banking and insurance. Brazil's
industrial sector is diversified and is the most advanced in
Latin America. Industries include automobiles and parts,

An impoverished woman stands in the doorway of her shack in Recife, Brazil. (Viviane Moos/Corbis)

steel, petrochemicals, chemicals, aircraft, iron ore, and consumer durables, among others.

Brazilian agriculture, while representing a relatively small proportion of the GDP, has undergone dramatic growth and transformation in recent years; the country is endowed with tremendous agricultural resources. After centuries of monocultural booms and busts, in which the economy was dedicated to the export of one main commodity, most notably sugar and coffee, agriculture witnessed both relative neglect and exploitation to extract resources for rapid industrialization and to provide cheap food for urban workers. This has changed dramatically since the early 1990s as Brazilian agriculture has diversified and boomed. Brazil has emerged as the world's largest exporter of beef, coffee, orange juice, and sugar, and it is closing in fast on the leaders in soybeans, poultry, and pork. Other products include tobacco, cocoa, forest products, and tropical fruits and nuts. Unlike many countries, Brazil is by no means running out of land; without hurting the Amazon, Brazil still has huge expanses of land that could be dedicated to agriculture.

The service sector is also diverse and sophisticated, including a large and overhauled banking sector. Brazil is one of the few large countries in Latin America in which the banking sector is dominated by local players. In contrast, for example, Mexico's largest banks are owned by foreign—American and Spanish—multinational banks.

Brazil's government has made a huge push to reduce the country's dependence on imported oil; it now represents only about one-third of the country's oil needs, and many argue that Brazil will be self-sufficient in the very near future. The country has developed an impressive ethanol program that capitalizes on the country's huge sugar production; cars in Brazil use a mixture of gasoline and ethanol, a development that is even more interesting now that the United States is trying to develop alternative energy sources. The country is one of the world's leading producers of hydroelectric power. Existing hydroelectric power provides as much as 90 percent of the country's electricity; the massive Itaipú Dam on the Paraná River is the largest dam in the world. Brazil also has three nuclear reactors.

Brazil's mineral resources are also impressive. Huge iron and manganese reserves provide both raw materials for industry and important exports. For example, iron ore is used for domestic steel production and is exported in huge quantities. Other mineral resources include nickel, tin, chromite, bauxite, copper, lead, zinc, and gold. Coal needed for the steel industry, on the other hand, is in relatively short supply.

Brazil is still a somewhat closed economy, the legacy of decades of state-led policies pushing closed economic borders to support domestic industries. To illustrate, despite being a top-ten global economy, Brazil accounts for only around 1 percent of global trade; its average tariffs also continue to exceed other developing economies. However, Brazil's international trade has grown dramatically in recent years, as the closed development model has shifted to more liberal trade policies. Brazil's top export partners are the United States, Europe, Argentina, and China. Likewise, imports to Brazil primarily originate in the United States, Europe, Argentina, Japan, and China.

These descriptive statistics and qualitative descriptions should give the reader a snapshot of the contemporary Brazilian economy. At a minimum they will hopefully help underscore the dimensions and complexity of this enormous economy.

GROWTH VERSUS DEVELOPMENT

We have already defined GDP as simply a way to measure the total market value of a country's goods and services. In order to correct for the impact of inflation, economists also measure real GDP, which identifies the true economic output of an economy by correcting for changes in prices. One way to compare global economies is to simply look at the absolute size of real GDP; some might even argue "the bigger the better."

However, looking only at the size of an economy can mask important details. Most significantly, a nation's people can become better off only if their country's real GDP grows faster than its population grows. In fact, many economists define modern economic growth as the long-term growth in average real GDP per person. Qualitatively, modern economic growth involves the systematic application of scientific and technical knowledge to economic pursuits, in the process developing and transforming agriculture, industry, and commerce.

While this description of modern economic growth is important, focusing specifically on growth may miss important components of the economic development process—in fact, many have argued that it misses a large part of today's world, where modern economic growth is absent. In general, there has been a shift over time in analysis from a pure focus on growth to a more general focus on development. This shift includes qualitative assessments and value judgments. For example, more and more qualitative assessments of development include explicit calls for the elimination of poverty and the alleviation of income inequality.

The concepts of growth and development are not mutually exclusive. Modern societies typically strive for both growth and equity. But before digging deeper into the subject of Brazil, it is important to point out that Brazil specifically represents a case of growth *without* equity. At a minimum, Brazil underscores the fact that growth of per-capita product alone is not enough to achieve economic development; specific qualitative goals—like poverty reduction and lessening of inequality—must also be targeted.

In this sense, modern Brazil presents a fascinating window into these complicated issues. Having pursued rapid economic growth, which in many ways exacerbated inequality, the Brazilian economy entered a difficult phase characterized by high inflation and low growth (and an enormous foreign debt). As we shall see, the Cardoso era was dedicated to overhauling the economy, but many argued that not enough attention was paid to problems of poverty and inequality. More recently, President Lula has pledged to retain mainstream economic policies, but he has also promised to try to reduce poverty and income inequality.

OVERVIEW

Brazil, like the rest of Latin America, experienced a long colonial history as a territory of Portugal. Unlike the rest of Spanish America, though, it initially appeared to possess neither dramatic mineral wealth nor densely populated native populations. As such, it was relatively neglected by Portugal. The country's economy developed primarily as an agricultural exporter, with an early emphasis on sugar. While we will look at Brazil's sugar boom in more depth below, this represented just the first in a string of so-called monocultural export cycles.

The discovery of gold in 1690 set off a tremendous gold rush in Brazil, and another export cycle. Importantly, the development of the gold industry acted both to shift the economic and political center of the colony from the Northeast to the South-East and to spur a more intensive exploration of the country's huge interior. The tremendous mineral wealth in Brazil led Portugal to focus much more on the colony, not in the least to make sure the mother country received her fair share of the windfall.

This would lead to growing resentment in Brazil, especially as the colony became more important economically than Portugal itself. As discussed in chapter one, these tensions did not develop into an independence movement due to unusual historical developments—namely that the French invasion of Portugal led the royal family to move the seat of the empire to Brazil. This eventually led to a relatively nonviolent independence in 1822, avoiding the massive physical and economic destruction seen in the Spanish American countries (not to mention the period of violent political struggle following independence).

Brazil's role in the nineteenth century was straightforward. The country produced a few agricultural commodities for export and used the foreign exchange it earned to buy manufactured products from the more advanced economies. In effect, the defining economic policy was free trade. The biggest commercial crop for most of the century was sugar; however, the development of the coffee industry played a much more important role in defining the direction of the nineteenth-century Brazilian economy, as it turned into the engine of growth.

The nineteenth century would see the very beginnings of industry as well as a growing role of the government in the Brazilian economy. Early industrial growth would continue into the 1920s, fueled by the steady expansion of the coffee sector and heavy immigration of free labor. Still, agriculture remained the leading sector of the economy.

Industrialization began in the 1930s, accompanied by significant structural changes in the Brazilian economy.

Specifically, industry became the leading growth sector. And government increased dramatically its role in the economy, including efforts to intervene in the coffee sector. A phase of "spontaneous industrialization" began in the mid- to late 1930s, strengthened by additional forms of state intervention in the late 1930s (import controls, quotas, etc.). The state then began active public investment in industries and infrastructure, leading to a new phase of active industrialization. We will discuss below the role various external shocks—like the world wars and the Great Depression—played in the industrialization process.

By the 1950s, Brazilian officials became convinced of the need to diversify the economy and consciously industrialize; in essence industrialization became the government's principal tool to increase the growth of the economy. At this point perhaps the most salient feature of Brazil's postwar economic history was the dramatic increase in government participation in the process of economic development. The principal mechanism was import-substitution industrialization (ISI), in which international trade was restricted so Brazil could begin producing the industrial goods it had previously imported.

As we know, while rapid growth was achieved, economic and political instability grew by the early 1960s, ultimately resulting in the end of civilian rule and twenty years of military government. After a brief period of relatively orthodox economic policies, the military expanded further still the government's role in directing the economy. The military years would see strong growth, rising inequality, growing foreign debt, and ultimately economic chaos. Ironically the military, which had taken power to assert control over the economy, left power in the midst of economic crisis largely based on a failed model of state-led development.

The 1980s witnessed both political transition back to democracy and ongoing economic difficulties, underscored most importantly by the debt crisis and the so-called lost decade it generated. Brazil's generals had borrowed heavily to finance their huge development program, and in the 1970s this borrowing came cheap. The world changed as the second oil crisis led to a dramatic rise in global interest rates and ultimately global recession.

Brazil simultaneously faced a dramatic rise in the price of oil imports, a big rise in its foreign debt service (most of its massive foreign debt was at floating interest rates, and so adjusted upward), and falling demand (and prices) for its exports. The end result was default on the foreign debt and economic crisis. The first three civilian presidents proved incapable of solving Brazil's economic crisis; multiple stabilization programs were attempted, and all failed. Brazil's rate of inflation reached astronomical rates.

It can be argued that the economic chaos of the 1980s and early 1990s laid the foundation for a new development model—ISI and state-led development had clearly failed. While Brazil lagged in the region in moving to more market-oriented policies, these gained momentum with the appointment of Fernando Henrique Cardoso as finance minister for President Itamar Franco in 1993. Cardoso and his team created the first successful stabilization plan in Brazil since 1964, the Real Plan.

The success of the Real Plan catapulted Cardoso to the presidency, and he would begin an attempt to create a new development model for the country. While many of Cardoso's ambitious reform goals were not met, reflecting both political resistance in Brazil and a number of external economic shocks, the economic achievements were impressive. His achievements are particularly notable when contrasted with the resounding economic failures preceding him.

As mentioned, one of the main criticisms of the Cardoso administration was that it focused excessively on stabilization and macroeconomic reform, with relative neglect of poverty alleviation and the reduction of income inequality. At least in part Lula was elected to move the policy agenda in this direction. On this score, Lula's administration is still a work in progress.

THE COLONIAL ECONOMY

The Portuguese claim to Brazil came under the Treaty of Tordesillas in 1494 and originally represented mostly the northeastern coast of modern-day Brazil. The Portuguese began their explorations at roughly the same time as the Spanish were conquering Mexico and Peru. Unlike the Spanish, who encountered large settled populations, the Portuguese encountered indigenous groups that were relatively small and dispersed. Likewise, since the native populations had not developed an interest in precious metals, Brazil's huge deposits of precious minerals would lay untouched for nearly 200 years after discovery.

As a result of these two factors, Brazil was not seen as a rich prize by the Portuguese—there was no windfall gain like the Spanish received; thus development in Brazil would occur relatively gradually. The earliest economic activity centered on the collection and exportation of brazilwood (*pau-Brasil*), from which the country derived its name. Valued in Europe as a dye for use in the growing textile industry, the wood attracted the French to Brazil. Not surprisingly, the French interest in Brazil did not sit well with the Portuguese—in fact it motivated Portugal's rulers in the 1530s to stimulate the colonization of Brazil to better secure its claim to the territory.

Brazil's Sugar Cycle

The Crown allocated huge tracts of land to a relatively small group of settlers, and sugar rapidly became the single most important cash crop for the colony. Since the indigenous population was insufficient to serve as labor on the sugar plantations, a massive importation of African slaves began by the late 1500s. The importation of slave labor enabled Brazil to become the largest producer of sugar in the world by the mid-1600s, and considerable economic prosperity was created in the process (although the lion's share of the benefits went to a small minority; for the rest, sugar production was an unpleasant, often brutal activity). The rapid growth of the sugar trade turned into the first of Brazil's numerous primary export cycles, which would define the country's economic growth until the twentieth century.

Brazil's advantageous position was not to last, however. The Dutch unsuccessfully attempted to invade and occupy Brazil's Northeast in 1624 in order to control the sugar trade. While they managed to establish themselves for a time, they were ultimately repelled by locals. After their defeat the Dutch set up their own sugar plantations in the Caribbean, as did the English and the French. The resulting competition eroded Brazil's market power and sent the world price of sugar tumbling by the end of the 1600s. Brazil also lost access to European markets, as colonial powers gave preferential treatment to their respective colonies.

Importantly, the scarcity of labor and the seemingly limited economic benefits offered by Brazil to Portugal meant that early organization of the colony was relatively decentralized; trade for the most part was left to private parties, and while a governor-general was appointed to rule from Salvador in the mid-sixteenth century, affairs were typically handled at the local level. The general policy guidelines were crafted in Portugal, but interpretation and implementation were left to the governors and municipal councils—and the latter were dominated by powerful owners of large plantations and sugar mills.

Brazil's Northeast was ideal for sugar, with good growing conditions and a location suited both to receive slaves from Africa and ship sugar to Europe. The main economic linkage was with the interior of the Northeast, whose surplus agricultural output helped feed people in the plantation zone. A number of prominent Brazilian economists—Celso Furtado was one of the first and most well-known—have pointed out the sharp differences between Brazil's early productive structure and that developed in England's colonies in North Amer-

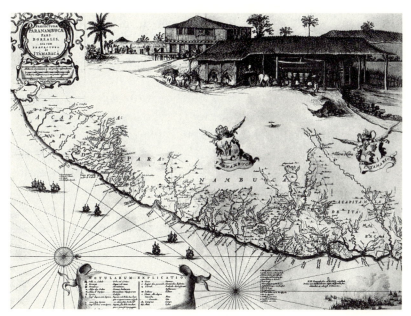

A seventeenth-century map of Pernambuco, Brazil, with a vignette of a sugar plantation. In 1630, the Dutch West India Company seized Pernambuco to control the lucrative sugar district. (Library of Congress)

ica. The latter consisted in large part of small agricultural properties, while Brazil's sugar exports depended on huge plantations. Income in North America was therefore more evenly distributed, allowing the development of an internal market early on in the colonies' existence (laying the foundation, in turn, for early development of commerce and industry). By contrast, the concentration of property and income left Brazil's colonial economic structure relatively stagnant.

From roughly 1580 to 1680, then, Brazil was the world's largest producer and exporter of sugar, and it was in this context that colonial society was developed. Estimates put Brazil's population around 1580 at 60,000, with half being European. The colony was based on the plantation. It was also capitalized by Europe and supplied European demand for its tropical crop.

In turn, the labor system was based on slavery—first of native populations and later of imported African slaves. Most economists conclude that the sugar export cycle was, on the whole, negative for Brazil. Economic organization and production techniques were fairly primitive, and slavery inhibited any sort of development of human resources. Likewise, the distribution of land and income was extremely concentrated. finally, much of the profit from sugar was spent on imported consumer goods rather than on upgrading technology or infrastructure. After the boom the Northeast entered a period of relative decline; sugar plantations did not disappear, but the crop never again regained its former prominence.

The Gold Boom

At about the time that Brazil's economy was suffering from the loss of sugar revenues, in 1690, gold was discovered in what is now the state of Minas Gerais. Huge amounts of gold were discovered, sparking a gold rush that was augmented by the discovery of diamonds in 1729. The revenues generated by the two were tremendous, driving an era of unprecedented wealth that would last into the second half of the eighteenth century. Not surprisingly, the Portuguese Crown took renewed interest in Brazil, moving to increase control of trade as well as taxing output (in the same way the Spanish had done earlier in their American colonies).

It is important to note that before the discovery of gold, Portuguese mercantilist policies had been less constraining to Brazil than Spanish policies had been elsewhere in the region. Mercantilist policies focused on accumulating bullion and establishing colonies; mercantilism fell out of favor by the mid-eighteenth century as the benefits of the industrial revolution became more apparent. But mercantilist policies would continue to impact Brazil's economy for some time.

The previous lack of mineral wealth meant that agriculture was the foundation of the colonial economy—and the basis of Portuguese taxation. The Crown promoted the various crops and believed that diversification of the colonial economy was an important way to defend its claim to Brazil. Still, the Portuguese monopolized the most important export industries and prohibited any economic pursuits that might compete with Portuguese products (e.g., wine production).

While direct trade with Africa was allowed for slaves, the rest of Brazil's trade was restricted to Portuguese ports; however, given the large number of ships trading in the South Atlantic, it was hard for the Portuguese to enforce their restrictions, and contraband trade flourished. As mentioned, the discovery of gold and diamonds caused the Portuguese to tighten up their control of Brazil—they went as far as prohibiting all manufacturing in Brazil in 1785.

Portugal's power to monopolize trade in its South American colony was forever altered in 1703 by the Treaty of Metheun with England, which allowed the British access to Portugal and its colonies in return for favorable treatment of Portuguese products, such as wine, in Britain. The treaty, combined with rapidly growing Brazilian demand for manufactured goods during the gold rush, led to significant and growing British involvement in Brazil's eighteenth-century economy. While the improved access to English manufactured goods reduced Brazilian impatience with Portuguese controls, it also signified a move away from colonial control toward more independent trading.

Compared with the preceding sugar cycle, the gold boom produced significant economic linkages. For example, the rising demand for food acted as an impulse to agriculture. Likewise, pack animals were needed for transportation. In turn there was growing demand for imports, both of consumer goods and mining supplies. However, because goods that could be supplied to the colony by the mother country were not allowed to be produced in Brazil, local manufacturing remained in a very primitive state. In fact, transportation was purposely kept in a rudimentary state by the Portuguese to better control smuggling.

Not everyone in Brazil was pleased with the newly discovered mineral wealth. Specifically, the gold discoveries represented a threat to the Northeast, with many municipal councils pointing their fingers at the gold rush as the source of their economic woes. In particular they argued that mining siphoned away whites and free men of color, who otherwise could have been involved in the Northeastern agricultural economy. Another problem concerned slaves—since the miners could pay higher prices, and pay in cash, there was a shift in slave labor away from the Northeast toward the mining regions. Importantly, mining, and the internal migration it caused from the coast to the interior, also stimulated urbanization, which agriculture had failed to do for the preceding two centuries.

Significantly, the gold boom caused Rio de Janeiro to boom as well, resulting in its emergence as a major Brazilian port— in fact the main port for the export of minerals and the import of manufactured goods from Europe. This shift was significant to Brazil's development. In 1763 the viceregal capital of Brazil was even transferred from Salvador to Rio de Janeiro. The shift represented, in part, Portuguese efforts to tighten their administrative control of the colony (not in the least to ensure the payment of one-fifth of the mineral wealth to the Crown).

Importantly, despite the attempts to tighten control of the colony, the population movement west, the opening of new territory, and the development of mining itself stretched administrative resources considerably. In fact, large segments of the colonial population lived beyond effective control of the Crown, and popular challenges to Crown authority grew as a result. Another dramatic change occurred as the colony became wealthier than the mother country; gold wealth gave the demands of miners greater weight than those of planters. And demands were increasing, reflecting simultaneously

Baroque church in Ouro Preto in the state of Minas Gerais, Brazil. In the late-seventeenth century gold was discovered in Ouro Preto, spurring intense mine exploration and a subsequent surge of wealth. (Rogério Medeiros Pinho)

growing populations, increased urbanization, and stronger purchasing power of the free population.

The gold boom, like the sugar cycle before it, ultimately came to an end. For gold the end came toward the end of the eighteenth century, as key mines became exhausted. The population of Minas Gerais shifted to other occupations, especially agriculture, as well as migrated to other parts of the country, but the boom was over. However, to this day a legacy of the tremendous mining wealth remains in the churches of Minas Gerais, with their carved pulpits, painted ceilings, and even alters covered with gold leaf serving as remaining symbols of Brazil's golden age.

The Waning Years of Colonial Brazil

Napoleon's invasion and occupation of Portugal in 1807 led the Portuguese royal family, under the protection of the British, to sail for Brazil, at which point the capital of the Portuguese Empire was established in Rio de Janeiro in 1808. The court's move to Brazil brought with it significant creation of jobs, which had a positive impact on both the service and nascent manufacturing sectors. Combined with major construction projects to improve the city's infrastructure, the net effect was to stimulate economic growth.

The Crown, once based in Brazil, scrapped the stifling mercantilist controls on trade, resulting in significant growth in trade. The Crown's arrival resulted in a number of additional benefits to Brazil. For example, the printing press was brought over for the first time, and higher educational facilities, previously in scarce supply, were established. In turn, the Portuguese rulers imported technicians and scientists and tried to stimulate industry. Unfortunately, the attempts to grow industry failed, in large part due to the flood of English manufactured goods.

The monarch returned to Portugal in 1821, leaving his son as regent. It then became increasingly apparent that Portugal intended to return Brazil to the second-class status it held before the Crown relocated to the colony. Locals voiced increasing discontent, leading the regent to declare Brazil's independence in 1822. Brazil then formed an independent monarchy, which lasted until 1889, ruled first by Dom Pedro I and then by Dom Pedro II, who assumed power after a nine-year regency lasting from 1831 to 1840.

BRAZIL'S POSTINDEPENDENCE ECONOMY

Perhaps the most important difference between Brazil and the rest of Latin America in the era of independence was the relatively nonviolent nature of Brazil's independence. First, the economy avoided the destruction seen in other countries during wars of independence. In addition, the country managed to stay together as a distinct country, rather than breaking up into separate countries, again as happened in Spanish America (many point out that boundary disputes and violent internal conflict in Spanish America between 1830 and 1850 hurt their economies as much as Spanish taxes and restrictive trade policies had before independence). One year after independence, Brazil's population was estimated to be 3.9 million people, with 1.2 million being slaves.

The world economic order at the time was dominated by Great Britain, and Brazil fit well into the economic system. Britain represented the dominant economy of the newly industrializing world and exchanged manufactured products for food and raw materials from the "periphery," which was made up of largely agricultural and/or extractive economies like Brazil. As a typical peripheral economy, Brazil depended on a major primary export product (by this time coffee) and a few minor products (such as sugar, cotton, and cocoa).

During this period, Brazil's economy was open to European, mainly British, manufactured products. Likewise, it was open to foreign, mainly British, capital. This foreign investment targeted attractive opportunities to build the commercial, financial, and transportation infrastructure necessary to link Brazil to the global economic order of the nineteenth century.

Not only was England the key player in this economic order but it was also Brazil's protector as a new nation. This protection did not come cheap; Brazil was forced to pay Portugal's debt to the English that was incurred fighting against Brazilian independence. The British also pushed for preferential tariffs and made Brazil commit to ending slavery (although this promise would take some time to fulfill).

In short, after Brazil declared independence from the Portuguese, the British filled the void, becoming the dominant foreign player in Brazil's economy, actively pursuing both trade and direct investment. The British played a dominant role in arenas such as banking, insurance, and shipping. As some historians suggest, Brazil passed from direct control by the Portuguese Crown to the British sphere of influence, involved in a more indirect relationship often referred to as "informal imperialism."

During this time period, the United States also began a process of rapid industrialization that created growing demand for Brazil's raw materials and tropical commodities; by midcentury Brazil's exports were dominated by coffee.

Brazil's Coffee Cycle

The key to Brazil's coffee cycle—like sugar and gold before it, another example of Brazil's historical dependence on single commodity exports—was the rapid improvement in living standards in the industrializing world (specifically in Europe and the United States). This improvement, based on the industrial revolution, led to rapid growth in the demand for coffee. While coffee had been introduced in Brazil as early as the eighteenth century, it did not take off until the nineteenth century. By the middle of the century coffee was the main export item of Brazil. In fact, by the 1890s coffee had grown to account for 63 percent of Brazil's exports. Up to the late 1800s coffee production techniques were rudimentary, relying, for example, on mule trains and based on slave labor that

Gathering coffee on a Brazilian plantation, about 1870. (Mary Evans Picture Library/The Image Works)

remained outside the money economy. Plantation owners were powerful politically, perpetuating the status quo.

Early coffee production in Brazil centered on the Paraíba valley, relatively close to Rio de Janeiro, but these lands were increasingly exhausted by the 1880s. As a result coffee production migrated south to the rich lands of São Paulo, and then westward within the state. Importantly, by the 1860s construction of railroads had begun, and the rail lines would increase dramatically over time. In fact, by 1890 the amount of coffee passing through Santos, the closest port to the city of São Paulo, was equal to that exported from Rio. By 1894 Santos became the most important coffee export center in the world.

The westward expansion within the state of São Paulo led to the establishment of huge coffee estates (few small landholders had the resources needed to prosper in this line of business). While early coffee production was based on slave labor, São Paulo's planters increasingly turned to free laborers. And while European immigration was promoted before

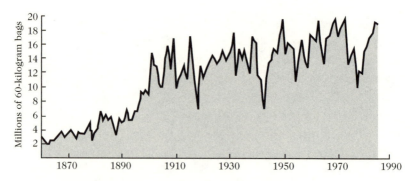

The key role of coffee exports.

slavery was abolished in 1888, its end resulted in a huge wave of European immigration.

It is clear that throughout the nineteenth century, exports of coffee were the engine of Brazilian economic growth. While the development started closer to Rio, the coffee economy shifted in the direction of São Paulo. Just as the gold cycle caused the economic center of the country to shift from the Northeast southward to Rio and Minas Gerais, so the coffee cycle drove the economy to move to São Paulo. The region remains the economy's center to this day.

Economists point out that Brazil's coffee economy exacerbated regional inequalities, in particular between the Northeast and the Center-South. The dynamic impact of free immigrant labor, investment in the infrastructure, and accumulation of capital by coffee plantation owners led to rapid development of the Center-South, while the Northeast stagnated.

Another issue deserves discussion, as it links the growth of the coffee industry to Brazil's poverty and income inequality—landownership. By the 1850s the growth of commercial agricultural exports, particularly coffee exports, made landownership more lucrative than ever. In turn, heightened immigration of free workers from Europe led landowners to try to figure out ways to keep wage laborers on their plantations, rather than see them settle in abundant unused land.

Brazil's answer to the conundrum was a law passed in 1850 decreeing that public land could be obtained by purchase only from the government or by paying taxes to regularize land agreements already made. The net effect of the law was to make access to land more difficult for small landholders.

The law thus favored large landowners, especially those involved in commercial exports, and most economic historians argue that this was precisely the law's intent (in other words, to promote the country's large plantations and their agricultural exports). There were some calls at the time to tax unused lands, in part to reduce the power of the large landholders, but these were effectively blocked.

Brazil's 1850 law contrasts dramatically with United States history. Twelve years after Brazil implemented measures to make small landholdings difficult to acquire, the United States passed the Homestead Act of 1861, which encouraged small landholders by making land grants to farmers who promised to actively cultivate their land. Brazil's chosen path reverberates today, as it institutionalized the concentration of land ownership, a contributing factor to the persisting economic inequality.

The Rubber Boom

Coffee reigned supreme among Brazil's nineteenth-century exports, but other exports did make their way to world markets. Among the most important were cotton, tobacco, and cacao. The country also witnessed a tremendous boom in the last decades of the nineteenth century in rubber exports. The boom took place in the Amazon basin—Brazil at the time was the world's main source of natural rubber, and demand for the product was ballooning in the early days of automobile production. Brazil's rubber exports grew from some 6,000 tons in the 1870s to 21,000 tons in the 1890s to a remarkable 35,000 tons in the first decade of the twentieth century.

By this time, Brazil supplied around 90 percent of the world's rubber, but the boom would unfortunately turn into a crash. At some point in the 1870s seeds from rubber trees were smuggled out of Brazil (most point to the British), and by 1895 rubber plantations were started in Asia. By 1899 Asian rubber hit the world market. The rapid growth in the supply of rubber on the world market by the 1920s caused a deep decline in prices. Remarkably, by 1921 rubber prices were one-sixth their 1910 levels, leaving Brazil unable to compete with the much cheaper Asian rubber. As a result Brazil lost its entire share of the world rubber market. While the boom was spectacular, leading to dramatic displays of conspicuous consumption (including the building of a famous opera house in the jungle city of Manaus), it had little long-term impact on the Brazilian economy.

The Manaus opera theater was built in 1896 and reflects the massive wealth created by the turn-of-the-century rubber boom. The theater was featured prominently in Werner Herzog's film Fitzcarraldo *(1982). (Wolfgang Kaehler/Corbis).*

GOVERNMENT AND THE ECONOMY IN NINETEENTH-CENTURY BRAZIL

Many of Brazil's early industrialization efforts were unsuccessful due to policies keeping the economy open to industrial imports from Europe, and especially Britain. However, one major developmental stride was taken in the second half of the nineteenth century, as the government actively promoted railroad construction. The government supported the process using subsidies and guaranteed rates of return—most of the lines were built by British firms. While the effort represented an important step forward in Brazil's economic development, there were a number of problems. For example, different rail lines were built using different gauges. As a result, transportation was improved, but Brazil failed to build a linked transportation system that could create a more unified national market.

Another government initiative concerned immigration—throughout the nineteenth century the government had intermittently promoted immigration and colonization. With the end of slavery in 1888 (followed by the establishment of the republic in 1889), a wave of immigration to Brazil's South began; this would have a positive impact on the economy.

By the end of the nineteenth century the government also grew more active in promoting Brazilian exports, guaranteeing earnings and offering import tariff exemptions for equipment imports. São Paulo state also began to get involved in coffee production, starting in 1908 the first of Brazil's "valorization" plans. In effect, the state would buy up large amounts of coffee and withhold it from the world market in order to stabilize prices.

BRAZIL'S EARLY INDUSTRIAL GROWTH

Latin America in general saw economic expansion between 1880 and 1910, the so-called golden age of export-led growth.

That growth supported early efforts to industrialize; for example, textile factories, food packing plants, processing plants for exports, and plants for construction materials started up to meet growing demand. At the same time, growing government bureaucracies, transportation services, financial markets, and other service-oriented jobs drew Brazilians to the cities. This golden age of export-led growth, accompanied by early industrialization, would break down by World War I. Brazil's experience during the two world wars, and the Great Depression in between, would irrevocably change the direction of its economic development in the years to come.

Early industrialization in Brazil became significant around the 1880s, and then continued to expand for the subsequent three decades. The early period of industrial growth was dominated by light industries, like textiles, food industries, clothing, and shoes. In effect, the driving force was the coffee boom based on free wage labor, much of this founded on immigrants. There was substantial investment in infrastructure to service the coffee sector—railroads, power stations, and so forth. This investment was financed by both domestic planters and foreign investors and supported growing local industries.

Significantly, the large and growing immigrant population in the coffee (and coffee-related) sector provided an important and growing market for inexpensive, locally produced consumer goods. Many early Brazilian industrialists began as importers, who at some point figured out they could make attractive profits by locally producing the goods they were importing.

Like other commodity booms of the past, the coffee export boom supporting early industrialization also experienced busts—most importantly in the early twentieth century. The downturn was primarily the result of Brazilian overproduction as well as the fact that other countries, like Colombia, began producing coffee. At its prime, however, Brazil was the largest coffee producer in the world, producing as much as 75 percent of the world's coffee from 1900 to 1911. As a result, Brazil used its market power in an attempt to manipulate the price of coffee using the valorization schemes mentioned above. While the move was started by governors in coffee-producing states, it was soon taken over by the federal government. This was an early sign that Brazilians were increasingly willing to use the power of the government to shape market outcomes.

World War I

There is considerable debate about the impact of World War I on Brazil's economy. A number of economists and economic historians have argued that the war acted as a major catalyst to industrial growth. More recent studies suggest that this is not the case. Rather than prompt industrial growth, the interruption to shipping caused by the war made it exceedingly difficult to import the capital goods Brazil would have needed to increase its productive capacity. Brazil at the time was simply incapable of producing these types of goods. So rather than causing any expansion or change in Brazil's industrial capacity, the war most likely led to an increase in the utilization of existing capacity that had been created in the years leading up to the war.

In fact, the argument has been taken one step further, to suggest that the drop in important capital imports caused by the war most likely delayed Brazil's industrialization. But an important change did take place due to the war: Brazil was able to accumulate significant amounts of foreign exchange during wartime. These foreign reserves were used after the war to help finance a sharp increase in capital goods imports after 1918.

The 1920s

Economic expansion in the 1920s was based on booming coffee exports. Coffee's share of exports rose from 56 percent in

1919 to more than 75 percent in 1924. Industry resumed its growth, albeit at a relatively slow rate. Several factors supported industrial growth, including government assistance given to firms in new sectors such as tax exemptions for equipment imports. Foreign investors also contributed to the growth of industry, entering areas like steel and cement. Domestic firms, like repair shops, which had expanded their activities during the war years, also reinvested their profits following the war to expand capacity. Still, industrial growth was slow and steady—Brazil's great boom would come later.

The 1920s witnessed a dramatic change in the global economic order, as Great Britain experienced relative decline compared to the United States and Germany—foreign investments from the latter would grow dramatically as a result. Global prices for Brazil's commodity exports were strong, allowing the country to effectively double its imports of capital goods, the foundation of industrialization. In essence, then, Brazil was diversifying away from its traditional dependence on agriculture, using commodity export earnings to build industrial capacity.

The relatively prosperous times came to an end in 1929 with the collapse of the world economy. For Brazil, this meant a drop in coffee export earnings of 50 percent in the short period between September 1929 and January 1930. The country also lost all of its foreign reserves, as Brazilians cashed in local currency for gold, dollars, and sterling. Brazil was facing bleak times, as the collapse in the industrialized world left few options for recovery in the periphery.

The Great Depression

Brazil seemed to have little in the way of options to drive recovery. Ironically, however, Brazil did not comply with conventional prescriptions of the time, which suggested cutting government spending and balancing the budget. One very important area of government spending was the policy of buying excess coffee stocks—the valorization policies. The program's net result was an expansion of the money supply and a stimulus to overall demand. This would lead to an earlier and stronger economic recovery in Brazil than in the United States—it would also serve as a new stimulus to urbanization. But first, let's look at economic conditions during the great depression.

The most immediate impact of the stock market crash of 1929 and the ensuing depression was a severe shock to the price of Brazil's exports, which fell precipitously. The lack of foreign exchange earnings, coupled with the need to service external debt, forced the government to take drastic actions, including suspending service on some of its foreign debt. Brazil was the first country in the region to implement foreign exchange controls. The country was also forced to devalue its currency.

The sharp decline in imports coupled with inflated domestic demand reflecting the coffee support program led to a shortage of manufactured goods and a rise in their prices compared with other goods in the economy. This proved to be an important catalyst to industrial production. Just as industrial growth in World War I reflected growth in the use of existing capacity, growth in the first half of the 1930s was |generated by increased capacity utilization. However, by the second half of the 1930s, industrial growth was increasingly supported by the expansion of capacity.

World War II

Similar to the years corresponding to World War I and the first half of the 1930s, World War II saw an important increase in economic output. However, this advance was again based on the more intensive use of existing capacity. Except for the cement and steel industries, the war years saw little in the way of expanding industrial capacity. As a result, by the end of the war Brazil's existing industrial capacity was deteriorating, with much equipment having become obsolete. The war years did see growth in Brazil's manufactured exports, such as textiles. However, as the war ended and traditional sources of supply returned to world markets, Brazil's manufactured exports essentially disappeared.

THE POSTWAR PUSH TO INDUSTRIALIZE

Economists tend to distinguish between industrial growth and industrialization. Industrial growth applies to Brazil up through the 1920s, when the growth of industry essentially depended on the growth of agricultural exports. While industry grew steadily, there was no real structural reshaping of the economy. In turn, the argument goes, industrialization takes place when industry becomes the leading sector of the economy, with concomitant structural changes in the economy. In Brazil's case, in the 1930s industry became the leading sector of the economy, with a dramatic increase in its influence on Brazilian economic growth. Growing diversification of industry led it to become the locomotive of the Brazilian economy.

It is important to note that until the 1930s, Brazil's government did not actively try to plan the country's economic development, including its industrial development (the coffee support program is a notable exception). The 1930s and 1940s would usher in new systematic analyses and evaluations of the Brazilian economy. For example, the Neimeyer report in the early 1930s was the first to point out that Brazil's main economic weakness was its dependence on the export of one or two commodities. The Cooke Mission followed in 1943, in a joint effort between the United States and Brazil to examine Brazil's role in the allied war effort. The mission also pointed out Brazil's structural weaknesses and obstacles to development. Still, these had little influence on the direction of Brazilian policy.

However, the war greatly accelerated the process of economic centralization; for example, the need to ration supplies like petroleum put new power in the hands of President Getúlio Vargas. Vargas wanted both to build a strong central government and to push an ambitious economic program, including state control of the petroleum industry. Over time the concept of pushing economic development grew increasingly popular. Governments wanted to achieve high rates of growth, with the government itself playing an active role in attaining this growth and channeling it into desired economic activities.

By the 1950s industrialization no longer reflected Brazil's reaction to external events. Rather, industrialization had become the government's principal vehicle to modernize the economy and increase the rate of economic growth. Policymakers had over time become convinced that the country could no longer rely on the export of commodities to develop. This conclusion was based on a growing number of analyses at the time that underscored the dim long-term prospects for commodity prices and overall demand for raw materials.

The government decided, over a period of time, that it was necessary for Brazil to change the composition of its economy through the promotion of import-substitution industrialization (ISI).

Developmentalism took off as a politically popular state-led effort to push growth. Perhaps the pinnacle of Brazil's developmentalism came with the administration of Juscelino Kubitschek (1956–1961), which launched a massive development program containing huge projects in infrastructure development and energy. Among Kubitschek's projects was the building of the new interior capital of Brasília. Kubitscheck's ambitious plans aimed to bring together the government and the private sector to produce high growth rates, accelerated industrialization, and infrastructure development.

In terms of growth, the postwar industrialization process was a success as it resulted in very high rates of growth: from 1947 to 1962 the average rate of growth was more than 6

Import-Substitution Industrialization

For fifty years Latin America pursued a strategy of development called ISI, or import-substitution industrialization, and Brazil was one of the leaders. As the name implies, the idea was to replace previously imported industrial goods with goods produced domestically. The strategy was inward looking and supported by Raul Prebisch, the head of the United Nation's Economic Commission on Latin America. The strategy relied on exchange rate and trade restrictions, such as multiple exchange rates, import licenses, quotas, protective tariffs, and export taxes. The goal was to limit trade and reserve the domestic market for local producers, providing a protected "training ground" for domestic industry with the hope that it would eventually compete internationally. Unfortunately, the policy typically led to inefficient firms and high-cost industrial substitutes. In general, local industry failed to become internationally competitive, and Latin Americans were forced to pay high prices for poor-quality goods produced domestically. In turn, by deemphasizing exports the countries lacked foreign exchange to pay for much-needed imports. While ISI did play a meaningful role in stimulating the economic development of the region, by the 1980s the process was exhausted. During the 1980s and 1990s Latin American countries were forced to introduce a host of reforms to open their economies, reduce the size of government, and improve efficiency. While Brazil was a laggard on reforms, it was also forced to remake its economy.

percent). However, the import substitution of the 1950s also saddled Brazil with a number of serious problems that would surface by the 1960s. For example, agriculture was typically neglected, causing problems in food supply as well as contributing to the persistent shortage of foreign exchange. Another major problem was inflation—by the 1960s inflation was rampant and causing serious distortions in the Brazilian economy, in large part caused by the government's use of "inflation financing," or covering public-sector deficits by simply printing money. An additional problem was inequality. Industrial growth increased Brazil's serious inequality, as the benefits of growth were unequally distributed both in terms of income groups and regions. Finally, ISI caused significant balance-of-payments pressures. In the 1950s the excess of imports over exports was financed by inflows of foreign capital; as a result, by the 1960s the foreign debt had ballooned.

As a result of these factors, then, by the 1960s, Brazil's growth boom had faded. Stagnation set in after 1961, in part due to the political crisis that began with the resignation of Jânio Quadros in August 1961. At least in part his resignation reflected the difficulties of trying to fix the country's serious economic imbalances. Brazil would not see consistent economic policies from the resignation of Quadros until the military overthrow of the Goulart presidency. Goulart in particular started from a weakened position institutionally, but then turned out also to be an ineffective leader. Additionally he

Construction of Brazil's new capital, Brasília, in 1960. The futuristic city was built on undeveloped land 600 miles from the old capital of Rio de Janeiro as part of an ambitious development program. (Frank Scherschel/Time Life Pictures/Getty Images)

grew increasingly nationalist and populist in his rhetoric, although this stance did not turn into much in terms of real policies. With the economy nearing chaos, the military opted to topple Goulart. This time they took power for themselves, aiming specifically to bring the economy under control.

BRAZIL'S MILITARY DICTATORSHIP

The military regime established in 1964 took immediate aim at inflation, arguing that any path to recovery had to be predicated on the control of inflation. In addition, the regime sought to modernize Brazil's capital markets to accumulate savings and to create a system of incentives to channel investments to targeted sectors deemed essential by the government. The military sought both domestic and international capital to finance its ambitious program, not to mention aggressive public investments in infrastructure projects and state-owned corporations.

The early effort at stabilizing relied on standard policies, like reducing public spending, increasing tax revenues, squeezing wages, and tightening credit. The government also sought to correct price distortions of the preceding inflationary period, for example by raising public utility rates.

The military regime in Brazil took an increasingly activist role in managing the economy. For example, more and more use was made of tax incentives to direct the allocation of resources to favored sectors of the economy and regions of the country. One of the most important examples was the regime's attempt to direct resources to Brazil's poor Northeast. State-owned companies dominated many of the country's heavy industries, like petrochemicals, steel, and mining. Thus the government's role in the economy grew, as reflected by a sharp increase in government expenditures as a percentage of GDP. Many argue that the rapid growth of the Brazilian economy after 1968 was primarily due to government policy. Significant disagreement exists, however, as to whether this growth worsened the country's inequality and sacrificed efficiency in the all-consuming desire to push growth.

Importantly, after continuing its poor performance until 1968, Brazil's economy then entered a period of extremely strong growth, often dubbed the "Brazilian Miracle," in which over a period of seven years the economy averaged annual GDP rates on the order of 11 percent. The period lasted from 1968 to 1974. Industry led the growth boom, and leading sectors shifted from lighter industries, like food and textiles, to heavier industries, such as chemicals and consumer durables. Income inequality worsened despite the rapid growth; defenders argued that this simply reflected market forces and could be alleviated by investments in education. Critics were less convinced, arguing that government policies, like wage policies, were exacerbating the problem.

Regional inequality also continued to be a problem, in particular the major inequality between the industrializing South-East and the relatively backward Northeast. The

Transamazon Highway construction near Altamira, Brazil, 1971. (Bettmann/Corbis)

military government implemented a number of policies to induce investments in the Northeast; however, most of these required relatively little labor and did not provide much employment. By 1970, the Northeast accounted for 30 percent of Brazil's population but a meager 12 percent of national income.

One of the most well-known plans to alter Brazil's regional imbalances in growth was the Transamazon Highway project launched in September 1970. The idea was to induce significant internal migration, and huge sums of money were spent on construction and colonization. Unfortunately, the project largely failed to achieve its perhaps overly ambitious goals.

EXTERNAL SHOCKS AND BRAZIL'S DEBT CRISIS

The military dictatorship initially focused on orthodox economic policies to shake the economy of its inflation habit. However, by the 1970s, the generals increasingly deviated from orthodoxy, introducing, for example, indexation as a way to cope with inflation.

With the first oil shock in November 1973, Brazil chose an even more dramatic path away from economic orthodoxy. Rather than implement an "austerity" program to cope with the dramatic increase in its oil bill, the government chose an aggressive growth strategy—this would impact the structure of the economy, as well as contribute to higher inflation and a dramatic growth in Brazil's foreign debt. The return to inflation and Brazil's debt crisis would ultimately help build consensus in the country for economic transformation; the process was partially started by Collar, but it would be Fernando Henrique Cardoso who drove the biggest changes in the mid- to late 1990s.

The November 1973 oil shock quadrupled the price of petroleum, and at the time Brazil imported more than 80 percent of its oil. As a result, Brazil's import bill doubled, and the country went from surplus to deficit in its trade account. There were only a few options available for Brazil at the time. The orthodox option was to reduce growth to diminish imports. A second option, and the one ultimately chosen, was to maintain high rates of growth and cover the external deficit using foreign reserves and/or an increase in foreign debt. Importantly the shock corresponded to a change in the generals ruling Brazil; the outgoing government of Emílio Garastazú Médici had presided over the miracle years. However, income distribution had deteriorated, and political repression had grown. Given this environment, the incoming Geisel administration chose the politically easier path of maintaining high growth.

Geisel's main policy package was announced in 1975: the government would push growth with the Second National Development Plan, which outlined huge investment programs and focused on deepening the substitution of imported

Itaipú hydroelectric power plant; the dam at Itaipú is the largest dam in the world and is a good example of the lofty economic ambitions of Brazil's military rulers. (Itaipú Binacional)

industrial inputs (steel, aluminum, etc.), dramatically expanding the economic infrastructure (e.g., huge hydro-electric power projects), and diversifying exports.

The government's role in the Second National Development Plan was pervasive—not only was much of the investment taken on by state companies but the private sector received tremendous financial support from the government. In addition, international debt was used aggressively to finance the current account deficit. The level of economic growth did not return to the levels seen in the miracle years, but it was relatively high, averaging about 7 percent for the rest of the decade.

The push for growth, and to finance that growth by a tremendous increase in foreign debt, occurred within a relatively supportive global economic climate. Notably the world was seemingly awash in money, the so-called petrodollars that oil exporters recycled back into the global economic system via international banks. At the time banks were literally scouring the world to make loans, and Brazil, with its highly ambitious development plan, became a prime lending candidate.

The last military president, General Figueiredo, came to power in March 1979, with the intention of handing power back to civilian democratic leaders. This goal would prove very challenging as Brazil entered dire economic circumstances. Conditions were already difficult when Brazil was hit by the second oil shock in 1979, when oil prices skyrocketed again as the Organization of Petroleum Exporting Countries (OPEC) dramatically increased the price of oil.

The United States, in part as a reflection of the oil crises, was trying to reduce inflation in its economy and significantly tightened monetary policy in 1981. Given that much of Brazil's debt (and much of the debt in Latin America) was floating, its cost of servicing the foreign debt rose dramatically with the rise in global interest rates. Further, tightened money caused recession in many developed countries like the United States, reducing demand (and prices) for Brazilian exports.

An initial "economic package" came in December 1979, but as servicing the external deficits became increasingly difficult, the Brazilian government moved to reduce imports by forcing the economy into recession. By 1982 another external shock worsened the situation, as Mexico declared a moratorium on its own external debt in August—one result of this was the closing of international debt markets to Latin American borrowers. By that time Brazil had the distinction of being the largest debtor in the developing world.

Brazil was forced as well to default on its obligations to foreign banks and go to the International Monetary Fund (IMF) for financial help. Brazil was once again embroiled in economic crisis, stagnating through the "lost decade" of the 1980s, crippled by its huge foreign debt and runaway inflation. Notably, this time around the economic crisis could not be blamed on leftists or democratic rule; the very generals who marched into power in 1964 to restore order to the economy had actually brought it to its knees.

A RETURN TO DEMOCRACY AMIDST ECONOMIC INSTABILITY

Power was returned to civilian hands in 1985, as discussed in detail in chapter one. For the next nine years democratization would be accompanied by largely ineffective economic policies. In fact, in the years leading up to the Cardoso administration, Brazil would have three civilian presidents, two of whom started as vice presidential candidates: Sarney assumed the presidency when Tancredo Neves died before taking office, while Itamar Franco assumed power when Fernando Collor de Mello resigned just before being impeached. This political backdrop was accompanied by eight stabilization programs that failed to stop Brazil's inflation or steer the economy in a new, more effective direction.

Probably the best known of the stabilization plans was the Cruzado Plan, which was announced to the country by President Sarney in February 1986 in a television address. This plan would be the democratic New Republic's first attempt to fix the economic problems—especially inflation—that were the direct legacy of the authoritarian military regime. The Cruzado Plan was deemed a "heterodox shock" that would be based on social consensus as opposed to the standard "orthodox shock" that required certain social groups to absorb a decline in their share of the national income. Although initially successful in taming inflation, the plan ultimately failed, most importantly because it included a sharp wage increase at its inception, swelling domestic demand. The plan's failure was made worse by persistent public-sector deficits.

The costs of the Cruzado Plan's failure were high for Brazil. Sharp losses in international reserves forced a moratorium on interest on external debt. Inflation came galloping back, and workers' purchasing power was hit hard, contributing to stagnating growth. The Cruzado Plan foreshadowed poor economic performance in the future. After the Cruzado Plan the May 1987 Bresser Plan followed. These were then followed in 1989 by the Summer Plan, the last attempt at stabilization in the 1980s; continued failure worried Brazilians about their ability to contain inflation.

The anti-inflation programs adopted by Collor and then Franco met the same fate—until 1993—as the plans of the second half of the 1980s. Collar shocked the country with a heterodox policy that included temporary confiscation of bank deposits. Collor also began a push for liberal reforms, but these lost steam with the corruption scandal and Collor's resignation at the end of 1992. Itamar Franco would muddle through economically, until he named Cardoso finance minister.

POLITICAL AND ECONOMIC TRANSFORMATION: THE CONTEXT

Brazil stood out in the early 1990s as the only Latin American country that had failed to control inflation (Brazil was also a relative laggard in the region in terms of economic liberalization well into the 1990s). As many students of Brazil point out, the failure was essentially political, not economic. Stabilization plans involve economic pain as real wages fall, credit is tightened, and economies move into recession. Brazil's presidents (except Castello Branco, who was strengthened by an authoritarian military regime) consistently backed away from true stabilization.

The path to reform in Latin America was led by Chile as early as the 1970s, but in general a regional movement took place by the 1980s, as ISI became exhausted and the stagnation of the lost decade forced governments to look for new policies. In general, countries looked for ways to liberalize their economies, redefine and reduce the role of the state, and identify new strategies for development. The latter included privatization of public enterprises, liberalization of trade, deregulation, and increased foreign investment. These reforms went above and beyond initial efforts to stabilize economies and bring fiscal affairs under control.

One of the most important trends in twentieth-century Brazil was the dramatic rise of government involvement in economic affairs, especially during the period of rapid industrialization. As other countries moved to liberalize, Brazil seemed stuck with state-directed development. There was an important debate within Brazil about the merits of its state-led model. Over time those opposing state-led development grouped together, calling for an end to the centralized regime that originated with Vargas and ballooned during the military dictatorship. Additionally, the fall of the Berlin wall and the dramatic economic rise of the "Asian Tigers," Taiwan, South Korea, Singapore, and Hong Kong, contributed to pessimism surrounding statist policies and optimism surrounding market-oriented development.

While early civilian-government policies were largely ineffective, analysis of reform must start with 1985, when Brazil began a dual transition, from an authoritarian state to a democratic republic and from state-led development to economic liberalization. As discussed, the early years of democracy failed to conquer inflation or set a new course for the economy. However, Collor's short presidency represented the first time that the need for serious structural adjustment and liberal economic reforms entered the national debate. Fernando Henrique Cardoso's appointment as finance minister for President Itamar Franco would bring both successful stabilization and a new direction for Brazil's economy.

FERNANDO HENRIQUE CARDOSO AND THE REAL PLAN

Cardoso became Franco's finance minister at a time of severe pessimism among Brazilians about the state of their economy. Likewise, many doubted whether Cardoso's background had prepared him for the vicious battle ahead. However, Cardoso, as finance minister, would finally achieve stabilization, and then continue his efforts to reform the economy as president.

Cardoso's plan focused on a few basic policies. First, a balanced budget was drawn up; unlike predecessors' attempts, Cardoso's plan had no heterodox measures such as wage and price freezes. Cardoso also crafted a two-stage move to a new currency, first by creating a new unit of value and then by full conversion to the new currency, called the real, on July 1, 1994. These policies were accompanied by a mildly overvalued exchange rate and high real interest rates (the former helped fight inflation, and the latter helped dampen consumption).

Stabilization was the top priority, as Brazilian economic life had become chaotic. Inflation in 1993 had reached the astronomical level of 2,489 percent; it fell to 913 percent in 1994, 19 percent in 1994, 11 percent in 1996, until it reached just 4 percent in 1997.

The process was not an easy one, and several huge challenges stood in the way of success. For example, having lived through one of the most significant inflationary episodes in

A supermarket in Rio de Janiero updates prices as Brazil transitions to a new currency under Fernando Henrique Cardoso's 1994 Real Plan. (Julio Pereira/AFP/Getty Images)

the world, Brazilians had become sophisticated in protecting their economic interests against inflation. As such, the government knew that any resurgence of inflation would almost immediately signal the failure of the Real Plan. Inflationary expectations were critical to success.

The reduction of deficit spending was another monumental challenge. At all levels of government, deficit spending had become a way of life. Its reduction would constitute a major battle, first with Congress and then with the individual states. Another major challenge was the sheer size of the federal, state, and local bureaucracies, whose bloated payrolls and generous pensions were a major contributor to unsound fiscal policies.

Importantly, stabilization was envisioned as just the first in a series of steps to remake the Brazilian economy—structural and fiscal adjustment would lead to a reform of the state and a new development model, and protection, state-led development, and "heterodox shocks" were to be things of the past.

FROM STABILIZATION TO LIBERALIZATION

As Franco's finance minister and the architect of the Real Plan, Cardoso focused on fighting inflation by reducing the country's huge fiscal deficit, with fiscal reforms including a budget cut of some $6 billion, improved tax collection, and the collection of debt the states owed the federal government. Congress also approved a new emergency fund that would ensure fiscal balance for the next two years; Congress would then extend the fund numerous times in the years ahead.

As mentioned, the government then turned to the two-stage process of adopting a new and strong currency, the real. The IMF endorsed the plan, giving important support to its success. The country was also able to renegotiate its huge foreign debt. Growth returned to the economy.

Cardoso, riding a wave of popularity as the architect of the country's newfound economic stability, was elected president and assumed office in January 1995. Realizing that his popularity and electoral victory were the result of the Real Plan and its success, Cardoso continued to give stabilization top priority; a reflection of the plan's success, by 1996 inflation had fallen to single digits for the first time since the 1950s.

By this time there were a few early warning signs of complications to the plan that would surface down the road. For example, even though inflation had fallen dramatically, Brazil's inflation was still higher than that of its most important trading partners, leading to concerns about currency overvaluation and growing trade deficits. In addition, the plan depended on high real interest rates, which acted as a constraint on growth.

Trade

While Collor advocated trade liberalization during his short time in office, Cardoso took a more cautious approach on the matter. He pursued Mercosul, a trade union linking Brazil to Argentina, Uruguay, and Paraguay. Brazil continued to maintain tariff protection, though, with average tariffs well above the Latin American average. By 1996 Brazil went from trade surpluses to deficits, as growing currency overvaluation took its toll. In the context of growing international currency crises—first devaluations in Asia and then a financial crisis in Russia—Brazil would finally be forced to devalue in early 1999; this would lead to dramatic improvement in the trade balance. With its long history of state control of the economy, not to mention its huge domestic market, Brazil in general has taken a cautious approach to trade, pushing more for export promotion than aggressive import liberalization.

Privatization

In contrast to the cautious approach Brazil has taken with trade, the privatization program has been much more aggressive. Privatization brings resources to the state, helps reduce budget deficits, and contributes to the efficiency of the economy, in part by eliminating redundant jobs and reducing corruption. Given the large number of state-owned enterprises, policymakers realized by the early 1990s the amount of resources the state could take in through privatization.

While Brazil's privatization program began in the 1980s, it was under Collor that it really gained momentum; by the early 1990s Collor was focused on selling state-owned companies in the steel, petrochemical, and fertilizer industries. His resignation interrupted the process, but despite hinting at stopping it, Franco continued a modest privatization program.

With Cardoso's arrival, the privatization process in Brazil accelerated again, reaching its culmination in 1997–1998, when government revenues topped $15 to $20 billion in each year. One highlight was the privatization of the state's mining giant CVRD, which was the largest privatization to date and brought in almost $7 billion. This was then topped by the 1998 privatization of the telecommunications sector, with the sale of twelve companies netting the government just under $19 billion. The sale of some 120 state companies since 1991 brought in around $60 billion, leading Brazilians to consider it the most extensive privatization program in the world. States also got in on the action, and foreign direct investors participated in a significant way in Brazil's privatizations.

Deregulation

As with privatization, Collor pushed hard for deregulation of the economy. Cardoso then took the torch and pushed for an overhaul of the regulatory system. Probably the biggest step was the dismantling of Brazil's complicated system of indexation, which was one of the main ways Brazil had coped with high inflation—it had also acted as a mechanism that reinforced the country's so-called inertial inflation.

ROADBLOCKS TO REFORM

As mentioned above, critics of the stabilization program argued that it hampered growth, in part due to high real interest rates. But any strong growth would worsen the trade deficit by stimulating imports. Concerns about the strength of the currency were also voiced, with growing comments that it was overvalued. By 1996, budget and trade deficits began to deteriorate, because a strong currency makes imports cheaper and exports more expensive, contributing to trade deficits. The sharply deteriorating deficits contributed to a growing sense of crisis, and pressures from financial speculators increased. Another concern was finance—the external deficit had been financed by strong foreign investment, but as the sense of crisis spread, the government had to resort to more extreme measures as capital flows slowed. These included spending foreign reserves and raising interest rates to slow growth and discourage imports.

Despite the growing imbalances, devaluation was difficult, if not impossible, to contemplate. The real was the foundation of Brazil's stabilization plan, and there was widespread belief that devaluation would spark a return of inflation and thus signal the death of the Real Plan and a possible return to hyperinflation. Concerns grew in 1998 about Brazil's vulnerability to a currency collapse as had happened in a number of Asian countries. Russia's financial crisis and debt default in the summer of 1998 also exacerbated both fears and market speculation. There were growing calls from respected academics for Brazil to act more aggressively to prevent a crisis, and most of these were predicated on the idea that the currency was dangerously overvalued.

At the time, Brazil seemed trapped in a vicious circle: the overvalued real held back growth and exports while stimulating imports and worsening the trade deficit; at the same time, high interest rates used to defend the currency stifled both investment and growth. October 1998 (just before the presidential election) witnessed another market panic, as the country lost some $30 billion from reserves that totaled $50 to $60 billion.

This crisis made it very clear that more aggressive reforms were required—deep fiscal reforms were unavoidable. Speculators increasingly felt Brazil was vulnerable to the wave of financial crisis originating in Asia. With ongoing capital flight and a stock market collapse, the government continued to deploy billions to defend the currency. At this point the government reached an agreement with the IMF and a number of other governments, including the United States. Brazil promised aggressive reforms in exchange for $42 billion in loans.

In the end, even this enormous financial package would prove insufficient to prevent a collapse of the currency. Brazil finally had to float its currency in early 1999, which then depreciated by 45 percent. And with a new floating exchange rate, external and internal crises would spark further currency declines in the following years.

Ultimately, fears about the consequences turned out to be exaggerated. Calm returned to the markets after a few months of hand wringing. Interest rates also came down from extremely high levels. And early inflationary pressures generated by the devaluation declined quickly.

While the economic implications of the devaluation were nowhere near as dire as expected—in fact, there were positive repercussions, as exports began to grow and import substitution helped generate a quick economic recovery—the last two years of the Cardoso administration would encounter a number of external shocks, and two internal ones. In 2001 Argentina experienced financial collapse, in its case both a maxi-devaluation and default on its external debt. This affected Brazil, given Argentina's proximity and status as a major trading partner. This effect was exacerbated by external conditions, as the United States was experiencing economic difficulties, including crashing stock markets. The terrorist attacks of September 11, 2001, added to global risk aversion. As if things could not get worse, Brazil was hit with a domestic energy crisis, aggravated by drought. At its worse the country had to ration power, hardly a popular measure politically.

The next year, 2002, brought another major crisis centering on the 2002 presidential election. Cardoso's hand-picked candidate, José Serra, never had a chance in the polls, which were led by the Workers' Party (PT) candidate Luiz Inácio Lula da Silva (Lula). In fact, by July 2002 a third candidate, Ciro Gomez, assumed second position after Lula, with Serra well behind in third place.

The critical issue was the presumed leftist stance of Lula and the PT. As it became more and more evident that Lula would be Brazil's next president, markets panicked as investors feared an end to Brazil's reform program, a return to inflation, and even a default on Brazil's hefty public debt (most analysts did not anticipate a default on foreign debt). The impact on the currency was dramatic: by July the currency had fallen to 2.90 reals per dollar; by October the panic selling drove the real to 3.90 per dollar.

As we know, Lula won the election, and a sense of calm returned. Lula had already tried to reassure the markets before the elections, saying that Brazil had changed, the PT had changed, and he had changed. While his comments were encouraging, his actions were the deciding factor. For example, Lula appointed well respected and market-oriented individuals to run the central bank and the finance ministry, the two most important government posts for the markets and investors. Likewise, Lula made clear that they would not buckle under pressures from the militant wing of the PT, which wanted early signals of a shift back to the left in economic policy.

Still, the pressures exerted on the currency do highlight Brazil's vulnerability, and they demonstrate that there exists a widespread view that Brazil has yet to put its house in order (with a sustainable fiscal model) in spite of the Cardoso-era reforms. Chronic pressures on the budget remain in place, deficits continue to be significant, and public debt levels remain high. One of the major drivers of these problems is the 1988 constitution, which locked in a number of exaggerated entitlements. At a minimum the Fiscal Responsibility Law of 2000 puts significant limits on payroll spending and debt servicing, a big step forward in Brazil's long-held habit of overspending.

While Lula's presidency is now mired in a corruption scandal, which has dimmed prospects for his reelection, his first years in office have been for the most part uneventful. There have been no major economic crises, and in large part this has reflected a highly supportive international environment, with strong demand for Brazilian exports combined with high international commodity prices. Brazil has been running consistent—and large—trade surpluses, which has helped support the currency. In addition, while growth has not been spectacular, neither has the country experienced stagnation. Perhaps most notably, Lula's economic track record will probably be recognized for a renewed emphasis on the poor, without sacrificing the country's hard-won economic stability. Given Brazil's recent economic history this will be an accomplishment if Lula is successful.

CONTEMPORARY ECONOMIC ISSUES

The first sections of this chapter provide a good starting point for understanding Brazil's complex economy—both its basic structure today and the historical path the country followed to arrive there. In this final section on the economy, we survey a few issues that dominate the national policy debate or resonate within Brazil's recent economic history or both.

Inflation and Stabilization

Inflation has a long history in Latin America, and Brazil has experienced one of the region's most renowned inflationary episodes. Typically Brazil is classified as a high-inflation country: inflation averaged 45.8 percent from 1960 to 1969, 30.5 percent from 1970 to 1979, 142 percent from 1980 to 1985, and 795.6 from 1986 to 1989.

Brazil's inflationary experience led to a vigorous national debate about its origins, with two contrasting sides developing. The competing sides are called the monetarists and the structuralists. Monetarists in general are orthodox economists. They blame inflation quite simply on excess liquidity, which they argue is typically caused by lack of control over government spending. They advocate a low and steady rate of growth in the money supply. In their view the origin of Brazil's inflation lies in inappropriate fiscal and monetary policies.

The structuralists argue that the problem of inflation is more complicated. In their view the money supply is the dependent variable—it expands as a reflection of rising prices. To them, Brazil's inflation reflects the monopoly powers that firms, unions, and the state hold. In essence, each group tries to maintain its share of national income through the manipulation of prices, interest rates, and wages, resulting in "administered inflation." They also identify bottlenecks in the economy, which create shortages and price increases.

The structuralists tend to identify political causes of inflation, pointing to politically weak governments unable to resist the pressures to increase spending. Structuralists have also pointed out the inertial nature of Brazil's inflation, as a number of instruments and policies have led inflation to be self-propagating (for example, the indexation of wages).

In the end, there is some logic to both sides of the argument. High rates of inflation would not be possible unless governments allow growth in the money supply. The question is how to identify what causes money growth. The structuralists effectively identify the socioeconomic and political factors that help explain Brazil's inability to stop inflation. For example, the growing sense of illegitimacy surrounding the military dictators helps explain their increasing willingness to over-spend, using inflationary finance (printing money) to cover part of the bill.

The structuralists and the monetarists logically differ in their prescriptions for fighting inflation, just as they differ in their analyses of its origins. As we have discussed, mone-tarists tend to focus on orthodox stabilization programs, call-ing for budgetary discipline, tight money, and often exchange rate devaluation. Often these policies result in recession, and as such are never very popular.

Structuralists have tended to be critical of orthodox meas-ures—they are typically proponents of heterodox shocks. Focusing on the inertial nature of inflation they typically rec-ommend some form of wage and price controls to break the battle for income shares in a controlled manner. They also tend to recommend government intervention to overcome supply constraints in the economy.

While it is beyond the scope of this analysis to try to deter-mine which side is correct in prescribing policies to fight inflation, it is clear from Brazil's history that heterodox shocks have not worked—each of the many attempts ended in failure. Only with the arrival of Cardoso, and the Real Plan, has Brazil managed to solve its inflation problem. The Real Plan notably did not contain heterodox attempts to control wages and prices, but rather focused on getting the govern-ment's house in order.

Poverty and Inequality

As we have discussed, poverty and a relatively unequal distri-bution of income have been characteristics of Brazil for cen-turies—in fact inequality started with the initial distribution of enormous tracts of land to the "donatary captains" in the early colonial era. Not only did landholding policies in the nineteenth century exacerbate these problems but they were also worsened during the period of rapid industrialization (and the debt crisis). Economists who study the process of economic development point out that economic poverty reflects political poverty. In other words, the poor typically lack the means to voice their demands.

Death by starvation is rare in Latin America, and in Brazil, but millions suffer from malnutrition, hunger, insufficient

A favela stands in stark contrast to the modern highrises of Belo Horizante, capital of Minas Gerais, Brazil. (Rogério Medeiros Pinho)

medical care, and low-quality housing. The poor typically have larger families than the middle or upper classes. As a result, the incidence of poverty is usually higher among children than adults. Likewise, Latin American poverty is decidedly higher in rural areas than in urban centers.

In Brazil the rural poor are typically landless laborers who survive on temporary employment. For these rural poor, the urban informal sector represents a land of opportunity and drives migration from rural areas to cities. The informal sector is huge in Latin America, in essence a separate economy that operates in cash and exists outside of the official, taxed economy. Informal workers pursue a multitude of occupations, from selling their wares in the streets to working in households as maids, gardeners, and other services.

Importantly, average income levels in Latin America often exceed those seen in Africa and Asia, but extreme poverty exists primarily because of the unequal distribution of income. The region, including Brazil, clearly has enough resources to feed, house, and clothe its people.

As seen in the preceding pages, the debate in Brazil about growth and its relation to equality has been a sharp one, as rapid postwar growth exacerbated the country's inequality and as poverty remained pervasive. In essence the question is whether Brazil's poor benefited from rapid growth and whether they might have done better if the government had pursued different policies. Consider that in 1960, the wealthiest 10 percent of Brazilians earned 28 percent of the national income. By 1970 the same group earned 48 percent of income. In the same time period the bottom half of Brazil's population saw their share of national income drop from 18 percent to 15 percent.

Those less critical of Brazil's growth path argue that absolute incomes rose for nearly all groups in the country. In other words, the "pie" got bigger for everyone; the rich simply received larger slices over time. Some economists have even argued that inequality is a natural function of growth, although this seems dubious, as Taiwan and South Korea have achieved a level of growth similar to Brazil's while maintaining much greater levels of equality.

Brazil's share of social service expenditure as a percentage of GDP has been as high as, or even higher than, other developing nations, yet its indicators of social welfare have been lower (e.g., infant mortality, literacy levels). Historically there have been two key problems. First, public resources have been poorly managed. Second, they have not been appropriately targeted. For example, public spending on health care has been directed to high-cost curative hospitals rather than on preventive health care (such as immunization, maternal and child health, etc.). The problem can be seen in education as well, with Brazil's governments historically spending more to support free university education than on primary and secondary education. As mentioned, President Lula da Silva has promised to tackle these thorny issues. The next presidential elections will at least in part reflect Brazil's judgment on his progress

Foreign Debt

Latin America, and Brazil specifically, have had a long history of using debt to pursue national goals. Latin American countries have also proven to be susceptible to debt-related economic crises. Probably the single worst debt crisis experienced in the region was that of the early 1980s, which led to nearly a decade of economic stagnation and high inflation. In very general terms, this crisis was triggered by a sharp rise in global interest rates and a move into recession by the developed world, led by the United States. Many Latin American nations had increased significantly their international borrowing in the 1970s, taking advantage of "cheap money" resulting from the first oil shock. In effect, the oil-exporting nations were "recycling" their windfall gains from high oil prices by depositing them with big international banks, which in turn searched

Antigovernment demonstration requesting early elections, São Paulo,
Brazil in July 1987. (Paulo Fridman/Corbis Sygma)

the globe for customers looking for loans. The second oil
shock, as discussed, turned the Latin American economies in
a decidedly more negative direction, as it sparked both sharp
increases in oil prices and the inflation-fighting policies in the
United States.

Seemingly out of nowhere, Latin American nations faced a
sharp rise in external obligations, as they paid much more for
imported oil and the service on their foreign debt. In turn, the
move into recession in the developed world caused a decline
in the demand for Latin American exports, as well as a fall in
their prices. Many countries, including Brazil, then went into
default on their international obligations. A debt crisis arises
when a country fails to meet its interest payments, whether it
reflects an inability or an unwillingness to pay.

These crises arise for multiple reasons, from fiscal
profligacy to political weaknesses to international shocks.
There are two sides to every coin, and debt crises tend to
involve both excessive borrowing and overeager lending from

exporters of capital; not infrequently global shocks are involved, setting in motion surprisingly similar crises.

The debt crisis of the 1980s fit the general mold. Latin American nations borrowed excessively, while international banks willingly lent billions to Latin countries. High interest rates in the developed world increased the pain of debt service and induced recession, depressing the export earnings in the debtor nations. Default became nearly inevitable, especially as fragile domestic political environments made austerity measures impractical.

Once the lending stopped, service of debt could only be managed by exporting significantly more than was imported, and countries shifted to large surpluses in the exports of goods and services. This was typically generated by engineering economic slowdowns (to reduce imports) and devaluation (to make imports expensive and exports more attractive). The service of debt often leads to plummeting investment and inflationary government financing—the lost decade, for example, saw depressed living standards, a sharp increase in inflation, reduced investment, and stagnant growth. Eventually a number of plans were developed, including the Brady Plan in 1989, which sought for the banks to forgive part of their loans to Latin American nations in exchange for guarantees of repayment, backed by the World Bank and the IMF.

As has been suggested, the economic malaise caused by the debt crisis of the 1980s in general led Latin American countries to push liberal reforms. In general terms the region moved to open borders to freer trade and to reduce the size of government and its involvement in the economy. While Brazil was a laggard in the region's reform movement, it eventually moved to reform its economy.

Agrarian Reform

As mentioned above, Brazil's unequal land ownership is a direct result of its colonial heritage—the Portuguese Crown granted huge pieces of land to a small minority of people who came to Brazil, and later policies would reinforce the unequal distribution of land. Perhaps most importantly, policies in the 1850s would make small landholdings difficult to obtain, in direct contrast to the U.S. Homestead Act, which encouraged small farming.

In the modern era, Latin America has seen considerable violence associated with land reform. Brazil's National Landless Workers Movement and the church-related Pastoral Land Commission have both suggested that rural violence is often caused by gunmen hired by large landowners who oppose any kind of land reform. Peasants continue to demand land in rural areas of Brazil as a solution to rural poverty and inequality. They also continue to die in the process. A common call for land reform suggests that it can improve the productivity of land and bring idle land into use. Those opposed to land reform argue that any radical change in the structure of land ownership will reduce output. They also suggest that many peasants will simply engage in subsistence agriculture, thereby significantly reducing export earnings.

In practice, land reform in Latin America has witnessed both orderly transitions as well as chaotic disruptions as land has been taken from large-scale producers and given to rural peasants. Brazil looked for an easy way out: rather than take large quantities of land from current owners, it tried to promote the colonization of the Amazon River region. The scheme was an attempt to relocate landless peasants, primarily from the destitute Northeast. Unfortunately, small farmers did not have a clear priority over large commercial farmers. Likewise, receipt of title was often delayed, making it hard for small farmers to obtain credit.

Those who managed to obtain credit planted crops, but it turned out that the soil was relatively fragile and could not sustain continuous agriculture. Likewise, poorly built roads and huge distances made the marketing of crops difficult. By 1973 the government was already changing its approach, promoting large commercial farmers rather than small farmers. The government heavily subsidized commercial ranching, ironically making the most attractive opportunity for peasants the deforestation of their land to sell to ranchers.

In general Brazil's experience with land reform has been less than successful and clearly inefficient. The constitution of 1988 has made land reform more difficult by limiting expropriation to so-called nonproductive lands and requiring full payment in inflation-protected bonds. The absence of a strong government presence in rural areas has allowed considerable conflict. However, there have been a few success stories, and the land reform agency has distributed a considerable amount of government-controlled land.

References and Further Readings

Alden, Dauril. "Late Colonial Brazil, 1750–1808," in Leslie Bethell (ed.), *The Cambridge History of Latin America, Vol. III*. Cambridge, U.K.: Cambridge University Press, 1984: 601–662.

Baer, Werner. *The Brazilian Economy*, 3rd ed. Westport, CT: Praeger, 1989.

Bresser Pereira, Luiz Carlos. *Economic Crisis and State Reform in Brazil: Toward a New Interpretation of Latin America*. Boulder, CO: Lynne Rienner, 1996.

Bulmer-Thomas, Victor. *The Economic History of Latin America since Independence*. Cambridge, U.K.: Cambridge University Press, 1994.

Cardoso, Eliana, and Ann Helwege. *Latin America's Economy: Diversity, Trends, and Conflicts*. Cambridge, MA: MIT Press, 1995.

Coes, Donald V. *Macroeconomic Crises, Policies, and Growth in Brazil, 1964–1990*. Washington, DC: World Bank Publications, 1995.

Dean, Warren. "The Brazilian Economy: 1870–1930," in Leslie Bethell (ed.), *The Cambridge History of Latin America, Vol. V*. Cambridge, U.K.: Cambridge University Press, 1984: 685–724.

Dietz, James, and James Street. *Latin America's Economic Development: Institutionalist and Structuralist Perspectives*. Boulder, CO: Lynne Rienner, 1987.

Evans, Peter. *Dependent Development: The Alliance of Multinational, State, and Local Capital in Brazil*. Princeton, NJ: Princeton University Press, 1979.

Font, Mauricio A. *Transforming Brazil: A Reform Era in Perspective*. New York: Rowman and Littlefield, 2003.

Furtado, Celso. *The Economic Growth of Brazil: A Survey from Colonial to Modern Times*. Berkeley: University of California Press, 1963.

Mauro, Frédéric. "Portugal and Brazil: Political and Economic Structures of

Empire, 1580–1750," in Leslie Bethell (ed.), *The Cambridge History of Latin America, Vol. I.* Cambridge, U.K.: Cambridge University Press, 1984: 441–468.

Merrick, Thomas W., and Douglas H. Graham. *Population and Economic Development in Brazil.* Baltimore: Johns Hopkins University Press, 1979.

Purcell, Susan Kaufman, and Riordan Roett, eds. *Brazil under Cardoso.* Boulder, CO: Lynne Rienner, 1997.

Schwartz, Stuart B. "Colonial Brazil, c. 1580–1750: Plantations and Peripheries," in Leslie Bethell (ed.), *The Cambridge History of Latin America, Vol. II.* Cambridge, U.K.: Cambridge University Press, 1984: 423–500.

Sheahan, John. *Patterns of Development in Latin America: Poverty, Repression, and Economic Strategy.* Princeton, NJ: Princeton University Press, 1987.

Skidmore, Thomas E. *Brazil: Five Centuries of Change.* Oxford, U.K.: Oxford University Press, 1999.

Skidmore, Thomas E., and Peter H. Smith. *Modern Latin America.* New York: Oxford University Press, 2001.

CHAPTER THREE

Politics and Government

INTRODUCTION

Brazil has been governed as a democracy since its transition to civilian rule in 1985. Although the country got off to a rough start in its return to democracy, in part reflecting the economic crisis prevailing at the time, civilian democratic rule seems to have taken hold. For example, the institutional crisis in 1992 surrounding President Fernando Collor de Mello's impeachment could have turned out quite poorly, but the country's democratic institutions worked well during the difficult process and peacefully replaced the president. In turn, the two terms of President Fernando Henrique Cardoso (beginning in 1995 and 1999) contributed both to newfound economic stability and a deepening of democratic institutions. Cardoso was Brazil's first democratically elected president to be reelected to a second term and finish the full term.

This political maturation is also underscored by the election in 2002 of the current president, Luiz Inácio Lula da Silva, known as Lula. Importantly, the country peacefully elected a new president coming from a leftist background. While financial markets panicked that Lula's election would represent an end to reforms and perhaps financial stability, Lula and the Workers' Party (PT) reassured the markets and the country that both he and his party had significantly moderated their positions. While Lula is currently embroiled in a political scandal, making the reform process difficult, it has been clear from the president's words and actions that he has no intention of returning to the chaotic days of failed state-led development. More and more it looks like Lula will escape the crisis with his credibility damaged but largely intact; despite failing to win the 2006 presidential election in the first round, Lula managed a fairly easy victory in the run-off. Another term should give Lula the chance to become one of Brazil's most important leaders.

Brazil's democracy is not without its problems, as we will discuss below. Many of the problems originate from the Constitution of 1988, which was created to replace the constitution of the military dictatorship. One key problem is that the constitution mandates that a large portion of federal revenue be allocated to the states, without any corresponding commitment on the part of the states to spend on education or social programs. This means that despite important fiscal reforms, the country's fiscal position remains precarious. The constitution also supports economic nationalism and excessive regulation of the economy.

Another problem concerns the country's party system. A proliferation of parties and the proportional voting system have led to a lack of party discipline and, most importantly, to a lack of accountability of elected officials to constituencies of voters. We will discuss these main challenges and the prospects for political reform below.

Brazil's 1988 constitution granted broad powers to the federal government, which, like the United States, is split in three parts: the executive, the legislative, and the judicial branches. Brazil's president is elected to a four-year term, with the right to be reelected to one additional term. The legislative branch is divided between the Chamber of Deputies and the senate. There are 513 deputies and 81 senators. Senate terms are eight years, with elections staggered so that two-thirds of the senate are up for reelection at one time, then one-third four years later. Terms for deputies are four years, based on the complex system of proportional representation by states. Seats are allotted proportionally to each state's population, but each state can have a maximum of seventy seats and a minimum of eight seats; as a result the system is biased against the larger states, since the populations of states like São Paulo would have considerably more deputies without the seventy-seat cap. Constituents writing the constitution felt this bias could help overcome the traditional economic and political domination of Brazil's large states. There are approximately fifteen parties represented in Congress, but as it is common for politicians to switch parties, the number of seats held by each party varies.

Subnationally, Brazil is divided into states and municipalities. As in the United States, Brazilian states are semiautonomous; all states have the same form of government as set forth in the constitution. As mentioned, the constitution has given the states more financial independence from the central government; this has led to both heightened corruption and an increase in the power of state and local politicians vis-à-vis national politicians. The states are divided into executive, legislative, and judicial branches; in particular the chief executives at the state level, the governors, have increased their power as resource transfers mandated by the constitution pass through the statehouse.

In Brazil, voting is compulsory from the ages of eighteen to seventy and voluntary between the ages of sixteen and eighteen and over seventy (except for illiterate or disabled people, for whom it is always voluntary). A nominal fine is the penalty for failure to vote, although penalties for not voting are rarely seen. Elections for the president, state governors, and mayors of large cities and state capitals are held in two rounds. If no candidate obtains a majority (more than 50 percent), the two top candidates return to a second round of voting. Senators and mayors of smaller towns (less than 400,000 population) are elected in a single round. Deputies and city council members are elected by proportional elections with open party lists—the individual party candidates with the most individual votes take office.

THE HISTORICAL BACKDROP

Shortly after the discovery of Brazil in 1500, the Portuguese Crown created the first rudimentary form of government in the new colony by creating fourteen hereditary captaincies. As we discussed in chapter one, these were given to private individuals, the *donatarios,* whose territory extended inland to the edge of the colony's boundaries at the time. The donatarios assumed the financial responsibility, as well as the responsibility to colonize, in exchange for powers to govern and make economic profits. Only two of the original captaincies proved economically successful, São Vicente (south of present-day São Paulo) and Pernambuco (in the Northeast).

By 1549, the Crown decided to establish a centralized government for the colony in Bahia, in Brazil's Northeast. In that year the Portuguese Crown sent the first governor-general to direct the affairs of the colony, Governor Tome de Souza, who founded the city of Salvador, which remained the capital of the colony for more than two centuries. In 1572, in response to increasing threats from both the French and the Spanish near Rio de Janeiro, the Portuguese split the administration between Salvador and Rio, but this dual governorship was ended shortly thereafter, in 1578. However, it would foreshadow the later shift in the colony's political and economic center to the South-East.

In 1580, due to a lack of a legitimate heir to the Portuguese throne, Portugal entered a "union" with Spain in which Spain effectively took control of the Portuguese Crown; this would last until 1640, when a suitable heir was found. The Spanish did not take over Portugal's Brazilian colony, busy as they were trying to defend their own territorial claims. However, they did help the Portuguese colony by tightening up administrative and judicial procedures.

At the time the Portuguese regained their independence from Spain, the Crown began to cancel the concessions given to the donatarios, and public policy shifted in focus to the fiscal interests of the Crown. Early interest in brazilwood (used for dyes in Europe) expanded, while sugar became increasingly important; the discovery of gold in Minas Gerais in 1695 radically increased the mother country's interest in its New World colony. At this point economic profits became the driver of colonial policy. The seventeenth century in general witnessed significant expansion of territorial control by the Portuguese.

The nature of the colonial government had an important impact on Brazil's subsequent forms of political organization. Notably, power was extremely centralized, not always in reality but definitely on paper. Some have even called Brazil the "king's plantation." The state, in theory, was all-powerful, and its subjects looked to it for both direction and material gain.

Brazil's early society (and by extension its politics) was divided between the coast and the interior. The coastal communities were dominated by the merchant class, whose interests were typically aligned with the bureaucracy running colonial affairs. The interior was by and large the domain of the landed oligarchy. One of the central themes in Brazilian political history was already becoming evident—namely the battle between forces pushing for bureaucratic centralization and those pushing for regional and local autonomy; this theme has actually survived to the current era. Many analysts argue today that the current political system is excessively decentralized.

In colonial times, the Portuguese Crown was able to co-opt local landowners into the colonial system by using the public bureaucracy, using public positions as plums to gain the loyalty of the important families of the coast and the interior. While the Crown attempted to centralize authority, it did allow greater regional and local autonomy than did the Spanish at the same time in their New World colony. While many positions were occupied by Portuguese-born administrators, whites of Portuguese descent were also important. Family links were essential to gaining favor with the Crown, and important families regularly entered government.

Colonists nurtured their relationships with the Crown, and the benefits produced strong clans, which led to the regional oligarchies that began to dominate Brazil after independence.

By 1780, formal centralization by the Portuguese was setting in. One significant change, which reflected the importance of gold both to the colony and to the mother country, was the transfer of the colonial capital from Salvador to Rio in 1763. The result was a marked shift in population southward. The Northeast's early predominance faded, and the center of political and economic gravity shifted to the Center-South, where it remains to this day.

During the colonial period, church and state were united, but the Catholic Church, while important, was relatively small in size. The most important religious group in the early colonial period was the Jesuits, who controlled education and numerous Indian missions. There was a basic judicial system in place, with two main courts in operation—one in Bahia and one in Rio; major towns also had circuit judges to take care of local matters. At this point the variation between Brazil's regions was notable, with the Northeast based on plantation agriculture (mostly sugar) while the Center-South saw the development of the mining industry, in addition to a number of activities that supported mining.

As discussed in chapter one, the move toward independence reflected a growing divergence of interests between the colonists and their colonial rulers. It also reflected the fact that the colony had actually grown wealthier and more important than its mother country. Portugal's fate had become tethered to the wealth of its New World economy, rather than the other way around. As this became increasingly clear, Brazil's elite class would question its second-class status. Ironically, events in Europe would bring about a very different independence than seen in the rest of the Americas.

INDEPENDENCE AND THE EMPIRE

Driven out by Napoleon's forces in 1808, the Portuguese court relocated to Rio de Janeiro. Portugal's Prince João acted as the regent in the place of his mentally incapacitated mother. The move of the seat of power of the Portuguese Empire to the colony had a dramatic impact on Brazil. For example, ports were opened for the first time, allowing commerce and small manufacturers to benefit after the previously onerous restrictions were lifted. The all-powerful Portuguese state was effectively transferred to Brazil, and its bureaucracy merged with that of the colony.

This created tensions, as positions were increasingly occupied by Portuguese "guests." Rivalries took place between Portuguese immigrants occupying government positions, the local landed aristocracy, and merchants. Often the landed aristocracy was pitted against merchants and the Portuguese.

With the death of his mother in 1816, João became king, ultimately returning to Portugal in 1821. He left his son Pedro in his place to serve as regent. The Lisbon Constituent Assembly then attempted to return the colony to its previous subservient status, which had been upgraded with the arrival of the Portuguese court. The landed elite rallied around the regent to oppose Lisbon. King João ordered his son Pedro to return to the mother country, despite the fact that the king had told Pedro upon his departure to take the side of Brazil in any dispute between Portugal and its colony. Pedro refused, and in September 1822 he declared Brazil's independence from Portugal. His declaration marked the birth of the Brazilian Empire. While there was some resistance from Portuguese troops, Brazil avoided the violence and destruction seen in Spanish American struggles for independence.

The Empire

The decade following independence was marked by a compromise between three competing groups in Brazil: a conservative group favoring centralization of power and a unified government, a liberal group favoring a more loose federation under the control of the emperor, and a republican group opposed to royal rule. The Portuguese bureaucracy and powerful commercial groups favored strong central rule, while the landed aristocracy, who hoped for regional autonomy, pushed for a federation and decentralized rule.

Ultimately, Emperor Pedro I decided the direction for Brazil, opting for centralization. Pedro I maintained that in order to avoid anarchy and the possible break-up of the empire, a strong centralized government was essential; he dissolved the Constituent Assembly in 1824 and, with the help of his close advisors, created his own constitution—the Constitution of 1824.

This constitution called for a two-chamber legislature, with lifetime members in the Senate and elected officials in the Chamber of Deputies. One key feature of the new government was the emperor's *poder moderador,* or moderating power. This power gave the emperor the ability to approve or reject legislation, make appointments, and select the lifetime members of the Senate. The provinces had assemblies that were elected, but their power was limited to a consultative role; they also had an executive who was appointed by the emperor.

Notably, the elected lower chamber opposed efforts to centralize power from 1824 to 1831. At the same time there was growing dissatisfaction with Pedro's rule—both with what seemed excessive reliance on Portuguese confidants and his seemingly arbitrary decisions. Pedro I was forced to abdicate in 1831, leaving his infant son, Pedro II in his stead. Brazil was then ruled by a series of regents from 1831 to 1840. The regency period was an important one for Brazil, as a number of regional revolts occurred. These reflected dissatisfaction

A descendant of Portuguese royalty, Pedro I (also known as Dom Pedro) was the founder of the Brazilian empire and the first emperor of Brazil. (Ridpath, John Clark, Ridpath's History of the World, *1901)*

with the monarch and a desire for republican rule, as well a number of purely local issues.

By 1840 it was evident that the regency was both ineffective and weak—many argue that Brazil's unofficial experiment with republican rule had by then failed. For example, a number of constitutional amendments beginning in 1834 had allowed a sort of "creeping republicanism"; these were then reversed by the Interpretive Law of 1840. Despite the fact that he was not yet eighteen, Pedro II's majority was declared, and he became emperor of Brazil. Pedro II would rule Brazil from 1840 to 1889. This long period of imperial rule would be as important to Brazil's future political development as the long period of colonial rule.

During the time that Pedro II ruled as emperor, there were political rivalries between two parties, the Liberals and the Conservatives. However, the parties were essentially from the same social and economic class, and there was little to differentiate them in terms of political ideology. The new Brazilian monarchy, like the colonial rulers before, used honors and appointments to ensure political support. However, the imperial court designed its policies with little more than formal consultation of the landed aristocracy; the powerful imperial court and its bureaucracy would dominate Brazilian politics and society in the nineteenth century.

The War of the Triple Alliance (1865–1870), also known as the Paraguayan War, was quite significant for the long-term development of Brazilian politics. In particular, the war

Petropolis, Brazil's imperial summer palace, shown in a nineteenth-century engraving. (The Art Archive/Biblioteca National do Rio de Janiero Brazil/Dagli Orti)

caused the Brazilian armed forces to become politicized, in part due to frustration at their early poor showing. From 1870 until the coup by the armed forces that formally ended the empire in 1889, the role of the military in public affairs steadily increased. The Conservative and Liberal parties competed for support from military officers. Importantly, the ever-more-politicized officer corps also grew increasingly dissatisfied with the emperor and his performance.

By the last decade of the empire, the landed elite had also become unhappy with Pedro II—for them a major problem was Pedro's support for the abolition of slavery. The British had been pushing hard for abolition for some time, and this position was highly significant given their omnipresence in Brazilian trade and commerce. In effect, the landowners felt betrayed as abolition slowly advanced and their own economic and social status waned (slavery would finally end with the Golden Law of 1888, without compensation for slaveholders).

The last straw would be a break between the emperor and the Catholic Church, which battled over the issue of Freemasonry. The Crown went against the wishes of the Vatican and Brazil's bishops to wipe out the movement. While the church was relatively weak at the time—with only about 700 priests in all of Brazil, compared with some 8,000 in the United States, which had a much smaller Roman Catholic population—the loss of its support for the empire was significant.

So by the 1880s the key traditional supports for the monarchy had been steadily weakened. Likewise, many traditional supporters were not happy contemplating the eventual accession to the throne of Pedro's daughter Isabel. Finally, Pedro's personal prestige, so notable during much of his reign, was increasingly damaged by poor management—there were even rumors that he had become senile. The end came in a bloodless coup, led by Marshal Deodoro da Fonseca, on November 15, 1889. Fonseca was an army hero and headed the provisional government that followed on the heals of the empire's fall. The overthrow of the monarchy was largely the work of the military, and their role in Brazilian politics would remain critical throughout the twentieth century. In fact, from this point on the military assumed an active role as the "supervisor" of the nation's progress; they stayed on the sidelines when they felt things were going well, but did not hesitate to step in if they felt otherwise.

THE OLD REPUBLIC

The military thus ended the centralized regime of the empire, displaying its willingness and ability to change the direction of the nation's politics. In 1889, a constitutional regime was created, allowing some decentralization of political authority. The new system used federalism to distribute power to the various regional political machines, which ran the states according to local tradition. In the poorest and most backward states this unfortunately occurred often in a despotic manner.

The creation of the Old Republic represented a political victory for the parties supporting decentralization—most notably the landed aristocracy. And while the republic represented a break with the imperial order, it also represented a continuation of oligarchic rule. The actual level of participation in government by the people did not increase with the new government, and the key groups that were important during the empire remained in prominent positions during the republic—in short, power and influence remained concentrated in the hands of a select few.

The two most prominent groups of the Old Republic (dating from 1889 to 1930) were the military and the state governors. Early in the republic, the military dominated. And while the first civilian president was elected in 1894, the military never remained far from power and the political process. National leadership came primarily from the most powerful states, Minas Gerais and São Paulo, within the framework of the Republican Party, at the time the only national-level party.

The so-called *política dos governadores* (politics of the governors) was an agreement among state leaders that allowed São Paulo and Minas Gerais to dominate national affairs in exchange for a promise to the smaller states that the central government would not interfere in the states' internal affairs. In the pact, machine leaders—machines are unofficial systems of political organization, typically based on patronage; in essence they represent behind-the-scenes political control within an ostensibly democratic setting—agreed that the presidency would be exchanged between the two most powerful states.

Factions of the elite, both civilian and military, competed for control of the bureaucratic state, while regional and local elites looked for favors from the government. Society remained extremely hierarchical. The Constitution of 1891, which called for representative democracy, looked like the constitutions of other representative democracies in the world at the time. But at this point in Brazilian history, the reality was far removed—politics was a game played by a very limited group of elites.

The constitution called for twenty states, which would territorially be the same as the provinces of the empire, and a federal district in Rio de Janeiro. The federal government was created with three branches—executive, legislative, and judicial. The legislature was divided into two houses, with the Senate representing the states and the Chamber of Deputies elected on a population basis. Again, while substantively similar to the constitutions of other Western democracies, the reality of the Old Republic was very different. The franchise (or right to vote) was extremely limited; as a result, the absolute number of voters was low. Literacy rates were also low and social mobility was extremely limited. At this time an individual's loyalty was typically given to a patron or a region (or possibly a state) before it was given to the nation.

The Old Republic came to an abrupt end in 1930, the result of a dispute between presidential candidates. President Washington Luís Pereira de Souza of São Paulo broke with the unwritten agreement to alternate power and selected another paulista to replace him instead of accepting the nominee of the Minas Gerais political machine, Getúlio Vargas. Soon thereafter, Vargas led a military-backed rebellion that brought down the forty-year-old republic.

While the move by Luís to break with the old pattern provided the catalyst to the republic's downfall, there were other contributing causes. One of the most significant related to the 1929 stock market crash in the United States and the ensuing global depression. There was a widespread perception among the political class that Luís had failed to respond to the crisis; as a result, powerful political players had lost confidence in the government. As important, the military had become increasingly critical of the Republic and its seeming inability to accelerate development of the country's economy—officers in general were unhappy about Brazil's lack of progress.

What the various factions needed was a political figure who could unite them—from politicians to military officers to businesspeople and professionals. Getúlio Vargas turned out to be this uniting figure. Vargas was experienced in government and well-known, not to mention unhappy at having been denied the presidency. Vargas skillfully assured each of the players in the coalition that he would look after their interests. In return, they backed him, and the Old Republic was toppled. Vargas became the provisional president in November 1930.

THE VARGAS ERA (1930–1945)

Getúlio Vargas dominated Brazilian politics as the country's president for fifteen years. More content as an authoritarian than as a democrat, Vargas would over time highly centralize power and turn Brazil into an authoritarian state. Most scholars divide the Vargas era into three periods. The first period was characterized by the early provisional government, from 1930 to 1934. Vargas used this time to attempt to modernize the economy. He successfully put down a number of revolts against his moves to centralize federal power. One turning point came in 1932 with a serious confrontation with the state of São Paulo that Vargas helped in part to provoke. The leaders in São Paulo contended that Vargas was trying to postpone a return to constitutional government in order to increase his power vis-à-vis the state machines. They were accurate, but by starting and then losing the confrontation with Vargas, they actually enhanced his reputation as a hero defending the nation against rebels.

Once Vargas was in control, he called for a Constituent Assembly to write a new constitution in 1934. In the process, the assembly elected Vargas to his first presidential term. During this time, the Constituent Assembly became the Chamber of Deputies.

The second period of the Vargas era lasted from 1934 to 1937. Vargas ruled the period based on the 1934 constitution,

General Getúlio Vargas, head of the military junta and provisional president of Brazil (seated, center), with his companions in a railway coach as the group arrives in Rio de Janeiro to take charge of the new government on November 19, 1930. (Bettmann/Corbis)

but he consistently worked to undermine the constitutional process. The period was notable for the success with which Vargas manipulated and defeated all of his potential political rivals. For example, a communist uprising in 1935 gave Vargas the justification he needed to suppress the Communist Party and its leader, Luis Carlos Prestes. The only other major group that was politically organized was the fascist Integralists; Vargas managed to suppress this group in 1937.

The third period of Vargas's rule was ushered in when he ignored the constitutional ban on succeeding himself—this he justified by the need to maintain law and order. Vargas convinced the military to overthrow the constitutional regime and appoint him president, with indefinite tenure. He moved swiftly to abolish all political parties, canceled the 1938 presidential elections, and proclaimed with a new constitution the *Estado Novo,* or New State. This third period, dominated by the Estado Novo, lasted from 1937 to 1945.

Executive authority was significantly expanded during the Estado Novo. In general the period witnessed a dramatic expansion of state control over multiple facets of Brazilian life. Vargas was given the power to rule by executive decree. He also did not convene the legislature, avoiding in the process any sort of check on his authority. Vargas would intervene actively in the states; he replaced uncooperative governors with governors willing to follow his lead. Importantly, the state bureaucracy became the sole creator and implementor of government policies; in this period there was simply no check on executive power by an elected congress. The state nationalized economic institutions and natural resources, extending its power even further in the process.

Scholars point out that Vargas is perhaps more appropriately labeled an opportunist than a totalitarian. Most importantly, Vargas did not organize a party with a strong ideology the way the European fascists did. Vargas took a more paternalistic approach, using the presidency to consolidate influence with the urban working classes. As part of the process,

Vargas developed an extensive welfare system, created labor unions for urban workers, built elementary schools, and advanced public health programs; in paternalistic fashion these were presented as gifts from the state to the people. In return, Vargas, and the public bureaucracy, expected compliance (perhaps even obedience) from the Brazilian public.

The beginning of the end for the Vargas era came in 1943 with a secret but widely disseminated manifesto, the Manifesto Mineiro, written by politicians from the state of Minas Gerais, which called for a return to democratic rule. Once again, the military also played a critical role in radically changing the nature of Brazilian politics. Importantly, officers sent to fight in World War II in Europe were heading back to Brazil in 1945, having contributed to the effort to defeat totalitarianism. For obvious reasons, they favored an end to authoritarian rule in their own country and supported calls for presidential elections. Thus, simultaneously, political elites and members of the military of more middle-class origins supported the restoration of democracy and an end to the authoritarian Estado Novo. Vargas's opponents were helped by the fact that the United States had put Vargas on a short list of authoritarians whom it deemed should not be in power.

Getúlio Vargas organized elections to take place in December 1945. For many Brazilians calling for a return to democratic rule, suspicions mounted that the president would again try to subvert the elections, as he proved he could do in 1937 with the creation of the Estado Novo. The military chose to preempt this possibility, and issued an ultimatum to Vargas in 1945. Vargas quickly left the capital for his home in the southern state of Rio Grande do Sul. The Estado Novo had fallen.

Before moving to the discussion of the New Republic, which succeeded the Estado Novo, a few concluding remarks might be helpful, given the tremendous importance of the Vargas years to subsequent political and economic development in Brazil. Gary Wynia points out that Getúlio Vargas successfully combined two traditions of Brazil's nineteenth century. The first is the tradition of paternalistic central authority, which was perfected during the long reign of Dom Pedro II from 1841 to 1889. The second tradition that Vargas adopted was promoting the dependence of private economic groups on the Brazilian state. As he points out, the Old Republic had partially weakened centralized authority in Brazil, but it failed to eliminate the desire for it. Vargas was able to draw on the need and desire for a strong, centralized national leadership. In the process, he was able transform the presidency and the national bureaucracy into the single most important vehicles of the country's economic development.

When officers returning from the war and democratically inclined politicians began to demand a return to democracy, Vargas attempted to build mass support for the inevitable elections; as a result he turned in a populist direction, moving to mobilize labor through the Brazilian Labor Party. The move failed, as the military ensured that Vargas would not succeed yet again in subverting the constitutional order.

The body of Brazilian president Getúlio Vargas is surrounded by mourners at his funeral on August 24, 1954, in Rio de Janeiro. (Bettman Corbis)

Ironically, the coup-driven retirement for Vargas would prove short-lived, as he returned to power through elections in 1950. However, as we will see, this trip to power would prove complicated and unsuccessful, and ultimately end in Vargas's suicide in the presidential office on August 24, 1954.

THE NEW REPUBLIC

The New Republic proved to be no more successful or durable than the Old Republic that had been brought down by Vargas and his supporters. After Vargas's military-inspired move into retirement, elections took place to pick a successor. Vargas's former minister of war, General Eurico Gaspar Dutra, won the election as the candidate of the Social Democratic Party (PSD); he was also supported by the Brazilian Labor Party (PTB). The New Republic would see the party system expand to thirteen parties, but it was dominated by the PSD, the PTB, and the National Democratic Union (UDN).

Four elections were held in the years of the New Republic, with the PSD-PTB winning three of them—Dutra in 1945, Vargas in 1950, and Juscelino Kubitschek in 1955. Jânio Quadros won the elections in 1960, backed by the UDN, but he resigned the presidency in 1961, leading to the presidency of João Goulart of the PTB. Goulart's presidency proved to be the end of the road for the New Republic, as yet again the military stepped in to end what it considered an unacceptable civilian rule. The difference this time is that they took power for themselves, subsequently ruling Brazil for the next twenty years.

The brief period of the New Republic was marked by populist policies. Politicians focused on urban voters and developed patron-client style relationships with their constituencies. The patron-politicians needed access to the public bureaucracy to provide the patronage, which consisted of such rewards as jobs and contracts. In return, the client-voters provided electoral support. The main power contender was the military, which remained skeptical of the fragile electoral system, its unrepresentative nature, and the gradual move to the left that would culminate in the Goulart years.

The military saw at least one officer run as a candidate in each of the republic's four elections. Likewise, the military actively intervened in electoral politics, with military coups in 1954 and 1964, an attempted coup in 1961, and the beginnings of a coup in 1955 that sparked a countercoup by another wing of the armed forces. As we have discussed, the military held the view that it was their constitutional duty to intervene in the political process if they felt that civilian politicians were failing to govern effectively; these coups demonstrate that this belief ran deep.

It is important to understand that the Brazilian political arena had become markedly more complex under Vargas. A host of new political players had joined the political process, from increasingly powerful industrialists, urban professionals, and organized labor to foreign investors and state bureaucrats. Likewise, several new political parties were born with the return to democracy in 1945. This reality provides an important backdrop to understanding the fragile democracy of the New Republic—leaders tried to keep a balance between the key political players while at the same time promoting a rapidly growing economy.

The most successful president in the period at performing this complex task was Juscelino Kubitschek. However, he would leave at least part of the bill for his less talented (or lucky) successors to pay. Kubitschek initiated a dramatic program of economic development, which aimed to accelerate industrialization and build the economic infrastructure to sustain it. It included building Brasília, the new capital city intended to open up the vast interior. While Kubitschek succeeded in achieving rapid economic growth, the inflation kindled by his policies contributed to the political crisis that brought down civilian government. Kubitschek made it through his presidential term, but he left his successor with a bare treasury and the politically difficult task of tackling inflation.

Juscelino Kubitschek's high-growth strategy pushed, among other projects, the development of a national automobile industry. This photo shows the production line at a Volkswagen car factory in São Paulo, Brazil, 1975. (Diego Goldberg/Corbis Sygma)

The descent of the New Republic began in 1960, with the election of Jânio Quadros to the presidency. Quadros seemed determined to rule outside of the governing coalition that had dominated Brazilian politics since the arrival of Vargas. Quadros sought the support of the "man on the street" to help in his fight against corruption. Quadros was a charismatic leader and soon after taking office attempted to put together an effective stabilization plan. As the details leaked out, domestic opposition grew. Quadro's charisma was simply not enough to get the job done.

Quadros lasted only a short time—in less than one year in office he had managed to alienate several key political players. Quadros then made a completely unanticipated and unsuccessful move—he resigned from office in August 1961, apparently in an attempt to generate a show of popular support for his presidency. In theory he could then come back to the presidency with the "emergency powers" he needed to pursue his agenda. Quadros's bluff failed—his resignation was accepted and he lost the presidency. This bizarre turn of events would lead to even more turmoil. Brasília went into shock as it was left leaderless, and the political environment slipped into chaos.

Quadros's vice president was João Goulart. He assumed the presidency and proved even less able than Quadros to handle Brazil's tricky political environment. Most importantly, Goulart was not trusted by the military, not a strong starting position in Brazilian politics. To make his situation worse, the economy deteriorated quickly in 1962 and 1963, again a legacy of the populist policies of preceding administrations. Many scholars argue that the political environment of the time had overtones of impending civil war, as the left and the right simply could not agree on the direction the country should move.

Goulart attempted a few plans at bringing down inflation, but these ended in failure. By 1964, Goulart seemed desperate to build support for his obviously failing administration, and he made a huge bet by shifting dramatically to the left. He announced a major reform effort, complete with land reform (i.e., expropriations), nationalization of oil refineries, and the right to vote for illiterates. Amazingly, Goulart even entered a fight taking place within the military, taking the side of enlisted men protesting their treatment by their superior officers.

Goulart's gamble, foolish in hindsight, failed miserably. As historians point out, Goulart broke several basic rules that have guided Brazilian politics for decades, and some might say centuries. First, he attempted to redistribute property, in effect trying to take from the landed elite to give to the poor. He also tried to mobilize the masses against the ruling class, enlisting not only urban workers but also the rural poor. As

---

Latin America's Experiment with Bureaucratic Authoritarianism

The term "bureaucratic authoritarianism" (BA) has come to be largely synonymous with the repressive military regimes seen in Latin America in the 1960s and 1970s, notably in countries like Brazil, Argentina, and Chile. Such regimes exhibited a number of common characteristics. For example, people following bureaucratic careers, in areas like the military, civil service, and the corporate world, were commonly selected for public office.

Likewise, the working classes and popular sectors were largely excluded from politics—or at least they were highly controlled. In fact, political activity was often eliminated, especially early in such regimes. These governments considered the problems they faced to be technical in nature, rather than political, thus solutions were also deemed to be administrative rather than political (even if policies included "wage repression" of the working classes). One key feature of BA regimes was an intense focus on economic growth—and especially an emphasis on pushing growth by improving ties with the international economy (like multinational corporations). By the 1980s BA regimes became less prevalent, and Latin America experienced a transition to democracy.

Conservatives increased their attacks against Goulart, he in turn grew more obstinate. It became evident to Goulart's opponents that civilian rule was failing and that the military was the only political player that could swiftly solve the dispute. The coup that emerged to remove Goulart from power came as no surprise to anyone watching the political scene.

THE MILITARY REPUBLIC (1964–1985)

Like the empire, the Old Republic, and the Vargas era, the New Republic was brought down, as the military exercised its longstanding veto power to end the fragmented and drifting civilian regime. Note also that very limited civilian political participation made it easier to oust the civilian regime. This time around, however, the military took the helm, creating a bureaucratic-authoritarian regime to govern Brazil.

Many have argued that the military knew more about what they did not want than what they wanted regarding the type of political system they would put in place. There were many differences of opinion, with moderates wishing to rid the political system of the populists, restore stability and growth to the economy, and then return the government to conservative civilian leaders. Hardliners, by contrast, considered democracy a big part of the problem; they wanted to replace democracy with a permanent authoritarian state.

The military republic, which started in 1964, can be divided into three main phases. The first phase lasted until 1969 and represented a period in which foundations were laid, with new laws created and the executive branch reorganized. This was also the period of harsh inflation-fighting policies. The second phase took place between 1969 and 1973, in which repression saw a dramatic increase at the same time that civilian "technocrats" managed to produce the "Brazilian Miracle" of extremely high levels of economic growth. The third phase began in 1974, as the economy hit a rough patch due to the first oil shock. The military leaders of the time

wanted to start a process of "decompression" (political liberalization) to improve their own political legitimacy.

The first era, of laying down the foundations for military
rule and stabilizing the economy, was led first by General
Humberto Castello Branco and then by General Arthur da
Costa e Silva. During this period the 1946 constitution was
repeatedly modified by Institutional Acts issued by the generals. Many former civilian politicians had their political rights
suspended for a decade. The political party system was

*Brazilian military president General Arthur da Costa e Silva
(1967–1969). During his tenure, Costa e Silva greatly increased the
power of the president, silenced political opposition, and increased
media censorship. (Bettmann/Corbis)*

reorganized, including drastic changes to electoral procedures. Direct elections for governors brought in a number of winners who were opposed to the regime; the generals simply rewrote the laws to provide indirect election of governors. Two new parties were created: the National Renovating Alliance (ARENA) and the Brazilian Democratic Movement (MDB). ARENA attracted most of the UDN and the conservatives in the PSD, while the MDB served as the opposition party and appealed to PTB members and the left-wing of the PSD.

The Second Institutional Act of October 1965 further concentrated power in the hands of the generals. In 1966 General Arthur da Costa e Silva emerged as the military's candidate for president; he assumed office in 1967. At this time a new constitution was created.

By this time Congress had taken on a largely ceremonial role in the policymaking process; this minimal role was eliminated in December 1968 when Congress was put into indefinite recess due to a conflict with military leaders. In essence, Congress refused to remove the immunity of one of its members whom the military felt had defamed its integrity; the military simply closed Congress, which would not reconvene until March 1970. In this period, President Costa e Silva ruled by decree, while the public bureaucracy created and implemented policies, with very little regard for public opinion or legislative review.

Costa e Silva became incapacitated in August 1969. The event would spark the move into the second phase of military rule, which would be characterized by a sharp increase in authoritarian methods, including the arrest, imprisonment, torture, and even killing of alleged enemies of Brazil. Using additional Institutional Acts and a constitutional amendment, the generals further increased their power—in essence the regime now totally dominated Brazilian politics and society. Costa e Silva did not recover, and rather than turn to his civilian vice president, the generals declared the presidency vacant and selected another officer to fill the position.

Congress then rubber-stamped the selection of General Emílio Garrastazú Médici as president on October 25, 1969.

Ironically, while heading one of the most repressive administrations of the authoritarian regime, Médici was one of the most appealing leaders to the public; his administration would see a tremendous take-off in economic growth. Médici handed the presidency to Ernesto Geisel in 1974 (there had been an indirect election in Congress). Geisel then began the slow political liberalization process known as *abertura,* or opening.

Geisel and his political advisor, General Golbery do Couto e Silva, belonged to a more moderate wing within the military, which held that while military intervention was justified in origin, it represented a transitional phase of government—it was not meant to be permanent. Geisel lifted the harsh censorship of the press that was in place and announced that the political party structure would be reorganized. The most repressive Institutional Acts were also repealed.

The military faced a challenge in the sense that widespread and continued repression was simply unsustainable: they could not very well repress everyone in the whole country, especially if they wanted the economy to function properly. They were searching for a way to legitimize the state in the eyes of powerful civilian players; more elections were seen as an answer to their dilemma.

Geisel's successor was João Figueiredo, the fifth and final military ruler of the authoritarian regime. He would preside over the third distinct phase of military rule, taking the process of abertura to its conclusion, which was the handover of power to civilian leaders. The process of abertura included a broad political amnesty, further freedom for the press, restoration of habeas corpus (the right to have a court determine if a person is lawfully imprisoned and whether the person should be released), and finally direct elections in 1982 for municipal, state, and national offices.

The regime still planned to have one more military president in power in 1985, but the plan failed. Figueiredo proved

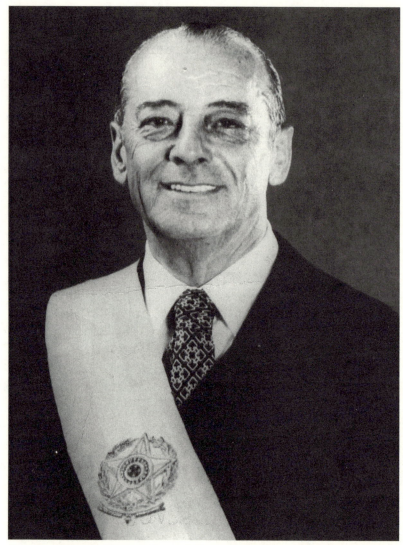

João Baptista de Oliveira Figueiredo was a military officer in Brazil who served as president of the country from 1979 to 1985. (AP Photo/Agencia Estado file)

to be a somewhat disinterested leader, and his health began to deteriorate shortly after taking office; he also proved to be an ineffective politician. This was unfortunate, as the economy entered increasingly dire straights, plagued by high inflation and excessive external borrowing; Brazil was then hit full force by the debt crisis in 1982.

By this point, inflation was rampant, budget deficits were massive, and debt service costs were huge. The soaring prices led to demonstrations and nationwide demands for direct presidential elections; the latter was avoided by the government, but there is no doubt that the economic chaos and rising political demands speeded up the return to civilian rule.

Opposition forces were determined to end the military regime, and they regrouped. An establishment figure named Tancredo Neves would lead the charge, chosen as the opposition candidate for indirect elections via electoral college in 1985. Paulo Maluf ran as the government's candidate. Neves beat Maluf in the vote, winning the race for the first civilian leader of Brazil since 1964. Neves became ill before his inauguration and did not live to assume the presidency.

It is hardly surprising that military dictatorship was attempted, and sustained, for so long. First, Brazil had a long history of authoritarian rule, including the long reign of Pedro II and the years of Getúlio Vargas—many argue that Brazilians were simply used to being ruled over, and the brief twenty years of the New Republic did not change this fact. In addition, there was a strong tradition of both the military exercising its option to change the nation's political direction if it was unhappy and also of powerful civilian players turning to the military to fix crises. As Goulart moved to incite the masses, it is no shock that the military stepped in.

The experiment with military rule reflects a chronic inability to resolve conflicts using agreed-upon rules. The working classes became ever more demanding, and the upper and middle classes were unwilling to accept the spreading populism and the changes demanded by the left. Civilian government could hardly be repressive, so the military took it upon itself to safeguard the country's direction and development.

The military government, in turn, grew increasingly illegitimate in the eyes of the nation. As discussed, abertura became one way to gain legitimacy. The government also felt that high rates of growth would guarantee approval. As discussed in chapter two, this led them to avoid painful economic adjustment to the first oil shock, instead using debt finance to push growth. It also led them to accept increasing levels of inflation—in large part a function of government policies. At some point the bill would have to be paid, and as the second oil shock occurred, Brazil effectively hit a brick wall. While the military leadership tried to replace national consensus and political unity with force, their experiment failed.

The economic turmoil in the early 1980s helped speed the military withdrawal from power by giving civilians political leverage. However, it also complicated the transition, as economic conditions for the new civilian leadership were abysmal. The early years of postmilitary rule were hardly an auspicious start to renewed civilian-led democracy.

TRANSITION TO DEMOCRACY

It has been argued that the forces of democracy, which won a major victory in 1985, nearly lost the war as Tancredo Neves fell extremely ill on the eve of his inauguration. The political elite, however, swore in Vice President José Sarney as acting president. Ironically, Sarney, a politician from the state of Maranhão, had been an important member of the military regime's team until late in the process of transition. His defection to the opposition late in the game angered his former military colleagues while at the same time making his new democratic allies suspicious of his motives.

JOSÉ SARNEY (1985–1990)

Neves died in April 1985. Sarney was simply not prepared to assume the presidency, and at the time did not appear interested in the job. He even wrote, "I told anyone who would listen that all I wanted was to wait for Tancredo Neves to recover so I could begin to serve as his second-in-command." The Sarney presidency was for the most part a failure. The president's motivation seemed to focus primarily on retaining office for a five-year term and passing the presidency to a civilian successor in 1990. His central task was overseeing the writing of a constitution for the New Republic.

As discussed, the economic conditions inherited by President Sarney were abysmal, far from an ideal situation to satisfy popular demands for increased political participation and economic benefits. Sarney attempted a heterodox shock (see chapter two for a detailed explanation) to bring inflation under control without the pain associated with traditional orthodox programs. The Cruzado Plan of 1986 seemed to be working well for a time, but wage and price controls were maintained for too long; the plan exploded just days after congressional elections that the government assumed would be won by its backers, reflecting the apparent success of the plan. The Sarney government never recovered from the disaster, nor from the appearance that voters had been tricked.

In 1987, Sarney declared a moratorium on Brazil's foreign debt, a decision not broadly followed by other countries in the region. While the move was in part designed to generate domestic political support, it also isolated the country internationally and served to reduce crucial lines of credit from international banks.

Sarney's years also saw the Constituent Assembly called to write a new constitution to replace the military's 1967 constitution. The process was cumbersome and confusing, not least because the constituents drafting the new constitution also served in Congress. Most importantly, the document was used as a political and social vehicle, and many nationalist and populist policies were embedded in the document. Most agree that the final document is unwieldy, even excessive, and in fact impedes rational economic policymaking. There were calls to change the document shortly after it was printed; those efforts continue today.

While the Constituent Assembly agreed to grant Sarney the five-year term he sought, little legislative progress was made. Many described his term as characterized by "systemic drift," vaguely reminiscent of the "inertial inflation" that plagued the economy. While there had been an important transition to civilian rule, much about the operations of government seemed to be "business as usual" in Brasília.

Sarney's economic programs led to little progress. However, their persistent failure helped build consensus among business and policy leaders that Brazil needed to move in a different direction—leaders had come to see a form of pragmatic neoliberal reform program as the way to go. At the time many called it "competitive integration" with an opening of the economy, privatization, and the like, but also with an eye to improving domestic competitiveness.

The campaign in 1989 for direct elections was a long one—this would be Brazil's first direct presidential election since 1960. Initially business preferred more moderate candidates from the Liberal Front Party (PFL) and the Brazilian Social Democratic Party (PSDB), but business in particular began to give its support to Fernando Collor de Mello, a young, brash political outsider. His fiery rhetoric also struck a note with the poor, and he quickly became the candidate to beat, and the most likely to beat Luiz Inácio Lula da Silva.

In the first round of elections, all but two candidates were eliminated, and as expected the two candidates for the second round were Collor and Lula. The contrast between the two candidates was stark. Lula had come from a labor union background, having been an important opposition figure to the military, and advocated a socialist policy stance. Collor, by contrast, came from a wealthy political family in the small Northeast state of Alagoas. Although some of his rhetoric was antibusiness, his policy proposals were pragmatic and aimed at improving Brazil's competitiveness—a largely neoliberal program. Collor won the elections in late 1989 and was inaugurated president on March 15, 1990.

FERNANDO COLLOR DE MELLO (1990–1992)

As discussed in chapter two, Collor attempted to implement a relatively dramatic economic reform program, founded on liberalization of the economy but also focused on stabilization. The inflation program worked for a time, but Collor's plan infuriated Brazilians, due mostly to confiscation of savings, but also to deindexation and wage and price freezes, which caused a sharp drop in real incomes. As the first Collor plan encountered problems, a Collor II plan was launched. But the new Congress taking office in early 1991 was basically unwilling to support the program. At this point, in mid-1992, a series of campaign finance scandals hit, involving allegations of corruption in the highest levels of government (they generated a Watergate-style investigation that eventually uncovered significant improprieties), and stabilization attempts generally stopped.

The political crisis escalated as the scandals deepened. While Collor tried, Richard Nixon–style, to defend himself publicly, his days were numbered. The Chamber of Deputies voted to remove Collor from office on September 29, 1992. Collor resigned the presidency before the actual vote to impeach; however, the Senate still voted to impeach on December 29.

Collor was obviously a political failure, but his brief presidency is important to understanding Brazilian politics. Most importantly, the national debate surrounding the 1989 elections focused on the presidential candidates and their policy prescriptions for the direction of economic policy. The country's voters were faced with a very clear contrast, and they

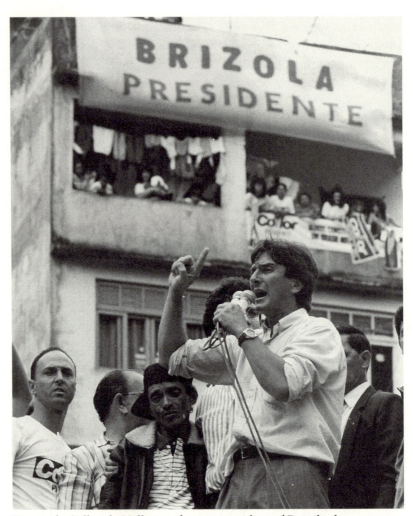

Fernando Collor de Mello is a former president of Brazil who was forced to resign in late 1992 after allegations that he had benefited from a massive kickback scheme. (Hulton Archive/Getty Images)

chose Collor. His administration was really the first attempt to change direction, and he accomplished a great deal in two short years; his impeachment cut short the possibility of following through with the program. In turn, it was a historic moment for Brazil, as it was the first time a president had been elected by orderly democratic means, rather than by military coup or ultimatum, and this time politicians lived up to their constitutional obligations.

Though Sarney had represented the first civilian to assume the presidency after the military, he did very little to change the direction of the country and its economy. Collor attempted this difficult task, hoping to open up the economy and most importantly reduce the pervasive role of the state in Brazil's economy. Much of Brazil's twentieth-century history is about the ever-expanding state; Collor was the first modern president to try to move the country in the opposite direction.

ITAMAR FRANCO (1992–1995)

Itamar Franco, Collor's vice president, was sworn in as president on October 2, 1992, following the vote in the Chamber of Deputies to remove Collor from office. Known as Itamar, Franco was a very traditional politician from the state of Minas Gerais, and most would argue that he simply did not have a fundamental grasp of economic policies and therefore of the immense problems facing Brazil. Franco permitted the

Itamar Franco served as Brazil's vice president from 1990 to 1992 and president from 1992 to 1994. (Paulo Fridman/Sygma/Corbis)

return of strong inflation in the economy, a move in line with his more populist instincts. Initially this allowed gross domestic product growth to resume. However, the uncertainty surrounding the Franco presidency caused business to put investment plans on hold.

Franco was not well-known—he was a regional politician with a reputation for mood swings and rash decisions. Unfortunately for Itamar, most students of Brazil think the most important decision he made as president was to appoint São Paulo Senator Fernando Henrique Cardoso to the position of minister of finance in 1994, after he had served a brief stint as foreign minister in 1993.

Franco appeared uncommitted to reform and quickly abandoned orthodoxy, slowed privatization, and pursued no visible strategy forward. The economy began to grow, but only as inflation and indexation returned. Brazilians had become adept at using inflation and indexation to their benefit, and they moved to take advantage of short-term opportunities the situation offered.

So with inflation rising rapidly, Franco appointed Cardoso as finance minister. Many argue that Itamar essentially turned over the reins of government to Cardoso, who then became a sort of "superminister." Cardoso rapidly put together a strong team of well prepared professionals to create the Real Plan, which was put in effect by July 1994. As finance minister, Cardoso made a concerted effort to resolve the country's fiscal problems by constitutional revision. However, few members of Congress were ready to change the distribution of benefits that the constitution had given to groups like public-sector employees, labor unions, and the elites in states and municipalities, as well as a large number of narrow special interest groups that benefited from the patronage. Still, several important amendments were passed.

Cardoso worked hard to advance his program, lobbying intensively in Congress. At one point he even threatened to quit if one of his measures was not adopted. The measure, which temporarily recovered some of the transfer payments to the states and helped stabilize the fiscal situation, then set the stage for the Real Plan. As we have seen, the Real Plan was not only an economic success, it was also a huge political success; Cardoso would ride this success to the presidency.

THE CARDOSO ERA (1995–2003)

The Real Plan was the foundation of Fernando Henrique Cardoso's ascent to the presidency. In addition, the political stature he gained through the process, combined with fears of the 1997–1998 financial crisis, most likely allowed him to win a second term. Cardoso won a decisive victory against his main rival, as once again Lula tried to reach the presidency. Cardoso beat Lula of the PT in the first round of voting in 1994 and was inaugurated president on January 1, 1995. He was reelected for a second term in October 1998, defeating his competitors—including Lula—quite handily.

Interestingly, in the run-up to the 1994 election, Lula maintained a big lead in the polls. Cardoso's party, the PSDB, lacked national strength, forcing Cardoso to construct an electoral coalition with other important parties. In the beginning, he approached the PT, contemplating a center-left coalition. The PT, of course, was not interested, given their own candidate's solid lead in the polls—why accept a vice presidency with Cardoso when they felt Lula could win the top office?

Cardoso ended up persuading the PFL, a remnant of the official party from the military dictatorship, and a traditional, conservative party from the Northeast, to join the coalition. The PT assumed that the PSDB's association with the PFL would open Cardoso to major attacks from the left. However, for Cardoso the power of the PFL, in particular to deliver votes from the Northeast, could not be passed up. Likewise, the PFL was a clear supporter of Cardoso's liberal reform program. While the Real Plan and its success played a key role in Cardoso's ultimate victory, many political analysts point to

Fernando Henrique Cardoso served two consecutive terms as president of Brazil (1995–2003). (UN Photo/Mark Garten)

the PFL's ability to deliver a large northeastern vote as a decisive factor in Cardoso's triumph.

The PT was ecstatic at the union with the PFL, believing the alliance with the right would doom Cardoso. In the end, however, the vote did not hinge on the partnership with the PFL, but rather on the success of the Real Plan and the sustained decline in inflation. The PT chose to attack the Real

Plan, despite public opinion polls clearly indicating its favor. Lula's poll numbers began to drop, and Cardoso was elected with an absolute majority in the first round with 54 percent of the vote.

Many scholars suggest that Cardoso represents Brazil's first "modern" president, one who steered away from politics as usual and took some historic steps to change the country and its political and economic system. Others suggest that while his accomplishments were significant, especially in getting rid of inflation and starting the reform process, the real record on reforms remains mixed. Likewise, the political foundations of Brazil's democracy, according to many, remain uncertain. We discuss this issue, and the need for *reforma politica* (political reform), below; the details of the economics reforms are outlined in chapter two.

There is probably some truth to both sides of the argument regarding Cardoso's impact on Brazil. However, Cardoso stands out as an effective leader and a statesman. Most importantly, Cardoso's fight against inflation worked, and Brazil has benefited tremendously. In turn, the move to reform the economy and to build consensus on the need for a new development model is important to Brazil's modernization. Finally, the stability of Cardoso's eight years in office has allowed political institutions to deepen, for Brazilians to truly participate in effective democracy and for the country to see what stability and real democracy can be like. Thus, while there is certainly some room for criticism of Cardoso, he accomplished a great deal. Those who denigrate Cardoso's role in changing Brazil need only look at the damage done during the previous years of military rule or the chaotic record of the first three civilian administrations to gain perspective.

When Cardoso took office in January 1995, he moved quickly to build allies to begin the reform effort. His central themes were to improve the competitiveness of the Brazilian economy and to reduce the role of the state in the economy,

Fernando Henrique Cardoso

Fernando Henrique Cardoso was a well-known intellectual before entering the Brazilian political scene. He had been a professor at the University of São Paulo, but went into exile in Chile after the military coup in 1964. While in Chile he coauthored with Enzo Faletto one of the most influential books on the theory of dependency, *Dependency and Development in Latin America,* still considered a must-read for students of Latin American development.

In brief terms, dependency theorists argue that certain characteristics of the global economy cause underdevelopment in poor countries. They maintain that there is a divide between the "core" and the "periphery," often simply a distinction between the rich northern hemisphere (the core) and the poor southern hemisphere (the periphery). Dependency is a condition in which the periphery can act only as a reflex of the expansion of the core economies. In dependency theorists' eyes, some economies are self-sustaining, while others can advance only as a reflection of the core economies.

Cardoso and Faletto took their analysis one step further, emphasizing the exploitive, unequal, and antagonistic patterns of social organization in dependent countries. In terms of policy descriptions the majority of dependency prescriptions—including those of Cardoso and Faletto—involve some kind of state intervention.

After writing his influential book, Cardoso moved to Paris, where he taught at the University of Paris. He returned to Brazil in 1968, where he taught, researched, and wrote extensively on the problems of economic development. After a distinguished academic career, Cardoso entered politics in the late 1970s. Ironically, Cardoso would reverse his earlier dependency-oriented thinking as he advanced politically, often joking publicly about the misguided ideas of his youth.

hopefully building a stable fiscal position in the process. Cardoso won some important victories early on, but then momentum slowed. Ironically, Cardoso's own party, the PSDB, was often reluctant to support his measures in efforts to protect special interests, while the conservative PFL supported his economic initiatives.

POLITICAL REFORM

One of the main reforms targeted early on, in addition to those discussed in chapter two, has yet to see any real progress: political reform, or the so-called *reforma política*. Many critics of the Brazilian political system contend that the lack of real political reform remains a huge obstacle to the country's future development. While the issue is complex and should be studied in more detail for full comprehension, we delve into the basics of the issue.

One of the most distinctive features of the system is that of open-list proportional representation, which is used to elect federal deputies and municipal council members. Each state in effect serves as a single, multimember voting district; there are no intrastate voting districts like those used for the U.S. House of Representatives. The number of seats per state is limited to a range from eight to seventy. Small states are deliberately overrepresented, with populations that sometimes do not warrant eight seats; large states are likewise underrepresented, as their populations would qualify them for considerably more than seventy seats (São Paulo, as the most populous state, is the most extreme case of underrepresentation). As mentioned, this system has been seen as a way to compensate for the economic power of the more populous states of the South-East.

Voters cast single ballots, either for a party, in which case the vote is added to the party's total, or for individual candidates. However, candidates' names are not printed on the ballots, so voters must write them in. Officials determine the number of votes each party received and then which party members, based on their individual totals, will receive one of the proportionately distributed seats in the legislature.

In this system, coalitions are very important. Partners in a coalition drop their party identities, competing in a basket of votes—this helps weaken the party system, as voters have little idea of the party affiliation of the candidates, or their policy agenda. Campaigns are often more about personalities than party affiliation or platform; this is especially so in coalitions, where voters vote for the alliance of personalities rather than the parties involved or their specific ideologies. Ironically, these coalitions often bring together a number of different parties with widely varying ideologies. The motivation is the potential reward—the promise of a leadership role—to parties for joining the coalition.

The system raises the issue of accountability, given that candidates are elected at large. Brazil does not have local constituencies that candidates must answer to. Most candidates therefore campaign statewide and are often competing against candidates from their own parties to make sure they receive enough individual votes to qualify for a seat when they are proportionately divided. This constrains efforts at party coherence, not to mention parties' policy stability. Importantly, the system minimizes constituent accountability after elections. Because of the absence of voting districts, citizens are unable to identify any given representative as their own. As many observers point out, deputies represent not the voters but the groups or party structures that produced the votes to ensure the representative's seat.

Another factor that weakens Brazil's political system is the ease of organizing a party. Small parties, which start in a weak position, can organize easily to send members to Congress; little thought is given to a party's platform or agenda. Cynics often call these small parties "rent-a-parties." Typically, the goal of obtaining office is to maximize the flow of resources to the state or municipality that sent you to the capital—deputies rarely view office as a permanent career but rather as a transitory one, before returning to the local power base. This reduces party coherence and means that nationwide parties do not really exist. Rather, parties in Brazil are regionally concentrated: the PFL is concentrated in the Northeast, the PSDB in São Paulo and Ceara, the PT in São Paulo, and so forth. Some contend that the legislative process is compromised by the regional nature of the system. There is high turnover, and often deputies have little legislative experience. In addition, little incentive exists to build experience or help strengthen the institutional process. The system reduces party discipline, encourages party switching, damages policy coherence, and minimizes representatives' accountability to their constituents. In fact, often lobbying the executive branch (for resources or "pork" to be sent back home) is more important than actually legislating. And the legislative process is extremely cumbersome. Constitutional amendments require two votes by majorities of 60 percent in each house; the final recommendation on a constitutional issue requires a vote by the full membership of each house in two sessions separated by an interval of five sessions. Clearly the system does not support swift moves on important national issues.

Typically, components of reforma politica include processes that make it more difficult to form parties, thereby reducing the number of parties and strengthening existing parties; increasing the incentives for party discipline, such as increasing the costs for not supporting the party platform; and reducing the bias against large states. Others also suggest a more aggressive approach to fixing the problems of proportional representation, most importantly by adding some form of district representation.

CARDOSO CONTINUED

Despite these constraints, Cardoso managed early on to get Congress to pass a number of important constitutional amendments, for example opening state monopolies in important sectors like petroleum and telecommunications. However, progress on "level two" reforms to social security, administrative operations, and the tax system was more painstaking. By mid-1996, for example, Congress rejected social security reform. Failures of this kind were a reflection of the weak political party system, as a number of key Cardoso allies defected to better serve the special interests they represented. The administration was again defeated on administrative reform in early 1997; along with some key defections, the PT's opposition was a very important component of defeat.

In 1997, President Cardoso began devoting his energies to reelection. This was not allowed by the 1988 Constitution, so his part of his focus was placed on mounting a difficult effort to amend the constitution. The already slowed reform process came to a standstill as the administration focused all of its attention to reelection. The thinking at the time was likely that vital fiscal reforms could be delayed until after the elections. In essence, securing another term would allow a deepening of the reform process. Cardoso's critics argue that too much effort was put into his reelection, taking the administration's focus from other important matters. Cardoso succeeded in winning the reelection amendment, despite opposition from former presidents Sarney and Franco, among others. One critical component of victory was popular support. However, progress on other reforms was very slow until 1988, when the threat of financial meltdown motivated Congress to adopt a more cooperative stance.

As discussed in chapter two, the so-called contagion effect hit hard in 1998. Cardoso launched a major legislative effort toward the end of the year and called for an extraordinary session of Congress for early 1999. The success of the stabilization program and the crisis environment combined to give Cardoso an advantage over his main contender—once again Lula. Cardoso successfully presented himself as the candidate of stability and fiscal responsibility, contending that the nation could hardly elect an avowed socialist in the midst of financial crisis.

At this time, Brazil was forced to obtain the aid of the International Monetary Fund (IMF), the World Bank, the United States, and other Group of Seven countries in late 1998; support was announced as Brazil promised a new fiscal adjustment program. Much was made of the fact that many of the reforms that had already passed through the Brazilian Congress had not been implemented, especially the level-two reforms such as social security reform.

Itamar Franco had over time become a sworn enemy of Cardoso, in part because he felt Cardoso received inordinate credit for the Real Plan. Despite the massive IMF program, Brazil could no longer support the currency, and Itamar played a crucial role: He declared a moratorium on his state's debt to the federal government, one of the last straws for the real. With massive capital flight, the government decided to float the currency.

A burst of legislative activity followed the devaluation, as legislators did not want to be blamed for the crisis. Important fiscal adjustments took place in the crisis environment, but Cardoso's plunging popularity constrained the overall reform process. No significant social security reform would be passed during his tenure, nor would there be much progress in terms of meaningful reform during the second term. Perhaps the most significant exception, after the flurry of legislation following the devaluation, was the Fiscal Responsibility Law of May 2000.

The second term for President Cardoso (1999–2002) was marked by a number of crises, including the Argentine financial meltdown, the domestic energy crisis, and the financial crisis associated with the transfer of power to a new president. Perhaps the biggest challenge was associated with the replacement of Cardoso. As the markets and investors contemplated the potential victory of Lula, an advocate of socialist policy in a country with still shaky fiscal foundations, the country entered yet another financial crisis. Interest rates skyrocketed, indicators of country risk shot up, and the stock market plummeted. The fear of an end to economic reforms, the return to unsustainable fiscal policies, and the possibility of a debt default were too much for domestic and international investors to handle.

The crisis was survived, in part because Lula and the PT reassured the country and important investors that they had modified their stance on economic policy. Cardoso had hand-picked his candidate for the 2002 elections—José Serra from Cardoso's PSDB. However, throughout the campaign, Lula from the PT maintained a lead. The prospect of the socialist's victory disturbed the domestic business community as well as the international financial and foreign direct investment communities. Lula adopted a pragmatic stance, promising a more moderate position (perhaps he had learned from his disastrous attempt to attack the Real Plan in the last election).

The key issue is that there had been a substantial degree of policy convergence. Most importantly, the PT, which had been the single most important obstacle to reform during Cardoso's years, had moderated its stance considerably in the run-up to the 2002 elections. In effect, the party moved from

Wearing carnival-like costumes, hundreds march through the streets of São Paulo, Brazil on March 26, 1999, protesting the deal Brazilian President Fernando Henrique Cardoso struck with the International Monetary Fund. (AP Photo/Mauricio Piffer)

advocating socialism to embracing social democracy, not too different from the stance Cardoso and the PSDB held. This moderation, coupled with the widespread view that more needed to be done to tackle Brazil's widespread poverty and income inequality, would give Lula the presidency.

The Cardoso administration experienced both important victories and disappointing defeats. While many important reforms were passed, many others never had a chance. A number of Brazil watchers also believe that too much energy was exerted in pushing for reelection: the second term was spent putting out fires rather than advancing reform, so, the critics believe, a crucial window for passing fiscal reforms was wasted on the effort to be reelected.

This is a difficult argument to support. First, Cardoso was already facing significant headwinds in the reform process, and there is little evidence to suggest it would have been easier without pursuing reelection. More importantly, had Cardoso not pursued reelection he would have been a lame duck in office by 1998; the fact that he pursued reelection and succeeded probably gave him as much power as he could have had at the time. Finally, the fact that many important fiscal adjustments were passed only in the midst of financial crisis underscores the political difficulties of advancing reform in Brazil—only when facing a dire situation offering limited options did Congress move to pass measures that were in the best interests of the country.

Cardoso's presidency was a turning point for the country, a time to discard the failed populist and state-oriented policies of the past. Much was accomplished, not the least of which was eight years without the nagging inflation of the past. In turn, political stability, with a successful reelection and then a peaceful hand-off to Lula, marked a political maturation for the country. However, the inability to pass crucial reforms during the Cardoso era also underscores the existing weaknesses of the political system. Without significant political reform in the future, Brazil will remain a very difficult country to change.

Cardoso's accomplishments are many. Among the most important were the stabilization of inflation, dramatic privatization of inefficient public enterprises (like Telebras, the huge state phone company), improved regulation, increased foreign direct investment, and economic restructuring. In addition, the simple fact that Cardoso successfully completed two terms in office while guiding the country through several financial crises and then passed the reins to the left-leaning Lula must be considered an important achievement.

LUIZ INÁCIO LULA DA SILVA (2003–PRESENT)

Luiz Inácio Lula da Silva finally achieved his goal of becoming Brazil's president on his fourth try, winning the 2002 elections and taking office in early 2003. While many pundits and financial market analysts argued that Cardoso's hand-picked successor, José Serra, would come from behind to win the elections, the polls showed throughout the campaign that Lula had a substantial lead and was most likely to win the elections. Several issues stand out in understanding Lula's victory.

First, Lula is a popular figure in Brazilian politics. Serra came across as a relatively stiff figure, while Lula seemed more genuine and enthusiastic. Second, there was a general perception that Brazil needed to move in the direction Lula proposed, focusing more attention on poverty and income inequality. Finally, a major factor in the PT's and Lula's victory was the moderation in the PT policy stance; as has been mentioned several times, Lula made it clear in the campaign that Brazil had changed, the PT had changed, and he himself had changed. Without this significant moderation, a victory during the financial crisis surrounding the elections would most likely have been impossible.

Lula's more moderate campaign promises proved to be more than rhetoric, and markets settled as Lula moved into his new job. Three early moves illustrate Lula's moderate and economically responsible policy stance. First, Lula immediately filled key economic positions with people who had considerable experience that the markets and investors would trust. The two key economic posts are the head of the central bank and the minister of finance. In both positions Lula placed strong candidates. The minister of finance in particular turned out to be a voice of rationality amid calls from more radical PT members for leftist policies. Second, Lula was able to pass a meaningful social security reform in his first year, something Cardoso failed to do in his eight years at the helm. This helped the markets gain further confidence that Lula would stick to tough-minded fiscal policies. Finally, in the early days surrounding the move to social security reform, Lula disciplined radical members of the PT who were not supporting the policy agenda. This signaled that the PT might have better discipline than Cardoso's own PSDB.

The corruption scandals discussed earlier have been a significant blow to the PT's reputation. While the party remains popular with the poor, the scandals have hurt its standing with the middle and upper classes. In short, the party long claimed to be above the corruption of Brazilian politics; the scandals now show that this is not the case. However, the scandals have brought some important housecleaning. There was a purge of the party's top officers, Lula's chief aid, José Dirceu, was forced to resign, and the minister of finance also later resigned. The fact that Lula won a second term to office, taking more than 60 percent of the vote in a second-round run-off, means that the PT will have another four years at the helm and the chance to further develop as the ruling party.

The Scandals

The campaign financing scandals managed to throw Brazil into its deepest political crisis since the impeachment

The Rise of Lula and the Workers' Party

Luiz Inácio Lula da Silva, the current president of Brazil and the leading figure of the Partido dos Trabalhadores, or Workers' Party (PT), was a former lathe operator and trade union organizer. He was born in 1945 in the poverty-stricken Northeast, and was himself raised in poverty. Lula has been his nickname since childhood. Before becoming president of the world's fourth largest democracy, Lula was the leader of a trade union that opposed the country's military dictators. He also led a political movement, the PT, that denounced the policies of the democratic leaders that followed the end of military rule.

The PT was founded in 1980, and by the 1990s it had grown into the largest opposition party in Brazil. Its constant and vocal opposition, as well as efforts to design a democratic socialist alternative to policy program have led many to question the party's contribution to Brazilian democracy. The party has many supporters, who focus on its efforts to both increase democratic participation and improve social justice. Its critics argue that the party's unfailing opposition during the Cardoso years has blocked critical economic and political reforms. Some even argue that the party is more interested in protecting relatively privileged urban workers and its party ranks than truly helping Brazil's poor.

Importantly, the PT and Lula have now been transformed from opposition party to the party holding power. While critics of the PT have some valid points, the PT appears to be beneficial to the development of democracy in Brazil. Most importantly, while acting as an opposition party until winning the elections, the PT has consistently used the institutions of formal democracy (e.g., electoral debate, parliamentary debate) to advance the party's progressive policy views on poverty alleviation and income inequality. Likewise, the party has served as a channel for more radical individuals to participate—legitimately—in the Brazilian political system, rather than rejecting it outright and engaging in less legitimate, and perhaps violent, means of political expression.

process involving Fernando Collor de Mello. The scandal has been dubbed the *menselão* in reference to monthly stipends congressmen allegedly accepted. The PT channeled large sums of money to PT-friendly congressmen through a campaign consultant. This type of off-the-books campaign finance is common in Brazil, but it is illegal. There are more serious charges, which have yet to be proven. Namely it has been claimed that the congressmen accepted the monthly stipend in exchange for backing the Lula government. Further, it is alleged that the money has come from state-owned enterprises or their pension funds. Further scandals have hit the Lula administration, including allegations that Lula's backers tried to buy a dossier implicating an ally of Lula's rival in the presidential elections. While Lula managed to win reelection, the scandal was likely a major factor in forcing the election to a second round.

As suggested, the scandals have been a blow to the PT, but Brazilians seem willing to give Lula the benefit of the doubt. First, there is a widespread (and cynical) belief that what occurred was not really any worse than what has occurred in the past. In addition, the population seems to trust Lula as an individual, as evident in his recovering popularity.

Lula: An Evaluation

Lula won a second term to the Brazilian presidency on October 29, 2006, winning more than 60 percent of the vote in the run-off after barely missing an outright victory in the first round on October 1. His term as president ends in 2010. The reviews of Lula's first term in office are mixed, but they leave room for optimism. Lula himself focuses on two main factors that have made the first term successful: social progress and economic stability. According to him, Brazil has never in history had the solid fundamentals that it has now. His approach is one that emphasizes incremental change—a "slow and steady" approach that can provide stable growth and further reform. This approach continues with Lula's growth-acceleration package, designed to set the tone for his second term in office.

On the social agenda front, there has been a significant net creation of jobs during the first years of the administration. Likewise a reduction has been seen in both inequality and poverty. By one often-quoted local measure of poverty, the percentage of Brazilians living in poverty dropped from 27.3 percent in 2003 to 25.1 percent in 2004. This reflects only partly Lula's policies; a number of policies from the Cardoso years have also contributed to the improvement. One important policy is the Bolsa Familia, or Family Fund, which transfers cash to poor families who in exchange must keep their children in school and promise to have them vaccinated.

Still, reform of the state remains in its infancy—the state remains bloated, inefficient, and, in many ways, unfair. Government spending must still be reduced, and the quality of its spending must be greatly improved. Lula did manage to push pension reform through Congress and has also suggested that he will resume a focus on fiscal reforms.

On the social progress score, then, Lula must be deemed successful, especially compared to the doomsday predictions of presidential disaster that were heard during the campaign. On the stability front, Lula entered office with a weak currency, extreme measures of country risk such as the yield on external bonds, and double-digit inflation. The central bank moved quickly to steady the currency and attack inflation by raising interest rates, proving to the market its seriousness about achieving stability. In turn, the finance minister indicated a tightening in fiscal policy, raising the target for the public sector's primary surplus, proving to the markets that Lula would honor public debt.

While these measures have been important, Lula has also had a bit of luck on his side. Namely, global demand for commodities, in which Brazil is a major supplier, has been unusually strong during Lula's term in office. This has led to an

Luiz Inácio Lula da Silva took office as president of Brazil in January of 2003. A former labor union leader, da Silva (known popularly by his nickname "Lula") was elected in a landslide following three previous tries at the presidency. He was reelected to a second term on October 29, 2006. (UN Photo)

inflow of dollars to Brazil, helping strengthen the currency and allowing the finance ministry to pay foreign creditors. While critics of Lula's hard-nosed approach to economic policy abound (even his own vice president has criticized the tight-money regime), the continuity of policy from Cardoso's era has benefited the economy.

The second presidential term for Lula is likely to be beneficial for Brazil. At a minimum, to have only two presidents in sixteen years will be a first for Brazil—the achievement represents an important foundation for a strengthened democracy. In addition, another two terms of economic stability under Lula should prove beneficial to the economy and Brazilian citizens. And finally, another four years of slow-and-steady economic reform can do much to strengthen both the state and the economy. Only time will tell if these forecasts will become reality.

A NOTE ON FOREIGN POLICY

It is beyond the scope of this chapter to provide a detailed analysis of Brazil's foreign policy and its development over time. However, a few brief comments on modern foreign policy can provide an introduction to this complex subject.

Following independence from Portugal in 1822, there were three principal components to Brazil's foreign policy. First, Portugal remained important to Brazil because of the two countries' strong historical and cultural ties. However, this importance would wane over the years. Second, England retained a very important role in Brazil's trade, commerce, and finance; this role would wane in the late nineteenth and early twentieth century as the United States and Germany slowly gained importance in Brazil's foreign policy. The overthrow of the Brazilian Empire in 1889 corresponded to a conscious shift away from the historical alliance with England—this would also mark the beginning of the special relationship with the United States. Finally, Argentina played a crucial role in foreign policy, as Brazil historically concerned itself with the balance of power in the Rio de la Plata region.

The years leading up to World War II were characterized by intense diplomatic maneuvering, complicated by the financial crash of 1929 and the ensuing Great Depression. Brazil would negotiate with the Allies and the Axis countries as fascists gained power in Europe; Brazil assured the Americans that its ties to the Germans and Italians did not affect its friendship with the United States.

As discussed in chapter one, Brazil eventually sided with the Allies in World War II, despite relatively close relations with Germany in the years leading up to the war. The country even sent forces to Italy to fight against Axis forces. In exchange for this support, Brazil received both arms and ships from the United States. The United States also contributed strong financial support for a huge steel plant at Volta Redonda, near Rio de Janeiro. President Franklin D. Roosevelt even stopped briefly in Brazil's Northeast during the war to meet with President Vargas.

Following World War II, Brazil witnessed a continuation of its special relationship with the United States. Relations with the Americans were largely defined by the Cold War, and disputes often reflected differing views on Latin America's (and Brazil's) role in the global balance of power. However, by the early 1960s, Brazil was increasingly unhappy with this relationship and began to articulate a more autonomous foreign policy. Such issues as Brazil's strong ties to Third World nations, the need to assert independence, and the need to control foreign investment stood out.

While the early military leaders explicitly supported U.S. foreign policy goals, a decisive shift took place under the military leadership of the late 1960s, which pushed a more nationalistic stance to defend Brazil's international interests. Brazil increasingly saw the South, which had the characteristics of a Third World country, as an area in which it could both trade and, more importantly, play a leadership role. In addition, there was a strong focus on national security, which emphasized colonization of Brazil's national territory; especially important was the notion that Brazil's tremendous natural resources should not be given away to foreign investors.

The 1970s were characterized by a policy of "benign neglect" regarding U.S.–Latin American foreign relations, as the United States focused its attention on the Vietnam War. Brazil's focus was on making the country attractive to foreign investors and generating increasing exports; this would help support the "economic miracle." As growth ramped up, the world began to pay more attention to Brazil. Brazil's stronger economic position in part supported the country's move to play a more assertive role in world affairs. The country began to distance itself from the United States, partially due to the military rulers' suspicions about U.S capital and the unequal partnership between the two countries.

One example of Brazil's more assertive foreign policy in the 1970s centered on nuclear power, important in Brazil as the country tried to develop domestic energy sources following the first oil shock in 1973–1974. In July 1974 the United States notified Brazil that it could not guarantee the processing of nuclear fuel for Brazilian reactors (which were being built by an American firm). Brazil quickly responded by signing a nuclear power agreement with West Germany. Relations worsened in the years of the Jimmy Carter presidency, as a human rights report critical of Brazil caused the country to break the military agreement in place with the United States since World War II.

The debt crisis ushered in a period of significant changes, and political and economic difficulties, for Brazil. The opportunities of the 1970s, from plentiful international capital to the ability to push more independent and assertive foreign policy, disappeared as economic conditions deteriorated. The second oil shock of 1979, and the associated debt crisis of 1982, led economics and finance to assume top priority in the international arena, rather than the traditional diplomacy and geopolitics. While the economic crisis dominated the agenda, issues like the environment (especially the Amazon), regional economic integration, and regional diplomacy became increasingly important.

The establishment of Mercosul, the common market of South America, in particular became an important foreign policy goal. In addition, the collapse of the Soviet Union in 1989 removed a central cause of friction in international relations, as the United States was able to reduce its focus on security and turn to economic affairs.

Fernando Henrique Cardoso's election in 1994 would prove significant. As discussed above, Cardoso was well-known outside of Brazil by the time he reached the presidency; Cardoso backed Mercosul but also pushed a number of additional foreign policy goals, including a much closer relationship with

The Amazon and Its Problems

The vast region has in recent years witnessed more and more explorers, wildcat miners, and landless peasants, attracted by mineral wealth and expanses of uninhabited land. One major problem has been constant invasion of Indian lands. Another big issue in the frontier is landless farm workers who invade unoccupied (or underutilized) lands; often the process leads to violence, with mass killings not uncommon. Both issues, as well as the ongoing destruction of the fragile Amazon jungle, have attracted international attention, reflecting poorly on Brazil. Cardoso, in response to international environmental concerns, set aside 62 million acres of rain forest for conservation.

The issue is complicated for Brazil, which must defend itself from foreign criticism but, given the hugely complicated nature of the issues, cannot move quickly to solve its problems. Not only are the issues complicated by circumstances such as illegal logging and mining and problems with land titles, but local and state opposition to meaningful reform is strong. As many have pointed out, Brasília's position is extremely difficult, as it is stuck between strong international criticisms to address these important problems and local and state pressures to maintain the status quo. Resolving these complex problems in the Amazon will require creative, unique solutions.

the United States. Cardoso took a more cautious approach to free trade, however, reflecting fundamental differences between the two countries on trade issues.

At the time of this writing, the proposed Free Trade of the Americas Agreement (FTAA), designed to include all thirty-four Western Hemisphere democracies, is effectively dead in the water. For now it seems Lula is focused on reinvigorating Mercosul—he has even stated publicly that neither the United States nor Brazil is making the FTAA a top priority. Rather, trade policy is focused on the Doha round of global trade negotiations—and the unresolved issues are many. In general terms, Brazil would like better access to developed markets, in particular for its agricultural products, but has been some-what reluctant to open further its own markets to industrial imports as well as liberalize its service industry. Negotiations will continue to be complex and intense, but Brazil will undoubtedly continue its slow and steady process of global integration.

References and Further Readings

Baer, Werner. *The Brazilian Economy: Growth and Development.* New York: Praeger, 1989.

Cardoso, Fernando Henrique, and Enzo Faletto. *Dependency and Development in Latin America.* Berkeley: University of California Press, 1979.

Dornbusch, Rudiger, and Sebastian Edwards. *The Macroeconomics of Populism in Latin America.* Chicago: University of Chicago Press, 1991.

Font, Mauricio. *Transforming Brazil: A Reform Era in Perspective.* Oxford, U.K.: Rowman and Littlefield, 2003.

Haggard, Stephan. *Pathways from the Periphery: The Politics of Growth in the Newly Industrializing Countries.* Ithaca, NY: Cornell University Press, 1992.

Kaufman, Robert. *The Politics of Debt in Argentina, Brazil, and Mexico: Economic Stabilization in the 1980's.* Berkeley: University of California Press, 1988.

Kingstone, Peter R., and Timothy J. Power, eds. *Democratic Brazil: Actors, Institutions and Processes.* Pittsburgh: University of Pittsburgh Press, 2000.

MacLachlan, Colin M. *A History of Modern Brazil: The Past against the Future.* Wilmington, DE: Scholarly Resources, 2003.

Mainwaring, Scott. *Rethinking Party Systems in the Third Wave of Democratization: The Case of Brazil.* Stanford, CA: Stanford University Press, 1999.

Purcell, Susan Kaufman, and Riorden Roett, eds. *Brazil under Cardoso.* Boulder: Lynne Rienner, 1997.

Roett, Riorden. *Brazil: Politics in a Patrimonial Society,* 5th ed. Westport, CT: Praeger, 1999.

Schneider, Ronald M. *"Order and Progress": A Political History of Brazil.* Boulder, CO: Westview Press, 1991.

Schneider, Ronald M. *Brazil: Culture and Politics in a New Industrial Powerhouse.* Boulder, CO: Westview Press, 1996.

Schwartz, Stuart B. "Colonial Brazil, c. 1580–1750: Plantations and Peripheries," in Leslie Bethell, ed., *The Cambridge History of Latin America, Vol. II.* Cambridge, U.K.: Cambridge University Press, 1984: 423–500.

Sheahan, John. *Patterns of Development in Latin America: Poverty, Repression, and Economic Strategy.* Princeton, NJ: Princeton University Press, 1987.

Skidmore, Thomas E. *Politics in Brazil, 1930–1964.* New York: Oxford University Press, 1967.

Skidmore, Thomas E. *The Politics of Military Rule in Brazil: 1964–85.* New York: Oxford University Press, 1988.

Skidmore, Thomas E. *Brazil: Five Centuries of Change.* Oxford, U.K.: Oxford University Press, 1999.

Skidmore, Thomas E., and Peter H. Smith. *Modern Latin America.* New York: Oxford University Press, 2001.

Stepan, Alfred. *The Military in Politics.* Princeton, NJ: Princeton University Press, 1971.

Stepan, Alfred. *Rethinking Military Politics.* Princeton, NJ: Princeton University Press, 1988.

Stepan, Alfred. *Democratizing Brazil.* New York: Oxford University Press, 1989.

Wynia, Gary W. *The Politics of Latin American Development.* New York: Cambridge University Press, 1990.

CHAPTER FOUR
Society and Culture

INTRODUCTION

Brazilian society and culture is without question a fascinating and complex subject. All of the preceding chapters, covering geography and history, economics, and politics and government, can be seen as providing the background and introduction to this largely contemporary topic. Over time these factors have helped create Brazil's culture—or soul, as some might call it. At the same time these factors have been shaped by this culture.

For the most part we focus on culture as defined by an anthropological perspective: the collection of beliefs, customs, traditions, and creative pursuits that make up and differentiate a given society. In the process we identify the factors that make Brazil unique, or its "Brazilianness."

We start the process by looking at the Brazilian people, focusing on the four main groups that make up the contemporary population: the Portuguese, Indians, Africans, and immigrants. We also take a critical look at the issue of race in Brazil today, particularly as we discuss the African contribution to Brazilian society and culture, and the reality of Afro-Brazilians today. While we will discuss the myth of Brazil as a "racial democracy," we also examine how different race relations in Brazil are from those encountered in the United States. A quick look at the Portuguese language, as it is spoken in Brazil, follows.

We then turn to look at social relations. Here we examine the hierarchical nature of Brazilian society, which mirrors our discussion of income and wealth inequality covered in the chapter on Brazil's economics. However, we also look at several social institutions, such as *parantela* and *panelinha,* which underscore Brazil's unique personalistic culture.

A final section in the first half of this chapter investigates religion in contemporary Brazilian society—like other issues in this chapter, a look at religion underscores Brazil's unique culture. While the country contains the world's largest Roman Catholic population and is the second largest Christian country in the world, it is also the home of several unique Afro-Brazilian religions, and we will take a close look at one of these, called Candomblé. Likewise, the country has witnessed a rapid rise in Protestantism in recent decades, in particular explosive growth in the number of evangelical Pentecostalists. Finally, and perhaps most interestingly, Brazil is unique in that a large number of its inhabitants actually practice, or at least claim adherence to, more than one religion. Perhaps the best example is the group of Brazil's population that practices one of the Afro-Brazilian religions while at the same time claiming to be Catholics, a concept sometimes hard for North Americans to grasp.

The second half of the chapter is dedicated to a number of specific topics that have been chosen to give insight into Brazilian culture and to illuminate the daily lives of Brazilians. We look at literature and the arts, popular culture, television, food and drink, women in Brazil, and education. While it must be remembered that this chapter is at best a quick introduction to the subject of Brazilian culture, it provides the foundation for those interested in further study.

THE PEOPLE

Our attempt to understand the uniqueness of Brazilian society and culture must begin with a look at the remarkable diversity of peoples that have come together to create the country's population. In very straightforward terms, four large groups of people have contributed to this society's unique and complex racial mix: the Portuguese, Indians, Africans, and immigrants. A more detailed look into each of the groups and their contributions to modern Brazil help us get closer to understanding modern Brazilian society. As we begin, however, note that each of these groups is far from homogeneous—great varieties of ethnicities exist within each apparently unique group.

The Portuguese

The Portuguese who "discovered" Brazil in 1500 were far from a homogeneous group. Portugal's location made it a natural crossroads between Europe and Africa and as such a target for numerous invaders. One group—the Iberians—came from the north some ten centuries before the birth of Christ, leaving a lasting mark on the region, including the name for the peninsula made up of both Portugal and Spain.

Numerous groups followed, including Celts, Greeks, Phoenicians, Carthaginians, and Romans. Rome eventually conquered the peninsula, naming it Lusitania, leading to the prefix "Luso" for things Portuguese. Further invasions followed, most importantly by the Moors from the north of Africa, who arrived in 711 CE. Portugal managed its "reconquest" from the Moors in 1249, several centuries before the Spanish were able to accomplish the same goal, but the ethnic legacy remained; after the reconquest the country's population included numerous ethnic groups, including Berbers, Jews, and Romanies (or gypsies).

Jewish people arrived in Lisbon and other port cities during the Moslem era. During the Portuguese Inquisition, many were converted to Christianity and became "New Christians." In addition, by the 1500s and the time of Brazil's discovery, a good 10 percent of Lisbon's population was made up of African slaves.

Not only was the population of Portugal at the time of discovery ethnically diverse but the Portuguese who settled the new colony were also a varied bunch. For example, members of the nobility were often the grantees of the original captaincies and owners of immense landholdings within the captaincies. Likewise, relatively prosperous commoners made the trip to the New World. They too often received large land grants. Peasants either became small landholders or moved to nascent urban developments. Like many colonies belonging to European powers, Brazil also received its fair share of exiles who had been banished from the homeland for violating its laws. New Christians also played an important role in early Brazilian society, migrating in particular to coastal cities and helping develop the burgeoning sugar industry.

The Portuguese brought to the New World a number of customs and attitudes that would contribute to the uniqueness of Brazilian culture. Among them, they brought Christianity and the Catholic Church to the colony. At the same time, adventurers heading to Brazil carried with them the materialism that drove their commercial endeavors, and these migrants to Brazil tended to disdain manual labor. Some might argue that this was a natural attitude resulting from Portugal's imperial history, but the reliance on African slaves to do most of the menial work was also a significant cause of this attitude. Another important institution the Portuguese brought with them was the emphasis on the family. This is somewhat ironic, since most Portuguese did not colonize as families, as the English would do later in North America. This fact led to the mixing of races, first with indigenous populations and then with African slaves.

While Brazil's population was becoming increasingly racially mixed, its manner of gaining independence from Portugal greatly contributed to Brazil's European foundations. As discussed in chapter one, the most dramatic event to take place after Brazil's discovery was the French invasion of Portugal in 1807, which caused the Portuguese monarch and

Rue Droit in Rio de Janeiro, about 1825. (Bettmann/Corbis)

the entire royal court to flee the country, crossing the Atlantic under the protection of the British.

Upon arrival in Brazil, Dom João (who had taken over as regent for his mentally ill mother, Queen Maria) moved to implement dramatic changes in Brazil. These included opening Brazilian ports to foreign trade and lifting bans on local industry. He also attempted to quickly transform his backwater colony, at least in Rio, into a European-style metropolis, establishing such institutions as an academy of fine arts, a royal school of medicine, a national library, and botanical gardens. The presence of the royal court in Brazil gave a boost to colonial morale, and among other things contributed to a passion for things European, especially French, among elites. This would have a significant impact on the historical development of Brazilian culture and can still be discerned today among Brazil's intelligentsia.

Independence from Portugal occurred in a relatively nonviolent fashion, in part since it was João's own son Pedro who declared "independence or death" on September 7, 1822 (he was crowned Emperor of Brazil on December 1). Two important points stand out on this score. First, this manner of independence has contributed to the belief—misleading at best—that Brazilians are a relatively nonviolent people. Second, the smooth transition from the colonial era to the empire contributed to national unity, avoiding the breakup seen in the Spanish Empire and allowing Brazil to remain a country of enormous size.

The end of the empire and the abolition of slavery were accompanied by enormous changes in Brazil, including the rapid growth of the coffee industry, the country's shift in focus to the South-East, early industrialization, and massive immigration. However, the Portuguese contribution to Brazilian society and culture by this time was indelibly set.

The Indians

One of the main factors that made the initial Portuguese experience in the New World considerably different from that of the Spanish was the lack of any so-called high civilizations of indigenous people. The lack of easily accessible treasure was another. Regarding the former, the key issue was that indigenous groups were for the most part dispersed in settlement patterns. This meant that the Portuguese, unlike the Spanish elsewhere, were unable to depend on large supplies of indigenous labor; while enslavement of Indians, in part led by the *bandeirantes,* was indeed undertaken, the relatively small and dispersed populations, the introduction and spread of disease and subsequent decline of the indigenous population, and the growing Portuguese need for labor would ultimately drive the move to slave labor.

It is commonly understood that the Indian contribution to Brazilian culture is less marked than either the Portuguese or the African, but it is significant nonetheless, influencing a range of elements from racial characteristics and customs to national mythology.

As discussed, the clash between civilizations has been nothing short of disastrous for Brazil's indigenous population. This disaster began in essence with the arrival of the Portuguese in Brazil, and to a certain extent continues to this day, most importantly due to internal migration to the country's frontier regions and efforts to exploit the resources of the Amazon Basin. To a certain extent, the plight of Brazil's indigenous populations has been aided by international concern for their welfare. However, recent history has also seen Brazil's elite leadership label these efforts as foreign plots aimed at impeding the country's progress, and in the process keeping the country in its poor and underdeveloped position in the world.

In general terms, Brazil's indigenous population now numbers only around 250,000, a small number in relation to

Yanomamo entertaining another clan's herald, who came to invite them to a manioc soup-drinking party in the Amazon rain forest, 1999. (Victor Englebert//Time Life Pictures/Getty Images)

the considerable international attention they receive. Their populations are located in peripheral areas, a fact that contributes to their relative unimportance to the vast majority of Brazil's population. Likewise, the lack of districts in the electoral system, described in detail in the chapter on government and politics, gives them scant importance in the policy arena.

Public policy regarding the indigenous is largely focused on creating reservations for them, as seen in the United States, but this process is complicated by a number of factors, such as tribal fragmentation and dispersed territories, not to mention tribal leadership that is often focused on selling mineral and timber rights. From time to time the government has resorted to using troops to clear prospectors from Indian reservations, but the draw of mineral wealth generally makes this a temporary solution. In the meantime, the Indian population continues to suffer, thinned by disease as well as acculturation.

Like other areas of the New World, one of the major contributions of the indigenous groups to Brazil centered on foodstuffs and cuisine. For example, Indians made a type of flour from the manioc root, which became a staple for colonists, who eventually preferred it to wheat flour. Other common foods included corn and cashew nuts. Indian names for locations, plants, and animals also found their way into Brazilian Portuguese. Indian forms of agriculture, especially slashing and burning, were merged with Portuguese techniques.

Indigenous beliefs in spirits and supernatural relationships between humans and animals eventually blended with similar beliefs and practices of African slaves. As we discuss below, the African influence in non-Christian religions in Brazil is dominant, but traces of indigenous beliefs can still be seen today as well.

Many observers point out that one of the most important roles played by Brazil's Indians was in contributing to the opening of the country's vast interior. Indians served as guides, bearers, and hunters. They were also involved as both participants in and victims of events taking place in Brazil's interior, the latter most notoriously as a result of the bandeirantes' slaving expeditions. For much of the 1800s most of Brazil's surviving Indians, located primarily in the North, were left alone. Many managed to avoid contact with the rest of the country, and many Christian converts actually reverted to native cultures.

During this time, Brazilian literature experienced an "Indianist phase," in which authors in general glorified the native Brazilian, played up character defects of the Portuguese, and ignored the harsh reality of contemporary indigenous life. The mid-1800s also witnessed the rubber boom, another disaster for many Indians that would last for roughly fifty years. As the Indians resisted encroachment on their lands by rubber trappers, bloody conflicts often ensued; some estimate that as many as forty thousand Indians were massacred in the period. As with current conflicts in the Amazon with indigenous populations, this provoked international outrage and condemnation. The end of the rubber boom brought a short-term end to this violence.

Some efforts were made to help the plight of Brazil's Indians. One famous figure who worked in this direction was Cândido Mariano da Silva Rondón, who convinced the government to set up an agency that aimed to protect Indians; the territory and now the state of Rondônia was named in his honor. However, most of the time, indigenous people continued to lose when they stood in the way of "progress." For example, during the military regime the generals set out to develop the country's vast jungles and rain forests. Perhaps the most dramatic project was the plan to build a transcontinental highway across the Amazon Basin. While further efforts were attempted to protect Indians, the military rulers were loath to let anything stand in the way of development; they preferred rapid assimilation to reservations and the preservation of native cultures.

By the late 1980s and early 1990s, international protests, both about the destruction of the tropical rain forest and the treatment of Brazil's indigenous peoples, aided in returning the policy focus to the creation of more reservations; still, pressures from outsiders to extract resources from Indian lands continue unabated to this day, and the ability of the federal government to enforce its own laws protecting the indigenous remains limited.

The Africans

Like the Portuguese who colonized Brazil and the indigenous groups already populating the territory, the African slaves brought to Brazil were also ethnically diverse and spoke a number of different languages. The number of Africans imported into Brazil was dramatic. While standard estimations vary, roughly speaking, 3.5 to 4 million slaves were brought to Brazil. It is interesting to note that Brazil received approximately two-thirds of the slaves sent to the New World, compared to what is now the United States, which received some 500,000. In Brazil, given the absence of immigrant Portuguese families, racial mixing was the norm. Portuguese colonists first mixed with indigenous populations and then with African slaves; although less frequent, some mixing also took place between Africans and Indians. In fact, scholars often point out that by the end of the colonial period one would have been hard pressed to find a "pure" European.

The first slave ship to arrive in Brazil landed in 1538. The boom in the Northeast's sugar industry created a demand for labor that colonists and Indians either could not or would not fill. While the notion is pervasive that Brazilian slavery was somehow more humane than in other parts of the world, the bottom line is that like everywhere, slavery in Brazil was based on the forced subjugation of black Africans by their colonial masters. Working conditions were often appalling, and brutal physical punishment was common, as was sexual domination of slaves by their masters.

Importantly, while Brazilian slavery was as brutal as that existing in North America at the time, there were undoubtedly more opportunities for blacks to advance. For example, attitudes toward the mixing of races were more permissive. In turn, this attitude, coupled with the shortage of white women in Brazil, led to both interracial cohabitation and sometimes interracial marriage. Often the offspring of such arrangements were both recognized and legitimized—property was even passed on to these legitimate children. Brazilian slaves faced much better odds of becoming free than their North American counterparts. Another way to gain freedom was through military service. Thus, while one must avoid the temptation to romanticize Brazilian slavery, this more permissive environment did help create Brazil's multiracial society, which is very different from that of the United States.

Mulattoes in particular took advantage of the availability of opportunity, often achieving remarkable success. One of the best examples of such success stories in Brazil was Joaquim Machado de Assis (1839–1908), a man often considered to be the greatest writer the country has produced and the offspring of a brown-skinned father and a Portuguese mother. Another oft-cited example is André Rebouças (1838–1898), an engineer and leader of Brazil's abolition movement.

From the moment of their arrival in Brazil, however, slaves searched for ways to gain their freedom. Early on, runaway slaves gathered in groups that were called *quilombos*. In the countryside these frequently reached considerable size, often replicating African villages in their organization. The most famous of the quilombos was Palmares, which thrived for decades in the interior of the Northeast. Not surprisingly, Palmares was viewed as a threat to the colonial order, and a number of attempts were made to destroy it. Eventually a military effort led by a famous bandeirante, Domingos Jorge Velho, succeeded in wiping out Palmares in 1695.

As discussed in the history chapter, the end of slavery in Brazil occurred in "slow motion." Likewise, the process was largely nonviolent, in part because slavery as an institution was established in the entire country, thus avoiding the regional conflict seen in the United States. Pressures to end slavery first came from Great Britain, but laws aimed at limiting the importation of slaves were largely ineffective. Still, by 1850 the transatlantic shipment of slaves became illegal. A number of laws followed in the middle of the second half of the nineteenth century. Finally, in 1888, Brazil ended slavery completely, becoming the last country in the Western world to do so.

Following abolition, the lives of Brazil's ex-slaves were not easy. To begin with, no substantive policy measures were adopted to help improve their condition. At the same time, the country's elites subscribed to certain European theories suggesting that Western "superiority" was the result of race. In applying these theories to their own context, these elite Brazilians found that their own country's backwardness and inferiority were the result of the large black and mulatto populations. Thus it was argued

"Whitening" European Racism

In the view of the elite class the answer to Brazil's problem lay not in creating a new mixed society but rather in gradually "whitening" Brazil's population. To facilitate the process, the government began to promote European immigration. As such, large numbers of new jobs in the country's South-East were filled by immigrants, while a large portion of the ex-slave population remained mired in abject poverty in the Northeast. These policies were also accompanied by efforts to discourage African culture. African religious practices were even violently suppressed, with these efforts peaking in the 1920s; by the 1930s the new spirit of Brazilian nationalism promoted by Vargas encouraged displays of Brazilian popular culture.

that a continuation of racial mixing, or miscegenation, would improve Brazil's development.

One of the most, if not the most, important contributions to the growing sense of Brazilian nationalism and the recognition of the role African slaves played in Brazilian popular culture came from Gilberto Freyre. His 1933 masterpiece, *Casa-Grande e Senzala* (*The Masters and the Slaves*) helped Brazilians come to grips with their racially mixed background and, many would argue, helped them replace a sort of national shame with a growing sense of national pride. In Freyre's view, postabolition Brazil was well on the way to developing a racial democracy that integrated whites, blacks, and people of mixed blood into a fairly egalitarian social structure, although he admitted that blacks had played a subordinate role. To take the idea further, Freyre felt that Brazil was a continuation of Portuguese civilization, a new "Luso-tropical," one that was capable of incorporating non-European and non-Christian elements. In short, Brazil was a "new world in the tropics."

Unfortunately, Freyre's term "racial democracy" soon came to be used by Brazil's governments and elites to dismiss racial issues and the miserable state of the country's masses of people of color. Later scholars have pointed out that the country is far from a racial democracy: Social and economic indicators consistently show to this day that the country's white population is significantly better off than either blacks or mulattoes, and that mulattoes are only slightly better off than blacks. A generalized correlation between race and socioeconomic status continues in Brazil, despite common denials of this fact by Brazilians themselves. Many take the argument another step, saying that Brazil has no "color problem" because blacks and mulattoes have simply accepted their position at the bottom of Brazilian society—to them, racial democracy is not only inaccurate but it may play a role in masking (and potentially legitimizing) the country's stark racial inequality.

One interesting question regarding race in Brazil is the peculiar lack of black movements, whether as vehicles for furthering racial justice or to develop Afro-Brazilian consciousness. The passivity of the underprivileged in Brazil has been striking, both historically and in modern society. One problem regarding race is the fundamental one of defining who is black, given the country's history of 500 years of racial mixing. Quite simply, color lines have been difficult to draw, in contrast to the United States, where one is typically considered either white or black. In Brazil there exists a huge continuum that ranges from white to black. Likewise, skin color is not the only factor used to categorize people. Education and employment are also used, often modifying classifications in everyday life and thus contributing to the mistaken notion that discrimination in Brazil is class based rather than race based.

Another point regarding minority status is that in several parts of Brazil blacks and mulattoes do not see themselves as a minority for the good reason that they make up a majority of the population. This attitude is often accompanied by the acceptance that their poverty is the result of Brazil's underdevelopment. Often there is a passive acceptance of underprivilege, a view that there is no obvious alternative to persistent poverty. Finally, it is often argued that this pervasive submissiveness is based on poor people's lack of access to the political system. As a result, poor Brazilians focus on individual efforts to escape poverty as opposed to political struggle.

It is important to point out, however, that a sense of racial consciousness is on the rise, especially in the cultural realm. While black political movements continue to be troubled in their efforts to gain mass followings, Afro-Brazilian identity is expressed in the cultural realm by participation in *blocos Afros,* or the percussion groups organized for Carnival activities. These groups arose in the 1970s in the poorer areas of Bahia as an Afro-Brazilian alternative to the white *trios electricos* that had dominated Carnival. One of the most popular of these groups is called Olodum, a name that comes from the African Yoruba language and the word "Olodumare," or "god of gods."

The group was founded in 1979 in the poor neighborhood of Pelourinho (meaning "whipping post"), a site once dedicated to the corporal punishment of slaves. The group is also widely credited with inventing "samba-reggae," a blend of Caribbean reggae vocals and the rhythmic drumming of samba. As such, it celebrates the peoples of the African diaspora, as well as "negritude" or "blackness." The group's success has spawned numerous other neighborhood groups in the Northeast as well as in Rio, further celebrating Afro-Brazilian culture and blackness. These groups stand as a powerful example of Afro-Brazilian identity in contemporary Brazil. In the discussion of modern religion below we explore another example.

The Immigrants

The Portuguese were not the only Europeans to populate Brazil, nor were Europeans the only immigrants. Some of the earliest non-Portuguese immigrants came from Switzerland and the Rhineland to establish small settlements in the state of Bahia in 1818. Two years later they founded Nova Friburgo, not far from the state's capital. During the 1820s, German immigrants also made their way to the South, responding to Dom Pedro's attempts to populate the territory bordering the newly independent countries of the Spanish colonial empire.

The biggest barrier to large-scale immigration was the existence of slavery (although for Protestant Europeans the country's Roman Catholicism was also an issue). Corresponding to the abolition of slavery in 1888, Brazil's need for labor on its coffee plantations drove the country to open its doors to European immigrants. Within Brazil the era was marked by a preference for Europeans, reflecting the desire to "whiten" the country's population, again, a reflection of racist theories of the time.

As mentioned, by the end of the colonial era, it would have been hard to find a "pure" European in Brazil. The onset of immigration did create a noticeably whiter population, as immigrants came from Portugal, Italy, and Germany, as well as Poland, Spain, Switzerland, Russia, and other European countries. Most of the immigrants headed to São Paulo, although smaller numbers spread out to such states as Paraná, Santa Catarina, and Rio Grande do Sul. Small groups even headed to the hinterlands, including Amazonas.

Assimilation into Brazilian society and culture occurred in varying degrees and at differing speeds. For example, Germans in Brazil's South remained almost completely unassimilated at the beginning of World War I; this caused tensions when Brazil joined the side of England and France. Brazil responded to the problem by requiring Portuguese to be the official language of instruction in all public schools. Despite this move, a similar problem was faced with the Japanese population in Brazil during World War II. Even so, this group became "Brazilianized" over time, especially in the second generation. In fact, many Japanese-Brazilians experienced culture shock upon returning to Japan in the 1980s, as well as rejection on the part of the Japanese.

In a clear contrast to Afro-Brazilians, most immigrant groups have fared relatively well in Brazil. The European immigrant populations of Italians, Germans, Poles, Spaniards, and Portuguese are strongly represented in Brazil's middle and upper classes. Likewise, their lifestyles, values, and religions are dominant in Brazilian culture. It is estimated that of the 5 million or so immigrants who entered Brazil between 1820 and 1930, nearly 35 percent came from Italy. Typically contracted to work on coffee plantations, skilled workers also made their way to São Paulo, playing an important role in the industrialization of South America's most economically significant city. Some observers note that the Portuguese spoken in São Paulo even carries inflections common to

Bavarian architecture in Blumenau, in Brazil's southern state of Santa Catarina. (Corel)

Italian. Perhaps more importantly, the Italians played a large role in organizing and unionizing urban laborers. German immigrants, while not nearly as numerous as Italian or Spanish immigrants, have also left their mark on Brazilian society and culture.

In its own way, Brazil has become a "melting pot," just like the United States. This can be seen in countless ways. A prime example is that numerous Brazilian presidents have come from many of the various groups. Just think of the names we have encountered thus far in the politics and history sections of this book: Kubitschek, Médici, Geisel.

Other non-European groups have played a major role in the flow of immigrants to Brazil as well. Most noteworthy are the Japanese. The first group of Japanese immigrants arrived in 1908 to work in the coffee fields, and as a result they are concentrated in the country's South-East, especially in São Paulo (in contrast to Afro-Brazilians, who remain concentrated in relatively backward regions). In general, the Japanese in Brazil have emphasized education for their children. This focus, combined with their favorable location in the country's most dynamic region, has allowed them to take advantage of educational and employment opportunities, leading them to significant social and economic success.

While many Japanese moved from the countryside to the city of São Paulo and its suburbs in the post–World War II era, others have continued in the agricultural sector, resulting in a number of dramatic success stories. It is estimated that the Japanese community provides 70 percent of the fruits and vegetables consumed in greater São Paulo. Many also point out that Japanese-Brazilians own and cultivate more land in Brazil than the total farm acreage available in all of Japan.

Another major group of non-European immigrants has come from the Middle East, and again their success has been noteworthy. Syrians and Lebanese began arriving in Brazil just after the turn of the twentieth century and have since seen several waves of additional immigration. Starting as peddlers, these groups have created an important presence in such areas as trade, industry, banking, hotels, and communications.

Brazil also has an important Jewish population, second in South America only to Argentina. For the most part the Jewish community is found in the major cities and is visible in areas such as business, banking, and communications (the print media, for example).

The influx of immigrants has largely ended for Brazil, and the ethnic composition of the country has remained constant for several decades. It is interesting to note, however, that the ethnic composition of the country is still somewhat fluid. Figures are essentially approximations, since individuals are free to choose their ethnic group in the country's censuses.

Regional Types

Interestingly, Brazilians vary not only according to ethnicity but also by region. It is common to classify individuals and their apparent behavioral characteristics according to their region of origin. The argument is often made that such distinctions are more noticeable in Brazil than similar geographic distinctions in the United States (New Yorker, Californian, southerner, etc.). Obviously, this kind of classification becomes a complicated process, given the degree of mobility and the widespread phenomenon of internal migration in Brazil. Still, a few basic comments about these generalizations could prove helpful; however, keep in mind that in many ways these are simply stereotypes—but stereotypes that contain meaning for Brazilians.

People from São Paulo are called *paulistas*. In general terms they are considered to be hardworking people, and often entrepreneurial. They are often considered materialistic, a bit pushy, and at times seen as displaying a sense of superiority (no doubt a reflection of São Paulo's status as the country's economic powerhouse). Residents of Rio de Janeiro are called *cariocas.* Cariocas are seen as fun-loving and carefree individuals, attitudes often associated with the beach lifestyle so typical of Rio. Some consider the cariocas to be somewhat devious, despite their laid-back demeanor. The inhabitants of Minas Gerais are called *mineiros.* They are considered to be taciturn, somewhat frugal, and cautious people. Some suggest that mineiros are also moody. *Gaúchos* are from Brazil's South and are thought of as very independent, even belligerent, a legacy of their cowboy (and separatist) past. Finally, *bahianos* are those from the country's northeastern state of Bahia. They are portrayed as somewhat introverted, but also sensuous and interested in food.

THE LANGUAGE

It is often pointed out that large numbers of people in the United States have no idea what language is spoken in Brazil. While it is understandable that people in England speak English, people in Russia speak Russian, and people in China speak Chinese, it is hard to understand why people who know perfectly well that Americans do not speak "American" might think that the Brazilians speak "Brazilian." They in fact speak Portuguese.

For Brazilians, language is a vital component of their cultural identity. Interestingly, the Portuguese spoken in Brazil is dramatically different than that spoken in Portugal; many argue that the two are substantially more different from each other than the English used in England is from that used in the United States.

One important reason Portuguese is so important to Brazil is the simple fact that Brazil's neighbors speak Spanish—this seems to give Brazil a sense of being unique and different from the rest of Latin America. In fact, Brazilians sometimes speak of Latin America as if it were another continent rather than the part of the Western Hemisphere to which Brazil belongs (obviously when used in this context Brazilians are typically referring to Spanish America). It must be pointed out that Brazil is a verbalistic culture, meaning that how one says things can be as important as what one is actually saying. The ability to speak well in public—with emotion and conviction—is a major attribute for politicians.

Portuguese is the world's seventh most widely spoken language (or eighth, depending on whether nonnative speakers are counted). While the language lacks the commercial importance of English or the political importance of Russian or Chinese, Portuguese is nonetheless one of the world's major languages. It is often noted that the Portuguese language is more complex than Spanish; at a minimum it is clear that Brazilians have an easier time understanding the Spanish spoken by its Latin American neighbors than vice versa.

Brazilian Portuguese is a relatively open language, like American English—new words enter the vocabulary relatively easily, in stark contrast to languages like French, which attempt to avoid the "corruption" associated with non-French words. Portuguese spoken in Brazil contains a multitude of words derived from both Latin and Arabic; it has also borrowed freely from other European languages, such as Italian, Spanish, and English, as well as words from Asia that reflect Portugal's maritime history.

There are two other major sources of words for Brazilian Portuguese: the Tupi and African languages. Tupi is the commonly used name for Tupi-Guarani, discussed in the history chapter. Importantly, Tupi-Guarani is a large language family rather than a single language; scholars note that the degree of linguistic variety at the time of discovery was tremendous. The multitude of indigenous languages made the work of the Portuguese somewhat difficult, as they aimed both to secure labor and save souls. The early Jesuits solved the problem by inventing a language based on the languages they most frequently encountered, in essence those from the Tupi group; this was called the *língua geral* (or general language). Interestingly the language flourished and was prevalent during the entire colonial period, used not only by clergy and converted Indians but also by the Portuguese settlers.

By the nineteenth century, which witnessed first the translation of the Portuguese Crown to its prized colony and then independence and the empire, Portuguese had become established as the national language. There were some calls for a return to the língua geral as the national language—in part a reflection of the anti-Portuguese sentiment that accompanied the move to independence—but these were largely ineffective. One major change that did take place was the elimination of the Portuguese system of given and family names. The new, more flexible Brazilian system is open to names from classical antiquity, Tupi, and invented or borrowed names (thus one can find Brazilians with names ranging from Aristóteles and Demosthenes to Iracema and Ubirajara to Hamilton and Wagner).

Tupi words are commonly found in Brazilian Portuguese for things like flora and fauna, but they often find their way into everyday speech as well. Words derived from African languages are common for foods, musical instruments of African origin, as well as for all aspects of African-derived religious ceremonies.

Brazilian Portuguese is now remarkably different from the Portuguese spoken in Europe; in fact "bilingual" dictionaries have been published to help speakers of the two versions of Portuguese bridge the gap. Two final points must be made regarding language, which relate less to the actual words and more to the manner in which Brazilians communicate. First, Brazilians are what Americans often jokingly refer to as "close talkers." In other words, Brazilians are used to being much closer to one another when in conversation than Americans—to a degree that would make many Americans uncomfortable (all the while they are likely to use a variety of hand gestures). In a related point, Brazilians greet one another in a very affectionate manner—again to a degree that might make Americans uncomfortable; kisses offered by women and male embraces are typical. The greater reserve of Americans is often interpreted by the Brazilians as a sort of coldness or excess of formality.

SOCIAL RELATIONSHIPS

Any discussion of social relationships in Brazil must begin with at least a short discussion of the country's social class system, as this defines the environment in which social interaction takes place. Brazil's social system, which has evolved considerably over time, is complex. The upper class includes both landowners and an industrial elite. The popular masses contain numerous groups, including a large peasantry and a rural workforce participating in wage labor. There is also an indigenous population, now rather small, that has relatively little contact with mainstream national society. An organized working class has grown in the country's urban areas, but this group stands in stark contrast to a huge group of chronically unemployed, or underemployed, urban residents. Over time Brazil has also witnessed the growth of its middle class, which many estimate to make up some 10 to 15 percent of the national population (but maybe as much as 30 percent of some cities).

In general terms, social status in Brazil reflects one's occupation and/or wealth. However, as discussed above, it is also a matter of race. There is a very strong correlation between race and social standing in Brazil: Most who are on top are white, while those at the bottom are largely black; some mixed blood people are in the middle, but not nearly as many as the proponents of racial democracy would suggest. Still, in Brazil (as opposed to the United States) race is not based only on physical features. Rather, categorizations of race are a social concept, and as such leave room for interpretation. Education, occupation—even manner of

Brazilian Portuguese

Brazilian Portuguese has been influenced by a host of factors, including both indigenous Brazilian and African languages. These influences have led the language to differ considerably from European Portuguese. Those readers interested in studying the language in detail must be certain to study Brazilian, as opposed to European, Portuguese—failure to do so could result in some unintended, possibly rather humorous, consequences. In the meantime we have added a short list of Brazilian Portuguese words and phrases to introduce the subject.

How are you?   *Como vai? Tudo bem?*

I'm fine!   *Tudo bem! Tudo tranquillo!*

Hello   *Ola!*

Hi   *Oi!*

Goodbye   *Tchau! Até logo!*

Good morning   *Bom dia!*

Good afternoon   *Boa tarde!*

Good evening   *Boa noite!*

Good night   *Boa noite!*

Thank you   *Obrigado* (masculine), *obrigada* (feminine).

You're welcome   *De nada.*

Yes   *Sim.*

No   *Não.*

Maybe   *Talvez.*

And   *E.*

Please/excuse me   *Por favor.*

Sorry (apologizing)   *Desculpe.*

Excuse me (making way, entering)   *Dá licença.*

No problem. It doesn't matter   *Não tem problema.*

No problem   *Não faz mal.*

My name is   *Meu nome é.*

What is your name?   *Como é seu nome?*

What's your nationality?   *Qual é sua nacionalidade?*

Pleased to meet you   *Prazer.*

Very pleased to meet you   *Muito prazer.*

Do you speak Portuguese?   *Você fala português?*

Yes I do/no I don't   *Falo/não, não falo.*

Yes, I speak a little bit   *Falo um pouquinho.*

How old are you?   *Quantos años você tem?*

I am 30   *Tenho 30 years.*

Pardon, I didn't understand   *Como? Não entendi direito.*

Speak more slowly   *Fale mais devagar.*

Repeat please   *Repita, por favor.*

Where is the restroom?   *Onde é o banheiro?*

How much is it?   *Quanto é?*

At what time?   *A que horas?*

How many?   *Quantos* (masculine), *quantas* (feminine)?

It was a pleasure speaking with you   *Foi um prazer falar come você.*

It was a pleasure meeting you   *Foi um prazer te conhocer.*

Have a good trip   *Boa viagem.*

Enjoy your meal   *Bom apetite.*

Have a nice weekend   *Bom fin de semana.*

Thanks/same to you   *Obrigado (masculine), obrigada (feminine)/igualmente.*

dress—are among the factors that allow for flexibility of interpretation.

Historically, Brazilian society, largely rural and based on agriculture, was split into two main groups: the aristocracy of the planter class and the peasants who worked for these elites. While there were some small groups of people that existed in the middle of these extremes, they were limited in number. To a large degree, the poor were dependent on the rich—they rarely owned property and were illiterate. Their survival depended on the protection of someone of elite status, called a *patron*. This dependence was often formalized in a ritual kinship, in which the wealthy patron became the *compadre*, or baptismal godfather, of the peasant's child, guaranteeing some degree of protection should the peasant die. Thus the lower classes were rarely organized or politicized—social organization in this sense was highly personal and based on the patron-client relationship. In some areas of rural Brazil this system of organization still exists; the power of the old aristocratic families has waned, but many remain important players in politics, especially in the country's Northeast.

The massive changes that have occurred in Brazil in the modern era, especially industrialization and urbanization, have also driven profound changes in the country's class structure. However, the dramatic contrast between rich and poor remains a fundamental feature of the country. The upper class has expanded to include groups such as industrialists, bankers, and entrepreneurs. The lower class has changed as well. For example, there is not only an urban working class but also a more marginal lower class, often made up of migrants, that participates in the "informal sector," engaging in low-productivity economic activities that remain largely "off the books." In Brazil, like in many countries in Latin America, the working class has become a sort of elite among the lower classes, with money to participate in the formal economy and some clout within the

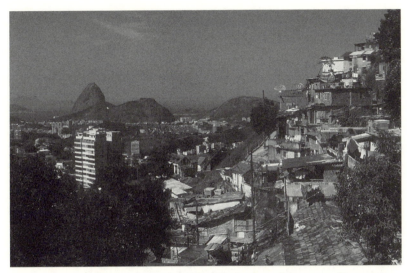

This picture captures the view of Rio de Janeiro from one of its many favelas. (iStockPhoto)

political system. Those less fortunate are often migrants to the cities, do not directly participate in the formal economy, and are marginal at best to the political system. These groups often live in slums (called favelas in Rio de Janeiro, and known by this name internationally).

The land on which the favelas are built usually belongs to someone other than its occupants. In turn, most homes do not have running water, electricity, or functioning sewers (although electricity is often "pirated" using illegal lines to existing power sources). Crude dwellings are constructed of anything that squatters can find, including cardboard and discarded lumber. Violence against squatters is not uncommon.

Along with changes to the upper and lower classes, Brazil's middle class has grown by leaps and bounds from the 1950s. This has reflected industrialization, the growth of the service sector, and the dramatic expansion of the government. Access to the middle class requires above all access to education, and it has only been in the twentieth century that higher education has become available to large segments of the population (there were no institutions of higher learning in Brazil until the nineteenth century; the printing press did not even arrive in the country until the Portuguese monarchy was moved to its colony). Still, despite growth of the middle class, the gap between the wealthy and the poor remains among the worst in the world.

In addition to the social class structure, there are other interesting and important features of social relationships in Brazil. A good place to start is to consider characteristics that are typically associated with national character. In the United States, characteristics such as rugged individualism and self-reliance are often glorified. Brazil is exceedingly different in this regard. Characteristics such as interdependence and cooperation are seen as important. Notably, Brazilians organize their lives around other people—social involvement is pervasive, and personal relations are paramount. These factors are so important in the lives of Brazilians that most people are rarely alone; in fact; being alone is often seen as a signal that something might in fact be wrong.

As regards social relations, the family is the single most important institution in Brazil, and *parantela* defines the network of relationships based on the extended family. Indeed, it is from the parantela that other relationships typically radiate. Given the dramatic changes associated with modernization in Brazil (e.g., migration, urbanization), parantela has become less important than in the past; however, extended family connections remain a key ingredient in Brazilian life.

Social life is defined by extended family groups, and membership in such groups implies both benefits and obligations. Weekends and holidays see family members gathered for food, drink, and conversation. These gatherings are intergenerational, and the focus is on the present. As for obligations, extended family members come to each other's assistance in a wide range of matters, from finances and personal problems to work issues and problems with government bureaucracy; strong loyalty is a given. Interestingly, given the importance of parantela in Brazil, few there claim to be "self-made" as is common in the United States; the need for connections is widely understood and recognized, and one's ties to an extended family provide the individual with identity and status at the same time. Indeed, without the identity and status of such a group, one could hardly be judged in terms of friendship, business relations, political office, or marriage.

Another important type of group in Brazil is called *panelinha* (little saucepan). Often the panelinha begins with one's class in school, and then becomes an extended network of people who share and promote common interests. In essence the group is informal, relatively closed, defined by personal ties, and made up of individuals from a wide variety of professions. Each then comes to the aid of the others, offering both professional expertise and contacts to members of the group. Of course, these benefits are offered in exchange for the protection and advancement one's own interests. Interestingly, the highly personal nature of the panelinha, as opposed to a bond based on political or ideological beliefs, has made for some extremely strange bedfellows in Brazilian politics, in which people of widely divergent beliefs and platforms become allies.

Attitudes about time in Brazil differ markedly from those in the United States, and often these attitudes reflect the country's unique social relations. For example, personal loyalty is more important than punctuality. Thus, if a personal acquaintance shows up, giving attention to this friend is seen as more important than making an appointment on time. Likewise, promptness varies depending on the importance of the events and its participants; dinners, parties, and the like often start well after the appointed time. As many observers of Brazilian social life point out, in Brazil time can bend to the needs of people.

One final characteristic of Brazilian social life must be mentioned, as it underscores the uniqueness of Brazilian culture. Called *jeitinho,* it is a uniquely Brazilian approach to solving an awkward or difficult situation or problem. It is a rapid, improvised response to a situation that at first glance seems impossible to fix. In essence, the jeitinho is a mechanism for dealing with society—a method or knack of getting something done. It is frequently referred to in Brazilian newspapers, literature, and travel books.

Often solving the problem involves using the one's parantela or panelinha to identify the appropriate person to intervene; at other times the individual attempting to overcome the problem will try to establish a connection or personal relationship between himself and the person needed to fix the problem—for the most part this is not considered bribery and does not involve money. Many argue that Brazil's arbitrary and often authoritarian system of government (at the local, state, and federal levels), the self-importance of office employees, and the rules and practices of most businesses make the jeitinho unavoidable. The wide gulf between the rich and poor extends to the jeitinho—the rich can often hire professionals to fix their immediate problems, while the less fortunate must search for alternative solutions.

RELIGION

As is apparent from much of the discussion above, Brazil is a country that defies simple definitions; a look at religion in the country further underscores this point. In essence, Brazil is a Roman Catholic country; in fact it is the largest on earth in terms of population and the second largest Christian country in the world. However, it is also a country in which many people also practice a second religion. Many see this as a great example of so-called Brazilian nonchalance. Afro-Brazilian religions have remained popular in the country, while Protestantism (especially evangelical movements) has surged in popularity, benefiting at least in part from the shortage of Catholic priests in Brazil. Also, various forms of popular Catholicism have persisted over time, which follow practices that are not typically Vatican approved.

Catholicism

Historically, the Catholic Church in Brazil was never as powerful an institution as it was in colonial Spanish America. For example, while the Jesuits joined the first royal mission to the colony and were largely responsible for education during much of the colonial era, they never played a major role in politics. Other orders competed with the Jesuits, both for lands and control of Indians. The Jesuits were expelled in 1759. Historians generally point out that Brazilian Catholicism exhibited a tolerance and flexibility unseen in Spanish America. For example, secular priests (the few who were there) often had female companions and children. Likewise, priests were often tolerant of both indigenous and African rituals. In general, the church remained fairly weak until independence in 1822, and then was weakened further during the long reign of Pedro II, from 1840 to 1889.

Even in modern times, the church has not always enjoyed influence at the local level, in large part because of the shortage of priests. Importantly, many Brazilians who consider themselves Catholic have little or no contact with clergy; this is especially the case in rural areas. Historically, traveling priests or circuit riders have frequently performed mass marriages for couples already living together. In turn, a good proportion of priests, perhaps as many as one-half, have not been Brazilian—they have been foreign born, another factor that has reduced their influence at the local level.

Despite these problems, the Catholic Church remains an important factor in Brazil and is one of a handful of national institutions. Roughly three-quarters of Brazilians consider themselves Catholic, even if the proportion of those actively practicing the religion is significantly lower. Brazil's Catholic Church has seen internal conflict in recent decades, in particular as a result of the growing importance (and outspokenness) of the progressive wing of the church. Starting in the 1960s and through the 1970s, this progressive wing grew in prominence, ultimately coming to dominate the National Conference of Brazilian Bishops (CNBB). Beginning by condemning the repressive military regime and its repressive tactics, church progressives then began to focus on the plight of average Brazilians.

During this time, liberation theology gained popularity in Latin America, and its radical "preferential option for the poor" was supported by important national church figures in Brazil, such as Dom Paulo Evaristo Arns, who after 1973 was the cardinal of São Paulo. Another development that did not sit well with the church's conservative leadership was the growth of ecclesiastical base communities (CEBs), which, like liberation theology, represented a move away from traditional Catholicism and toward a more active social role for the church (these CEBs multiplied in particular in low-income areas of Brazil's urban centers). At heart, these progressive movements were aimed at such goals as reforming Brazil's archaic land tenure system and its highly unequal social structure. In daily practice they brought together grassroots constituents to discuss the immediate needs and concerns of the community; this often led to political action.

As Brazil's transition to democracy took place in 1985, Pope John Paul II pushed the Brazilian Catholic Church back in the direction of the moderates and conservatives—he even warned the country's clergy against excessive focus on social problems to the neglect of its primary religious responsibilities. In particular, the pope used the power of appointment and assignment to tip the balance toward more conservative, Vatican-backed views. Some of the country's most vocal progressives even received cautionary letters from the Vatican in 1988. Other measures of this conservative reaction included splitting up the powerful archdiocese of São Paulo to reduce the power of Cardinal Arns. The progressive hold on the CNBB was also broken in 1988.

As mentioned, a serious problem faced by the Catholic Church in Brazil is the chronic shortage of priests; since many existing priests are involved in areas like education and administration, there are simply not enough priests to take care of spiritual needs. This problem is compounded by a low number of Afro-Brazilian priests and the inability of women to gain a more important role in the church. As a result of these factors, folk Catholicism has flourished in many areas, in essence unconstrained by clergy and the Vatican. One of the best examples of folk Catholicism is the popularity of pilgrimages to popular shrines throughout the country, like Bom Jesús de Lapa in the interior of Bahia and Nossa Senhora da Aparicida in the upper corner of the state of São Paulo. At the appropriate times of year the roads are dominated by trucks carrying pilgrims to such holy places. Among the lower classes (and even the middle classes) the belief in miracles is commonplace.

Folk Catholicism may also be evident in the cavalier attitude of many Brazilians toward official religion. Many people may participate in festivals, attend holy day activities and the like, but have little interest in devout worship or church doctrine. This is illustrated by a popular Brazilian saying, that "a man needs to go to church three times in his life—to be baptized, to marry, and to die."

Protestantism

While there were some early examples of Protestantism in the colonial era, the country's modern Protestant experience began in 1810, when the government allowed the practice of Episcopalianism. This was followed by the Lutheranism of many German immigrants. U.S. Protestant missionaries also began to arrive in numbers at that time. The early mainline

Bishop Edir Macedo, head of the Universal Church of the Kingdom of
God, prays during a giant mass in Rio de Janeiro in 1994. (AP
Photo/Samuel Martins)

Protestant denomination enjoyed fairly limited success in this
overwhelmingly Catholic country. However, more recent
arrivals, particularly Pentecostalists, have witnessed tremendous success.

Starting with relatively few in number, Protestants by
2000 represented more than 15 percent of the population.
As mentioned, the driving force of this growth has been the

Pentecostalists. One of the fastest growing churches is called the Universal do Reino de Deus (Universal Church of the Kingdom of God). This group was founded in 1977 by Edir Macedo and now has millions of members. As a neo-Pentecostal group, it emphasizes healing and exorcism and exhorts the faithful to believe that success and happiness can be attained on earth (perhaps particularly attractive in a poor and traditionally Catholic country in which the rewards for one's labor were always deferred to the next life).

Much of the growth and success of these groups has come as a result of television ministries. But they have also seen important progress at the local level, in neighborhoods and on street corners. They have more ministers than there are Catholic priests, and they are available in "easy to use" storefront churches. It is no surprise that these groups are capitalizing on the opportunities made available by the neglect of the Catholic Church in many highly populated neighborhoods, as well as large newly populated areas. In these areas, populations are often starved for organized religious activity and interaction with religious leaders. Thus, any new church opening usually attracts an immediate following.

Judaism and Eastern Religions

The history of Judaism in Brazil is as old as the colony itself. While most of the colonists from Portugal were Roman Catholic, Jews and New Christians have also been important in Brazil from the beginning of colonial times. The latter were converted or nominally converted Jews during the time of the Inquisition. By the end of the sixteenth century there were probably some 200 sugar plantations in Brazil that were owned by Jews or crypto-Jews.

The Portuguese Inquisition is considered to have been milder than its Spanish counterpart but was nonetheless responsible for forcing the conversion of Jews to Christianity;

Jews were also periodically repressed or expelled during the colonial era. One period of reprieve for Brazil's Jewish population occurred during the Dutch occupation of Brazil's Northeast; this period corresponded to the founding of the country's first synagogue in Recife in 1642. The Portuguese reconquered Recife in 1654, and the Inquisition continued its repression until 1773, when the distinction between Old and New Christians was abolished.

Another influx of Jewish immigrants took place in the latter part of the nineteenth century, with immigrants coming from the Middle East, Russia, and Poland. German Jews also began to immigrate to Brazil starting in the 1930s. For the most part this Jewish population is found in the country's large urban centers or in Rio Grande do Sul (the home of one of Brazil's best-known Jewish writers, Moacyr Scliar). As mentioned, today Brazil has the second largest Jewish population in South America after Argentina.

Brazil also contains perhaps half a million Muslims, most having come to the country upon the collapse of the Ottoman Empire after World War I. In Brazil, these people are called by the misleading name "Turks," despite the fact that they originate from not only Turkey but Syria, Lebanon, Egypt, and Iran. In certain cities this population is large enough that signs are posted in Portuguese and Arabic. Finally, the large population of Japanese immigrants in Brazil means that there are numerous practitioners of such eastern religions as Shintoism and Buddhism.

Candomblé and Other Afro-Brazilian Religions

As we have learned, the slave trade in Brazil was seen as the answer to the problem settlers faced concerning a scarcity of labor. The shortage caused by relatively sparse Indian populations, a disinclination on the part of the indigenous to do the work required, and then the tremendous demographic disaster brought on these populations by European diseases forced the Portuguese to look elsewhere for the labor they needed. Africa became their answer. The importation of African slaves took place on a huge scale, to the extent that slaves soon outnumbered their masters.

One technique the Portuguese used to keep an upper hand on the growing number of slaves was to mix the various ethnic and language groups—a sort of "divide and conquer" strategy aimed at preventing any sort of unity among slaves. However, despite these efforts, a variety of African religious practices survived. In particular these became established in the country's Northeast, where most slaves entered Brazil and where the African population is greatest. However, these practices, once taking root, spread throughout the country, to such an extent that many now consider them together to constitute a second dominant religion in Brazil. The names vary by region and state, but the most traditional are found in Bahia, where ceremonies and songs still take place in the Yoruba language of Africa.

Candomblé, as it is called in Bahia, is one of the most well-known. It is similar to Santeria, practiced in Cuba, to the point that the names of deities, called Orixás, are often identical. Each Candomblé group has its own *terreiro,* which is a square that resembles a churchyard, as well as a central building used for rituals. Most traditional Candomblés are matriarchies, where the *mãe de santo* (saint's mother) presides over the rituals (some have male *paes de santos*). The rituals follow a strict ceremonial calendar and are complex in nature. Initiates must undertake extensive periods of instruction and preparation.

Each deity has a particular area of influence, not to mention favorite colors, preferred foods and beverages, and a specific symbolic representation. Likewise, most deities are synchretized with Catholic saints that have similar characteristics. For example, *Iansã* is Saint Barbara; *Ogun,* the god of the hunt, is Saint Anthony; and *Xangô* is Saint Peter. In the early days the double representations probably

Practitioners of Candomblé sweep the steps of the Nosso Senhor de Bonfim. The ritual is part of the Festival of Yemanjá and symbolizes the cleansing of the soul for a new spiritual year. (Stephanie Maze/Corbis)

served the purpose of allowing practitioners to pray to African deities while giving the appearance of praying to Catholic ones. Now the double identities are deeply ingrained, and efforts to separate the two seem to have been abandoned. However, there are some who claim the "disguise" continues, with oppressed Afro-Brazilian populations continuing to practice their native religions. Still, one amazing feature of these Afro-Brazilian religions is that the vast majority of practitioners consider themselves to also be Catholic.

Terreiros usually have at least one sponsor, called an *ogan*. This ogan is typically a wealthy or prestigious person and can be useful to the terreiro in more ways than simply helping with finances. For example, in the past the ogan often convinced police not to interfere with religious ceremonies. Thankfully, police intervention is no longer an issue. Jorge Amado, one of Brazil's most famous authors, was a well-known sponsor.

Today Candomblé and other Afro-Brazilian religious practices are celebrated throughout the country. This can be seen particularly well in the month of February, when the faithful flock to the country's beaches by the thousands to make offerings to the sea goddess *Yemanjá*. In this celebration, participants stand on the beach or wade into the water, throwing bouquets of flowers and emptying perfume bottles, hoping to receive the blessing of the goddess in return.

Umbanda. Another important religious group in Brazil stands as a sort of mixture of traditions, a blend of African beliefs, Indian religions, Catholicism, and spiritualism that has resulted in Umbanda. (Spiritualism, often linked to the French writer Allan Kardek, is a diverse movement in Brazil tending to focus on communication with the dead and extrasensory perception). Umbanda originated in the early twentieth century among Afro-Brazilians in Rio de Janeiro but has now spread widely. Its name is derived from an Angolan word signifying religious practitioners.

Umbanda is particularly prevalent in Brazil's urban settings. It arose in part due to the historical repression of Afro-Brazilian religions like Candomblé and Macumba; as a result many observers of Brazilian culture and religion suggest that Umbanda represents a "whitening" of more traditional African religions. Many Umbanda rituals focus on calling forth Indian and African spirits, such as the *caboclo*, or indigenous spirit, and the *preto velho,* or old black or African spirit. Additional spirits are in essence the same as the Orixás seen in Candomblé, like Yemanjá and *Iansã*). Also like Candomblé, the legions of spirits in Umbanda are associated with Catholic saints, under whose guidance the spirits work.

However, there is considerable diversity in the practice of Umbanda—there are at least three subdivisions of Umbanda doctrine. Observers suggest that such an eclectic religion fits perfectly in Brazil, given its fluid and eclectic nature. Some also suggest that like other religions, Umbanda takes advantage of widespread dissatisfaction with traditional Catholicism in modern Brazil.

SELECTED THEMES IN BRAZILIAN CULTURE

The goal of this section is to expand upon the preceding discussion, using a number of specific themes as windows to look at contemporary Brazilian culture. Here we discuss literature and the arts in general, popular culture, women in Brazil, and education as we continue to explore Brazil's complex society and culture.

In this chapter, we have been focusing on the culture of modern Brazil by using a relatively broad understanding of the term "culture," working with the anthropological sense of the word to focus on such elements as custom, beliefs, and traditions that together characterize a particular population and make it distinct from others.

In everyday discussion, the word "culture" is often used in another sense—to refer to forms of artistic impression. This sense of the word is typically applied to the topics of the section immediately following, in which we discuss literature and the arts. However, as valuable as these topics are in helping us to understand modern Brazil, alone they are insufficient. In juxtaposing "high" culture with popular culture, the reader can come much closer to this understanding. The discussion of these two types of culture will then be followed by very important topical issues: women in Brazil and education.

Art and Architecture

Brazil's older cities are filled with cathedrals and churches, which in turn are filled with sacred art from the colonial era. Most of this art and architecture is Portuguese, although the

Northeast, and specifically Recife, contains some beautiful examples from the Dutch occupation. Among the cities in which the best examples of this national treasure remain well preserved are Ouro Prêto, Salvador, and Olinda (Rio de Janeiro also has a few examples).

One of Brazil's most famous artists was the sculptor known as Aleijadinho (or the Little Cripple, c. 1738–1814). Born Antônio Francisco Lisbôa, Aleijadinho is typically considered the greatest artistic talent of the colonial period. Many would argue that he is the greatest artistic talent that Brazil has ever produced. The sculptor was inflicted with leprosy but continued his craft even when his tools had to be tied to the stumps of his wrists. Perhaps his best-known works are the statues of the Twelve Apostles in Congonhas de Campo, Minas Gerais.

Among Brazil's best-known painters are Di Cavalcanti (Emiliano Augusto Cavalcanti de Albuquerque Melo, 1897–1976) and Cândido Torquato Portinari (1903–1962). The former is well-known for his paintings of Brazilian landscapes and people, while the latter is a highly renowned muralist, with masterpieces found at the United Nations

National Congress building in the capital city of Brasília, which was designed by Brazilian architect Oscar Niemeyer. (Corel)

building in New York City and the Library of Congress in Washington, D.C.

Architecture has been a particularly vibrant field in Brazil during the second half of the twentieth century. The movement began in the 1920s with a visit to Brazil of the Frenchman Charles-Éduard Jeanneret "Le Corbusier" (1887–1965). Many observers consider Le Corbusier to be the "high priest" of Brazilian architecture.

An explosion of new ideas and buildings took place from the 1930s through the 1960s, led by Oscar Niemeyer (b. 1907) and Lúcio Costa (b. 1902). While the two built their reputations independently, they worked together in the late 1950s in the design of Brasília, the capital built from scratch in the interior plateau. Neimeyer worked as the architect, while Costa acted as the urban planner.

Literature

One of the great ironies of Brazilian history is that the country, which has been largely illiterate for most of its history, has produced a long string of top-notch writers and some of the best literature in Latin America—indeed in the Western Hemisphere. Looking at this literary tradition in any depth is beyond the scope of this book; likewise, moving into any detail about such fields as music, architecture, painting, and cinema is not feasible. However, we provide a quick introduction to Brazil's literature, and then a few brief comments on these additional subjects to introduce the reader to Brazil's most important figures. In this realm of Brazilian culture one can discover truly unique windows into what is Brazilianness. Well-known and often internationally famous figures like Machado de Assis, Jorge Amado, Heitor Villa-Lobos, Oscar Neimeyer, di Cavalcanti, and many more are uniquely Brazilian. Interested readers should explore these figures and their work to gain a unique perspective on Brazilian culture.

As suggested, literature is a great way to explore Brazilian

Joaquim Nabuco was an influential Brazilian author and abolitionist during the nineteenth century. Through essays on the destructive nature of slavery, and his astute political instincts, Nabuco gained support for the antislavery cause in Brazil. (Library of Congress)

culture—in fact, Brazilian fiction can help interested readers gain a unique perspective on many of the problems and issues that have been discussed thus far in the book, such as regionalism, clientilism, and class and race relations. It must be remembered, though, that literature is not a medium of the masses, and audiences for fiction, like other arts, remain small for a country with such a large population.

Brazil's first internationally known author was Joaquim María Machado de Assis (1839–1908), who produced an amazing array of work ranging from poetry to short stories to novels. His works were often set in the Rio de Janeiro of his times, probing the relationships between the individual and society. Machado de Assis's *Memórias Póstumas de Brás Cubas* (*Epitaph of a Small Winner*) is considered the first masterpiece of Brazilian fiction, and many consider Machado de Assis to be Brazil's greatest literary figure.

Another important figure from the era was Joaquim Nabuco (1849–1910). From Pernambuco, Nabuco was a politician, a diplomat, and an outspoken abolitionist. Ruy Barbosa (1849–1923) came from Bahia; he was an essayist, an orator, and nearly elected the president of Brazil. Alberto Tôrres (1865–1917) helped found the search for Brazilian identity and destiny. Finally, Francisco José de Oliveira Vianna (1865–1951) followed with a call for Brazilians to look more closely at themselves, rather than imitate.

The 1920s and 1930s ushered in a new set of important figures, including São Paulo's Mário de Andrade (1895–1945) who wrote the famous poem *Macunaíma: O Herói Sem Nenhuma Caráter* (*Macunaíma: Hero without Any Character*). Andrade helped push the search for truly Brazilian themes. His poem included a character that embodied Brazil's strengths and weaknesses and was heavily influenced by Brazilian folk culture. Another great figure of the early twentieth century was Graciliano Ramos (1892–1953), who came from the northeastern state of

Alagoas. His most famous work was called *Vidas Secas* (*Barren Lives*).

Another great author of Brazilian literature was developing, somewhat in the shadows of Andrade and Ramos: Jorge Amado (who could very well be the best-known Brazilian author outside of Brazil, not least due to a number of popular films based on his books). Amado (1912–2001), who had written six novels by the age of twenty-five, seemed to focus in his early career on the political, but this appears to have faded over time, as Amado turned increasingly toward themes of human nature. He also had tremendous abilities in character development. Perhaps the best-known novel of Amado is *Dona Flor e Seus Dois Maridos,* which was translated into English as *Dona Flor and Her Two Husbands.* Like Machado de Assis in the nineteenth century, Amado is considered by many to be the country's top writer in the twentieth century.

João Guimarães Rosa (1908–1967) examined life in the vast and harsh interior of Bahia and Minas Gerais. His most famous novel was entitled *Grande Sertão: Veredas* (*The Devil to Pay in the Backlands*), a cowboy novel of violence and survival in the backland and at least partially indebted to Euclides da Cunha's description of *Canudos in Rebellion in the Backlands* (while not fiction, the latter had a great impact on Brazil's literary tradition). Érico Verissimo (1905–1975) wrote a five-volume masterpiece called *O Tempo e O Vento* (*Time and Wind*). Around the same time, a number of well-known female writers began to attract recognition: Rachel de Queiróz was the first woman elected to the Brazilian Academy of Letters. Clarice Lispector (1920–1977) attracted attention with her novel *A Maç no Escuro* (*The Apple in the Dark*); however, many consider her short stories to be her most penetrating works. Nélida Piñon is another of Brazil's talented women authors, perhaps best-known for her 1984 novel, *A República dos Sonos* (*The Dream Republic*).

Music

Brazilian music has witnessed considerable creativity, as well as a unique blend of Indian, African, and European influences that has helped create unique Brazilian styles. Several important musical developments, and their leaders, must be mentioned. First, Heitor Villa-Lobos is perhaps the shining star of Brazilian music, responsible for a huge body of compositions, including operas, symphonies, chamber music, and piano pieces. Villa-Lobos played a leading role in the modernism movement seen in the 1920s; he ultimately gained adoration in Brazil, as well as international acclaim. In fact, it can be argued that Villa-Lobos helped put Brazil on the map musically. His "Chôros" and "Bachianas Brasileiras" uniquely combined Bachian compositional techniques with Brazilian folk and popular music.

Chiquinha Ganzaga (1847–1935) composed in 1899 the song "Abre Alas" (Open Wings), which was instrumental in popular music for developing samba in song form. Gonzaga was followed in the 1930s and 1940s by Ari Evangelista Barroso (1903–1964), who continued the development of samba and composed the well-known "Arquarela do Brazil."

In the 1960s, Brazil ushered in bossa nova, which became an international sensation and launched the careers of many well-known Brazilian artists. Perhaps the best known of the bossa nova movement was Antônio Carlos "Tom" Jobim (1927–1994). Jobim is best remembered for the international hit "A Garota de Ipanema" ("The Girl from Ipanema"). Other famous bossa nova figures include Roberto Carlos and Chico Buarque. The latter was both a well-known singer and a famous composer.

A final important figure in Brazil's musical scene, from the 1950s through the 1970s, was Vinícius de Moraes (1913–1980). He was a poet, lyricist, and composer who could reach the masses. De Moraes, known simply as Vinícius, wrote the poem "Orfeu do Carnival," which became the French film *Orfeu Negro* (*Black Orpheus*). The film went on to win first place at the Cannes Film Festival in 1957 and an Academy Award for the best foreign film, another event bringing Brazil international attention. Vinícius was adored by the Brazilian people (not least due to his bohemian lifestyle).

Film

Brazil has witnessed a boom in both film and television; we cover television (and especially the *novela*) in detail in the section on popular culture below. For now, it suffices to say that due to the superior economic viability of television, most actors and actresses in Brazil survive doing television; film is not yet a medium for the masses.

Among the first Brazilian films, in the 1950s, to achieve international attention were Victor Lima Barreto's *O Cangaceiro* (*The Bandit*), which won best adventure film in Cannes in 1954, and Nelson Pereira do Santos's *Rio, Quarenta Graus* (*Rio, Heatwave*). A boom then took place in the 1960s, starting with Ruy Guerra's *Os Cafajestes* (*The Hustlers*) in 1961. In 1962, Anselmo Duarte won the best film at Cannes with *O Pagador de Promessas* (*The Given Word*). Another big film that year was *Assalto ao Trem Pagador* (*The Paytrain Robbery*), directed by Roberto Farias. In 1964, Nelson Pereira do Santos produced a critically acclaimed adaptation of Graciliano Ramos's masterpiece, *Vidas Secas*.

In the same vein, Joaquim Pedro de Andrade in 1969 brought Mário de Andrade's *Macunaíma* to the screen, ushering in Brazil's "new cinema." Next came Gláuber Rocha, a filmmaking genius who gained notoriety both at home and abroad. His masterpiece *Deus e o Diabo na Terra do Sol* (*Black God, White Devil*) was released in 1964.

In 1982, Jorge Amado's book *Gabriela, Clove and Cinnamon* was brought to the screen by Bruno Barreto, following up on the successful *Dona Flor and Her Two Husbands*. Hector Babenco, an Argentine working in Brazil gained world attention with *Pixote: A Lei do Mais Fracos* (*Pixote: Law of the Weakest*), a film about São Paulo's street children. Sadly, in a case of life reflecting art, the star of the film, born impoverished and picked for the role at age twelve, was killed by the police at age nineteen during an alleged robbery. Babenco, on the back of his success with *Pixote,* was able to land William Hurt and Raul Julia to star in *Kiss of the Spider Woman,* filmed in São Paulo in 1983.

Brazilian films continue to win international acclaim, with recent hits including *Central Station, City of God,* and *Carandiru.*

Popular Culture

In very general terms, popular culture refers to a sort of "people's culture" that can be found in any given society. Standing in opposition to the "high culture," which is typically the realm of elites, popular culture focuses more on the everyday pursuits of the masses and can include a wide range of things from cooking and clothing to mass media and other forms of entertainment. To better understand contemporary Brazil, we focus on Carnival and samba, soccer, television, and food. Obviously there are many more aspects of Brazilian popular culture that merit discussion. The following is merely an introduction to the myriad aspects of *Brazil's contemporary popular culture.*

Carnival. When non-Brazilians are asked to conjure up images of modern Brazil, Carnival is often one of the first to come to mind. It is an enormous pre-Lenten party, and pictures of the event can be seen on television worldwide as it takes place in Brazil. The most comparable event in the United States is Mardi Gras, French for "fat Tuesday," in New Orleans, which ends like Carnival on the day before Lent. Samba, a rhythmic dance and music of Afro-Brazilian origin, has become largely synonymous with the lavish Carnival parades staged by Afro-Brazilian samba "schools." Samba, a truly national form of popular culture, was repressed in late nine-teenth-century Brazil, along with other expressions of Afro-Brazilian culture. This gradually changed in the early twentieth century, and by 1935 President Getúlio Vargas began to actively fund samba schools, supporting a uniquely Brazilian tourist attraction.

Carnival has ancient roots in celebrations such as Greek Dionysian festivals and Roman saturnalias. This type of festivity made its way to Brazil from Portugal in the seventeenth century in the form of the *entrudo,* a street game in which celebrants pelted one another with food. It evolved over time into a sort of street dance with music and its own special songs, with samba schools being added in the late 1920s. Carnival is the most important religious festival in Brazil and is celebrated in the days leading to Ash Wednesday, the first day of Lent.

As can be garnered from the glossy photos of Carnival, everyday rules of behavior are abandoned during the celebration, as Brazilians enjoy a degree of exhibitionism and playfulness unseen during the rest of the year; common social restraints and class divisions seem to melt in the festive environment. The event is celebrated throughout Brazil, and there are logically some variations by region. However, the atmosphere of permissiveness during Carnival is pervasive throughout the country.

While many outsiders associate Carnival with Rio de Janeiro, it also takes place throughout Brazil, and some form of celebration is seen in many Roman Catholic areas throughout the world as well. In fact, the French and Spanish heritage explain its origins in New Orleans. International tourists began to arrive for the festival in Rio in the early 1960s, and the city began to invest to promote its Carnival—the tourist infrastructure put in place in Rio is nothing short of tremendous. As a result, internationally Rio is now synonymous with Carnival.

Samba school parade at the Sambadrome during Carnival in Rio de Janeiro. (iStockPhoto)

In Rio de Janeiro there are at least three different *fantasias* (or costumes) associated with Carnival—those of the samba schools, those of the ballroom dances, and those of neighborhood street bands. The samba schools prepare year-round for the spectacular parade during Carnival's culmination, raising money, making costumes, and rehearsing dance steps and drum rhythms. Since 1984, the schools have paraded to the giant "Sambadrome," a parade grounds with specially designed seats to accommodate the huge crowds that watch the spectacle. As the schools enter the Sambadrome, loyal supporters increase the noise level in support; it can take an hour for each school to move through the grounds, and the two nights of competition can last well past dawn the next day. Each samba school follows a theme, often taken from Brazilian history. In a well-known story, a designer was once criticized for his lavish Carnival costumes. He replied that "the poor like luxuriousness. It is the intellectuals who like misery."

The balls in Rio are more exclusive and include competitions for the most elaborate costumes; these appear in popular photo magazines, along with pictures of celebrities in attendance. Finally, a more spontaneous form of Carnival celebration can be found in the neighborhood bands and dancing groups that are called "*blocos*" and parade through various parts of Rio. Often costumes satirizing contemporary politics and popular culture are part of the celebration; in fact, the street carnival often targets the excesses of the samba schools and balls in its humor.

As mentioned, Carnival is a nationwide event; Rio is simply the biggest and most well-known celebration. Salvador, in Bahia, has another well-known Carnival celebration, touted by many as a more traditional festival still untainted by Rio's excesses. This Carnival celebration is marked by more spontaneity, as well as its "*trios elétricos,*" flat-bed trucks playing music as they travel around the city for dancers and other organized groups. Several of the blocos are dedicated to preserving Afro-Brazilian heritage. Recife, the capital of Pernambuco (and home to the Dutch occupation during the colonial era), preserves remnants of its heritage in its *frevo,* a style of music reminiscent of polka which is combined with Carnival dances and costumes.

Brazil's Carnival image was portrayed in the 1958 film *Orfeu Negro* (*Black Orpheus*). While somewhat exaggerated, the film does highlight Carnival's chaotic, raucous, and sometimes dangerous nature. Interested readers might use the film as a starting point to a better understanding of Brazil's Carnival culture.

Soccer. Called *futbol* in Brazil, soccer is without a doubt a top national pastime. To illustrate, students of Brazil point to a visit in 1994 by Pope John Paul II to Rio. The pope, wildly popular in all of Latin America, drew a crowd of 300,000 for his visit. However, when the Brazilian national soccer team returned victorious from the 2002 World Cup, having won an unprecedented and unrivaled five championships, the turn-out was 500,000. Rio de Janeiro also boasts the world's largest soccer stadium, called the Maracana.

Brazilian soccer started in the 1890s. The game was brought to Brazil from Great Britain and began as a fairly elitist game. However, over time it developed into a national passion; one can see Brazilians playing soccer in nearly every corner of the country—from organized games on soccer fields to impromptu games on street corners or in empty lots. The world's most famous soccer player, Pelé, is Brazilian; about 200,000 loyal fans filled the Maracana to watch Pelé play his last game before retirement.

While the English invented the game, many soccer aficionados argue that Brazil perfected it. Brazil has without doubt perfected its own style of soccer, which has become known internationally as the *jogo bonito,* or beautiful game, a style of play that combines exuberance with spontaneity. The Brazilian style of game is currently embodied in perhaps the best player in the world, Ronaldinho, who wore the canary yellow shirt of Brazil's national team, known as the *canarinho,* in the World Cup. Brazil's national team is a great

Brazil's national soccer team celebrates its victory over Germany in the 2002 World Cup final played in Yokohama, Japan. It was a record fifth World Cup title for Brazil. (FIFA)

illustration for the world of the country's unique racial blend—some players are black, some are white, but most are a blend of the two.

Pelé, born Edson Arantes do Nascimento, led the Brazilian national team to its first World Cup in 1958 with six goals. He is typically considered to have been the world's best soccer player, although some argue that the title should be given to Argentina's Maradona and commentators are beginning to ask if Ronaldinho could overtake Pelé. Pelé retired from Brazilian soccer in 1974, having scored more than 1,300 goals. He then came to the United States to help promote soccer, a difficult task in a country dedicated to sports like football and baseball.

Soccer is a natural fit for Brazil, given the country's large and relatively poor population. The game is easily accessible and can be played with very little equipment. In turn, it has become an important vehicle for socioeconomic advancement, as relatively poor individuals use the game to get ahead. Unfortunately, as a poor country, Brazil often loses its better players to richer teams in Europe, where players can earn five to ten times the amount of money they can earn in Brazil.

Loyalty to teams is fierce, games are loud and often emotional, and celebrations of victory are often spontaneous, with singing, dancing, and drum beating. Brazil's best players often become international celebrities, and Brazilians are likely to follow the overseas careers of their favorite players. In very Brazilian fashion, players are referred to by their nicknames, and players' nicknames or first names appear on the backs of their jerseys rather than the more traditional last names seen elsewhere—this occurs even in the World Cup.

Television. As mentioned above, television is more profitable than film in Brazil, and as a result most of the country's actors and actresses earn the bulk of their wages in that medium. In particular, Brazil's *novelas*, or *telenovelas*, are highly popular and reach a vast majority of the country's population—from the poor in rural villages to the wealthy in urban centers like São Paulo. Whether one sees this as positive or negative, one result is that television has a huge cultural impact on Brazilians, far greater than other media. In fact, many Brazilians are only familiar with their country's literary heritage because of the works' adaptations for television. Likewise, they are only likely to see movies when they are played on television. As such, televisions have become a consumer necessity, even within the country's large segment of poor households..

Brazil's novelas can best be understood as a sort of blend of afternoon soap operas and nighttime shows like *Dallas* or *Knot's Landing*. However, the acting is typically superior, as is the writing. These shows are avidly watched throughout the country and in fact are exported throughout the world, from other Latin American countries to places as far away as Italy and China. The novelas run six days a week and dominate the country's prime time programming. Brazil's Globo network is the fourth largest in the world, just behind the "big three" in the United States—its eight o'clock p.m. show is typically a main feature. Shows often run for nine months and can be shortened or lengthened based on viewer response. Interestingly, plots can even change direction based on the whims of viewers.

While the novelas dominate Brazilian television, other formats exist, and other TV personalities permeate popular culture. One is Sílvio Santos, who owns the SBT network and is Brazil's most popular game show host. Another highly popular figure is known as "Xuxa" (Maria de Graça Meneghel). Starting with a highly popular children's program, she has built an international career, though her attempts to break into the U.S. market have had limited success. Critics of Xuxa do not hold back, likening her to some sort of bizarre combination of Mr. Rogers and Madonna—hardly appropriate, in their view, for an audience of children.

Food and Drink. Brazilian food, like its population, is a blend of the numerous groups that make up the country. In a sense the history of food and drink in Brazil mirrors its overall history. For example, many of the foods come from the native Indians that populated the territory when it was discovered by the Portuguese. Examples of native foods include cassava meal, sweet potatoes, a variety roots, smoked and/or dried meats, and corn porridge. The Portuguese brought many of their own cooking techniques, which had evolved to include North African cooking traditions reflecting the long Moorish occupation of the Iberian Peninsula. Examples include coffee, pastries, and dried fruits. These traditions were adapted to utilize local ingredients.

A huge influence on Brazilian cuisine came with the importation of African slaves. Examples include *dende* and coconut milk, which became staples in the New World. It is widely believed that Africans, who prepared the meals on colonial plantations, provided the most important influence to Brazilian cuisine. The country eventually became a melting pot, reflecting the arrival of various peoples from Asia, Europe, the Middle East, and other New World countries. Thus, not only can one find authentic Brazilian cuisine but it is also quite easy to find Japanese and Italian food in urban centers like São Paulo. In sum, the country's cuisine is a creative blend of the four groups of people that make up its population: Indians, Portuguese, Africans, and immigrants.

Like most countries, food and drink play a critical role in cultural life. In particular, food and drink help maintain personal relationships at the various levels of social organization. A few examples of the role food plays in cultural life help illustrate the idea that Brazilians are outgoing and fun-loving people.

As suggested in the sections dealing with social organization in Brazil, the various divisions between types of social relations largely dictate where Brazilians tend to socialize. For example, there is a big difference in Brazil between *amigos* (friends) and *colegas* (acquaintances or colleagues). Colegas typically gather at pubs or restaurants for lunch or a drink after work. The colega relationship can last literally for years without advancing to the amigo level. Amigos are typically members of an individual's extended family or others who have shared years of close friendship. Amigos, in contrast to colegas, are invited to visit in Brazilian homes, where food and drink abound.

One traditional group activity, usually reserved for extended families on Saturdays, is gathering to eat the national dish of Brazil, *feijoada,* a heavy black bean stew made with smoked and other meats and served with toasted manioc flour and a number of side dishes. The dish is usually consumed slowly and is eaten around midday. Often the dish is accompanied by the national drink, the *caipirinha,* which is a mixed drink made of lime, sugar, and *cachaca,* a sugarcane-based type of rum. Beer is also a popular national drink for these types of get-togethers. Rice and black beans are staples in Brazil, served both as side dishes to meats or as a stand-alone meal at midday. Typically, breakfast and dinner consist of lighter fare.

One unique feature of Brazil is the national obsession with coffee—drinking coffee, like playing and watching soccer, is a national tradition. Breaking during the day to drink coffee is critical to relationships at work and at home. Noteworthy to Americans is the fact that Brazilians do not leave their office building for coffee; servers circulate regularly in places of business, typically serving strong coffee laced with sugar in small paper cups. While the coffee is strong compared with that served at work in the United States, it is served in very small doses, more akin to an espresso than a standard cup of coffee. Coffee bars are found throughout cities and on neighborhood corners. The arrival of newcomers to a business or government office is typically marked by the serving of coffee. Foreign visitors are often surprised by the number of coffees they are offered during business trips to Brazil.

Feijoada is a typical Brazilian dish made with black beans and several kinds of meat, especially pork. (iStockPhoto)

Such a short introduction to Brazilian cuisine can hardly do justice to this fascinating topic. Cuisines vary by regions, even while social customs surrounding food and drink are more stable. Cuisines vary largely in reflection of the major regions of the country, thus there is significant variation among the North, Northeast, Central-West, South-East, and South. Still, certain staples are found throughout the country: rice, beans (*feijão*), manioc meal (*farofa*), salted shrimp and codfish, coconut, palm oil, lime and *feijoada*. This short discussion may serve as a starting point. Those interested in more information need only consult a few additional sources to find considerably more detail.

WOMEN IN BRAZIL

Despite winning the right to vote in Brazil sooner than in France and most other Latin American countries, Brazilian women have played a relatively small role in public life. Congress approved female suffrage in 1932, but this expansion of the franchise did very little to change the role of women in Brazilian society. Women, at least in stereotype, continued to be passive, submissive beings, defined most importantly by their roles as dutiful daughters and patient, caring wives. Such women lived in a male-dominated society and, if they ventured outside of the home to work, were limited to such "female" careers as nursing and teaching. For the vast majority of Brazilian women, however, life was considerably more difficult—nursing and teaching were "high-class" professions for most working women, who were forced to battle almost daily with issues like miserable wages, domestic violence, and single parenthood.

In general terms, not only did the status of women change very little in the decades after obtaining the vote but the period of military rule actually reinforced the view that women should remain in their "traditional" roles. The military enforced this through its control of politics and the media. Feminist organizations practically disappeared. However, the military's repression backfired, as women, especially mothers, began to protest the government's brutality.

At the very time that censorship ended in the late 1970s, women (at least white middle-class women) were beginning to enter the traditionally male-dominated professions. However, as the economically active female population surged, increasing from less than 20 percent in 1970 to 27 percent in 1980, the harsh wage policies of the military rulers also led to discontent, especially among urban, working-class women, who began to openly protest the government's economic policies. A similar phenomenon occurred in rural areas, as women working long, hard hours for very low pay began to demand better conditions. As a result, women of all classes were becoming increasingly active in criticizing the status quo and demanding better conditions—and organizing politically in the process.

Feminists began to focus on specific issues—perhaps most importantly on the issue of reproductive rights. They demanded free and accessible contraception and legalized abortion, but the results were mixed. Violence against women was another critical issue. Abuse against wives was a well-known problem in Brazil, but traditionally such behavior was rarely regarded as a crime. In fact, even in cases of murder, husbands were often excused from penalty when using a "defense of honor" claim that the wife had been, or intended to be, unfaithful. While social attitudes have been difficult to change, feminist groups at a minimum entered the public debate.

Another major problem centered on the role of women in Brazilian politics—or rather the underrepresentation of women in politics, whether in local, state, and national governments or in labor unions and professional organizations. One telling example centers on the Constituent Assembly that was elected in 1986 to write Brazil's Constitution of 1988, which had only twenty-six women. The women constituents pointed out that women represented a meager 5 percent of the assembly while making up more than 50 percent of the population and 53 percent of the electorate. Some progress has been made on each of these critical issues over time. Still, women continue to be underrepresented politically, and they earn less than their male counterparts.

It is often pointed out that despite facing considerable obstacles, Brazil's women's movement is the largest and most effective in Latin America. While this is an important achievement, the women's movement has also been pulled in diverging directions in recent years, by issues such as class and race. Likewise, while the movement played a very important role in the transition to democracy, the return of democracy has corresponded to a waning in its relative importance. Many observers thus point out that in a sense the return to legitimate politics took some of the momentum from the women's movement. In general terms, Brazil continues to be a country that is governed by a small, largely white, and largely male, elite. It is also a country that is plagued by widespread poverty. Solutions, logically, must be interconnected and targeted at such areas as improved political representation, poverty alleviation, and better education.

EDUCATION

Brazil's record in education has been one of the worst in the developing world. What was already an unenviable record worsened with the financial crises of the 1980s. Teachers' salaries were shockingly low, schools were falling down, and the quality of education deteriorated. Schoolchildren were repeating elementary school grades more than any other country in the world. One major problem is that the quality of primary education is generally low, and this is where the majority of Brazilians attend public schools. While this is a serious problem, it is often pointed out that this is the natural result of—or even the price to be paid for—increased access to such schooling.

The wealthy, of course, have better options, since they can send their children to private schools. Unfortunately, this only adds an educational component to the country's social class divisions. It has also added to the decline of the public school system. In general terms, the country has not made the transition successfully from preparing several hundred thousand students for university-level education to educating millions of Brazilians to take part in a complex society and economy, let alone in the global marketplace.

Observers were quick to point out that the deterioration seen in the 1980s was not the result of budget cuts, since in 1989 the country was spending nearly 18 percent of public expenditures on education, a reasonable figure by international standards (the same was true regarding education spending as a percentage of GDP). Rather, the problem seemed much more a reflection of issues like corruption and incompetence—not nearly enough of the spending on education was actually reaching classrooms and students.

As a result, dropout rates were high, while hordes of half-literate children entered the labor force. The "output" of public schools was so poor that businesses were forced to spend huge sums of money to train their undereducated workers. The country struggled to bring illiteracy below 20 percent (and this was probably on the generous side).

The most serious problem regarding Brazil's education system is twofold. First, despite large numbers of seven- to fourteen-year-olds enrolled in school, there are also many who are not enrolled. One major reason for this is an extremely high rate of failure in first grade, reflecting in part the fact that few of these children are able to attend kindergarten. This problem is then exacerbated by large class sizes and a relatively short school day (often several shifts are run each day). Furthermore, the high number of students repeating the first year then takes up scarce space needed for the next group of seven-year-olds. Only about a third then make it to the eighth grade. Conditions are significantly worse in rural areas and in the country's impoverished Northeast.

The current situation is clearly unsatisfactory, but it also represents a great improvement over the past. Brazil does have Latin America's largest system of higher education, with a number of internationally recognized universities, like the University of São Paulo. The way forward will need to focus on a few basic goals. First, the quality and availability of rural schooling must be improved. This will have to be accompanied by widespread efforts to convince the poor to keep their kids in school rather than helping increase family income. Another goal must be to increase the quality of primary schooling. While great steps forward have been made, significant work remains to be done—and as with so many of Brazil's problems, much of this effort must be targeted specifically at the nation's most disadvantaged populations, a big challenge given their relatively weak political voice.

References and Further Readings

Béhague, Gerard. *Music in Latin America: An Introduction.* Englewood Cliffs, NJ: Prentice Hall, 1979.

Blay, Eva Alterman. "Women, Redemocratization, and Political Alternatives," in Julian M. Chacel, Pamela S. Falk, and David V. Fleischer (eds.), *Brazil's Economic and Political Future.* Boulder, CO: Westview Press, 1988: 199–213.

Boff, Clodovis. *Feet-on-the-Ground Theology: A Brazilian Journey.* Maryknoll, NY: Orbis Books, 1987.

Conniff, Michael L., and Frank D. McCann, eds., *Modern Brazil: Elites and Masses in Historical Perspective.* Lincoln: University of Nebraska Press, 1989.

Fontaine, Pierre-Michel, ed. *Race, Class and Power in Brazil.* Los Angeles: University of California Press, 1985.

Freyre, Gilberto. *New World in the Tropics: The Culture of Modern Brazil.* New York: Vintage Books, 1963.

Gledson, John. "Brazilian Fiction: Machado de Assis to the Present," in John King, *On Modern Latin America Fiction.* New York: Noonday Press, 1987: 18–40.

Hess, David J., and Roberto deMatta, eds. *The Brazilian Puzzle.* New York: Columbia University Press, 1995.

Hulet, Claude L. *Brazilian Literature.* Washington, DC: Georgetown University Press, 1974.

Leff, Nathaniel H. *Development and Underdevelopment in Brazil.* Boston: Allen and Unwin, 1982.

Lemos, Carlos Alberto Cerqueira. *The Art of Brazil.* New York: Harper and Row, 1983.

Mainwaring, Scott. *The Catholic Church and Politics in Brazil, 1916–1985.* Stanford, CA: Stanford University Press, 1986.

Mattoso, Katia M. de Queiros. *To Be a Slave in Brazil, 1550–1888.* New Brunswick, NJ: Rutgers University Press, 1986.

McGovern, Arthur F. *Liberation Theology and Its Critics: Toward an Assessment.* Maryknoll, NY: Orbis Books, 1989.

Morse, Richard M. "The Multiverse of Latin American Identity, c. 1920–c.1970," in Leslie Bethell (ed.), *The Cambridge History of Latin America: Volume X, Latin America Since 1930, Ideas, Culture and Society.* Cambridge, U.K.: Cambridge University Press, 1995: 1–128.

Page, Joseph. *The Brazilians.* Cambridge, MA: Da Capo Press, 1995.

Patai, Daphne. *Brazilian Women Speak.* New Brunswick, N.J.: Rutgers University Press, 1988.

Perrone, Charles A. *Masters of Contemporary Brazilian Song.* Austin: University of Texas Press, 1989.

Schneider, Ronald. *Brazil: Culture and Politics in a New Industrial Powerhouse.* Boulder, CO: Westview Press, 1996.

Wagley, Charles. *An Introduction to Brazil.* New York: Columbia University Press, 1971.

PART TWO
REFERENCE SECTION

Key Events in Brazilian History

1415   Portuguese capture the North African port of Ceuta in Northern Africa; this event is usually considered the beginning of Portuguese overseas expansion. This expansion moved down the west coast of Africa and out to the islands in the Atlantic Ocean, eventually reaching the Indian Ocean as well as Brazil.

1493   Just one year after Columbus's first voyage and seven years before Cabral reached Brazil, the pope issues a series of papal bulls dividing the New World. The Portuguese resist the pope's demarcation, and an independent agreement is reached with the Spanish in the Treaty of Tordesillas, which moves the line farther to the west. The greatest early threat to Portugal's hold on Brazil came from France, which did not recognize the Treaty of Tordesillas.

1497–1499   The epic voyage of the legendary Portuguese explorer Vasco de Gama opens the sea route to India and stimulates further global exploration. From India, it was possible for the Portuguese to go all the way to China and Japan. Vasco de Gama's voyage marks the creation of the Estado de India, a network of Portuguese coastal trading enclaves.

1500   Pedro Álvarez Cabral arrives in Brazil en route to India. On March 9, Cabral's large expedition of thirteen ships destined for the East Indies set sail from Lisbon. The expedition was supposed to sail around the Cape of Good Hope and head to India through the Indian Ocean, but Cabral's lead ship swung off course sailing due west, reaching the coast of what is now the Brazilian state of Bahia on April 23. Some scholars debate whether they purposely headed to Brazil, but most evidence suggests the voyage was directed to India.

1511   The first indigenous people are brought from Brazil to Portugal; Brazil's indigenous population is made up for the most part of hunters and gatherers—estimates of the indigenous population at the time of Portuguese arrival range from some 500,000 to 2 million.

1530	The first Portuguese colonists arrive in the New World colony.
1534	The Portuguese monarch divides Brazil into hereditary captaincies, using this semifeudal system of land grants to strengthen its position in the Americas. Between 1534 and 1536 fourteen captaincies are granted to rich nobles in the hope that they will exploit brazilwood and other colonial resources. Only two of these original captaincies are successful: São Vicente and Pernambuco.
1539–1542	Francisco de Orellana explores Amazônia; the potential of this vast territory will remain a constant theme in Brazilian history.
1549	Arrival of first Jesuit missionaries as well as the first governor general, Tomé de Souza. The Crown creates the governor generalship in 1550, which Tomé de Souza founds in Salvador. It remains the capital of the colony for more than 200 years until it is moved to Rio de Janeiro (only in the twentieth century is the capital moved to Brasília).
1555–1560	French Huguenot settlement is established near today's city of Rio de Janeiro—in general the French did not recognize the Treaty of Tordesillas and threatened Portugal's early hold on Brazil, trading in brazilwood and at times practicing piracy.
1562–1563	A wave of epidemic disease wipes out perhaps as much as half the Brazilian native population. Brazil's indigenous population shrinks drastically as Europeans arrive, and epidemic disease is the central cause.
1565	The French are driven out of Rio de Janeiro by Portuguese and Indian troops the same year as the official founding of the city by the Portuguese. This puts an end to this part of the French attempt to build "Antarctic France" as a refuge for French Protestants, although further French incursions in Brazil continue throughout the sixteenth century.
1580–1640	The Spanish and Portuguese monarchies are merged, a sixty-year union that resulted from the lack of a royal heir in Portugal and the end of the Aviz dynasty; Spanish control of Brazil lasts until 1640, when a successor to the Portuguese throne is again found. The Iberian Union also leads to a temporary disregard for the Treaty of Tordesillas.

1607–1694 This period marks the lifespan of *quilombo* Palmares, which is populated by fugitive slaves and led by chieftain Zumbi, who is caught and killed in 1695. At the time the destruction of Palmares is seen as important as the expulsion of the Dutch from Portugal's Brazilian possessions.

1624–1654 The Dutch invade Brazil's Northeast. Dutch invaders take advantage of the "Iberian Union" by invading Brazil's Northeast coast and manage to maintain control for thirty years. A coalition of Brazilians of all social classes drives the Dutch from the coast in 1654. Some historians identify Brazilian resistance to the Dutch, and their ultimate success in expelling the invaders, as the birth of Brazilian nationalism.

1695 The first discoveries of gold in Minas Gerais; the eighteenth century is dominated by the rise and decline of the mining industry. The corresponding shift in population to the South has a significant effect on the administration of the colony—in fact the colonial capital is moved from Salvador to Rio de Janeiro in response to these changes.

Brazil becomes the largest gold producer in the world in the eighteenth century; the mineral bonanza allows Portugal to enjoy the kind of wealth Spain had experienced earlier with its colonies. The wealth also finances a cultural boom in Brazil's center-south (like the baroque-style churches in the eighteen-century mining towns of Minas Gerais).

1727 Coffee is introduced into Brazil. It takes coffee a century to become a major Brazilian export. Coffee is successfully commercialized in the province of Rio de Janeiro in the late eighteenth century—by the 1830s and 1840s it becomes the center of coffee cultivation. The product then dominates the Brazilian export economy for well more than 100 years after that.

1750 The Treaty of Madrid ends the Treaty of Tordesillas; this treaty for the most part also ends open conflict with Spain, which agrees to recognize Portugal's claims to areas that it has already occupied (in effect all territories west of the imaginary line drawn by the Treaty of Tordesillas). The treaty was based on *uti possidetis,* or ownership by possession—also a key feature in successor treaties in 1777 and 1801. Important Brazilian territories included in these new agreements were the Amazon Basin, parts of Mato Grosso, São Paulo, Paraná, and Santa Catarina, along with all of Rio Grande do Sul.

1763   Brazil's colonial capital is moved from Salvador to Rio de Janeiro, in large part to keep better control of the important mining areas.

1777   The Treaty of San Ildefonso alters Portuguese–Spanish territorial boundaries.

1788–1789   One of the first and most serious anti-Portuguese plots arises in Minas Gerais. Led by a group of prominent citizens in Ouro Prêto, Minas Gerais, the Inconfidência (conspiracy) was a plan to assassinate the governor and declare an independent republic. Authorities quickly learn of the plot. Six defendants are sentenced to hanging, but only Tiradentes is actually hanged on April 21, 1792. The plot is typically considered the most important historical antecedent of Brazilian independence.

1807   In November the entire Portuguese court and the royal family move from Lisbon to Brazil (a result of the French invasion of the Iberian Peninsula); no other European monarch ever sets foot in the New World, let alone rules an empire from a New World colony. The fleet arrives in Salvador in January 1808 and moves to Rio in February.

1810   Commercial treaty gives Britain effective control of Brazilian trade—a direct result of Britain's protection of the Portuguese Crown.

1815   In response to the demand for the Portuguese court to return to Portugal, not least due to Napoleon's defeat in 1814, Prince Regent João compromises in 1815 by elevating the Estado do Brasil to equal status with Portugal in a new "United Kingdom." This legitimizes his continued residence in Brazil. One year later his mother, still the formal monarch but mentally incapacitated, dies, leaving the prince to become Dom João VI.

1821   Dom João VI returns to Portugal with some 4,000 Portuguese, less than half the number that left Lisbon for Brazil in 1808. João leaves his son Pedro, named prince regent, to rule Brazil—João tells his son that in the event of a break between the two countries, he should choose Brazil.

1822	Brazil gains independence from Portugal under Pedro I. On September 7, 1822, Pedro proclaims Brazil's independence; he is then crowned Emperor Pedro I on December 1, 1822. Brazil is the only former colony in the New World to name as its monarch a member of the ruling family of the country it was rebelling against—this is truly a unique historical path.
1824	First Brazilian constitution is written; another revolt occurs in Pernambuco, where militant republicans want a Brazil that is free of any royalty; the rebels proclaim a "Confederation of the Equator" and gain additional adherents; the confederation, like other revolts against the Crown, is ultimately crushed.
1825–1888	War breaks out between Brazil and Buenos Aires over the attempt by Brazil's Cisplatine Province to leave Brazil and join Argentina. The Brazilians are incapable of winning the war, and English intervention resolves the conflict. One result is the creation of the independent country of Uruguay in 1828, designed to act as a buffer state between Brazil and Argentina.
1826	Britain pushes Brazil into a treaty that is aimed at ending the slave trade by 1830; the treaty also gives the British generous commercial terms in Brazil. By this point the British are the dominant foreign actor in Brazil, replacing the Portuguese.
1831	Pedro I returns to Portugal and abdicates the throne, leaving his five-year-old son, Pedro II, as the claimant to the Brazilian crown; Brazil is ruled from 1831 to 1840 by a succession of regents; during the period wider powers are given to the provinces, and separatist movements gather strength.
1832–1835	These years witness the outbreak of the first regional revolt, called the War of the Cabanos in Pernambuco, which is fought for the return of Pedro I and the suppression of the regency. Rio Grande do Sul is the site of another revolt, called the War of the Farrapos, in 1835–1845, which is inspired by federalist ideas. An extremely violent revolt also occurs in the Amazon (War of Cabanagem, 1835–1840). Estimates suggest that as many as 30,000 people were killed out of a total population of 150,000. While a number of other regional conflicts occur in this era, the last major regionalist challenge is crushed in 1850.

1834   The most important item increasing the powers of the
          provinces is the Additional Act of 1834, which amends
          the Constitution of 1824 and is approved by Parliament.
          Each province is allowed to create its own assembly,
          which can control taxation and expenditures, as well as
          appoint local officials. Historians often refer to the act as
          the regency's "experiment with decentralization."

1840   Pedro II ascends the Brazilian throne at the young age
          of fourteen, as liberals and conservatives alike look for
          a way to promote stability. Many elites feel that the
          installation of the hereditary monarch will solve the
          country's problems of instability. Parliament also
          revokes the Additional Act of 1834 in an attempt to
          recentralize political power.

1845   Rio Grande do Sul's revolt, in which rebels declare in
          1838 the independent Republic of Piratini, is put down
          by the Baron of Caixias; he soundly defeats the sepa-
          ratist revolt but also reconciles with the rebels (includ-
          ing a general amnesty), an approach the central gov-
          ernment will copy in later regional revolts.

1850   The slave trade ends under threat by Britain via the
          Eusebio de Queiroz law. A land law is also passed that
          favors large landholders, particularly those dedicated
          to the large plantation system; access to land for small
          landholders is made more difficult. Many contrast this
          support for concentrated landownership to the United
          States's Homestead Act of 1862, which encouraged
          small landholdings.

1858   Coffee becomes Brazil's principal export. As the soils of
          Rio de Janeiro become increasingly depleted by intense
          cultivation, the center of coffee production moves to
          more productive areas to the south and west, especially
          to the provinces of São Paulo and Minas Gerais.
          Heightened coffee production causes a demographic
          shift in Brazil to the south.

1865–1870 The Paraguayan War, also known as the War of the
          Triple Alliance, dominates Brazilian politics. While
          Brazil gained some territory and asserted itself as an
          important military power in South America, the war is
          also very costly for Brazil. It also leads to questions
          about slavery and the role of the military in public
          affairs.

1870	Manifesto of Republican Party—The Republican Party is founded in 1871 by members of the Liberal Party. Republicans begin to openly question whether monarchy is the appropriate political system for Brazil. Discontent with the status quo mounts.
	Parliament passes the Law of the Free Womb, freeing all children born of slave mothers after this date. Still, "free" children are required to render service to their mother's master until the age of twenty-one. Abolitionists are unsatisfied, calling for an immediate and a complete end to slavery.
1873–1875	Church–state conflict brews over the royal privilege of naming bishops. In general the relationship between church and state is tense during the 1870s—some historians consider this simmering dispute to be a factor contributing to the eventual fall of the empire; others, although not denying the conflict, say its role in the triumph of republican government should not be overemphasized.
1885	Saraiva-Cotegipe Law, also called the Sexagenarian Law, frees slaves at the age of sixty-five, with no compensation for their owners (few slaves survived more than sixty years); in 1887 the military formally refuses to hunt down fugitive slaves.
1888	Parliament approves total abolition of slavery without compensation to owners. Since Pedro II was traveling in Europe, the law is signed by Princess Isabella. Abolition contributes to a wave of European immigration.
	A military coup, led by Marshal Deodoro da Fonseca, topples the empire; Dom Pedro II accepts the military ultimatum and heads into exile in Portugal. A republic is proclaimed on November 16, 1889, and begins as a military government. Coffee interests are dominant in the new government.
	President Deodoro da Fonseca dissolves Congress and is then deposed; Marshal Floriano Peixoto becomes president.
1890–1891	The newly elected Constituent Assembly writes Brazil's second constitution; the most important feature of the Constitution of 1891 is a dramatic decentralization of power—Brazil becomes a federation. One result is greatly fragmented federal authority. A new flag is cre-

ated, bearing the motto "Order and Progress." Symbols of the empire are eliminated, as are many records of the slave trade.

1893   Naval revolt threatens the republic; civil war breaks out in Rio Grande do Sul.

1897   A three-year war in the backlands ends with the massacre at Canudos. This communal settlement, in effect a messianic peasant movement, is led by Antonio Conselheiro. The settlement is seen as a threat to the new Republican government and is wiped out (after three unsuccessful military expeditions). The conflict is immortalized in Euclides da Cunha's 1902 classic, *Rebellion in the Backlands* (Os Sertões). One of the main themes of the book is the vast divide existing between the elites of the coast and the masses of the interior.

1900–1910   During this time period Brazil is the only producer of natural rubber in the world; it would eventually lose its monopoly on rubber exports when the British and Dutch were able to produce their own rubber trees in the East Indies. The rise and decline of the rubber industry is another example of the boom-bust nature of Brazil's commodity exports.

1904   Vaccination riots occur in Rio de Janeiro.

Price supports via the valorization agreement are given to the coffee industry. The governors of Brazil's three leading coffee-producing states, São Paulo, Rio de Janeiro, and Minas Gerais, sign a "valorization" treaty called the Treaty of Taubaté, which is aimed at limiting production and exports with the goal of raising international prices, one of the earliest signs that Brazil is willing to use the government's power to interfere with the workings of the open market.

1910   The first seriously contested presidential election of the new republic occurs as a result of the death of the officially designated candidate and the inability of the Republican Party bosses of the leading states to agree on a new candidate. The election pits Marshall Hermes da Fonseca against Senator Rui Barbosa (chief author of the Constitution of 1891 and a leading orator and legal thinker). Barbosa frames the election as a choice between military and civilian government, infuriating many military officers; he ultimately loses the election.

1917	Brazil belatedly declares war on Germany, after initial neutrality—the move makes Brazil the only Latin American belligerent in World War I. During the war the Brazilians cooperate with Allied efforts, furnishing foodstuffs and raw materials (as well as sending a hospital unit to France and a few officers to join the French army).
1922	Copacabana Fort uprising of cadets starts the *tenente* movement, which calls for social reform and a stronger state; the Brazilian Communist Party (PCB) is founded. The city of São Paulo hosts its "Modern Art Week" festival of poetry readings, plays, concerts, and expositions, marking Brazil's entry into what becomes known as "modernism."
1924–1926	Tenente rebellion continues; the suppression of the insurrection includes the bombing of neighborhoods in São Paulo. The last revolt, in Rio Grande do Sul, becomes the most famous and is led by Captain Luiz Carlos Prestes, who also leads the "Prestes Column" that eludes state and federal forces during a three-year march through the Brazilian interior and demonstrates the government's weak hold on large parts of the country.
1926	Paulista Washington Luís is elected president, but divisions among the various state political machines by this time are strong; the lack of consensus regarding the political system comes to a head during the next presidential campaign in 1929.
1929	Brazil's economy proves quite resilient in the postwar 1920s, and industry begins to grow rapidly. The good times end with the collapse of the global economy in 1929, leaving Brazil to face bleak prospects and no obvious recipe for economic recovery. Brazil's failure to follow the conventional, orthodox policy prescriptions, however, helps induce an eventual recovery and further industrialization.
1930	Vargas takes political power following coup d'etat; this follows President Washington Luís's break with tradition in choosing a fellow *paulista* as his successor, breaking the unwritten alliance between Minas Gerais and São Paulo. Vargas moves quickly against his politi-

cal opponents, strengthening the central government, dissolving Congress, and assuming emergency powers.

1932 The state of São Paulo revolts against the provisional government, calling for the constitutional assembly Vargas promised; Vargas puts down the revolt (which is called the Constitutionalist Revolution). The revolt ironically aids Vargas and the cause of centralism. The paulistas' perceived disloyalty severely weakens the state's strength in national politics for decades.

1934 A new constitution is promulgated following a Constituent Assembly that meets from 1933 to 1934. The assembly produces the Constitution of 1934, Brazil's third. Under the terms of the new constitution, Vargas is a given four-year presidential term.

Revolts break out in three cities. The uprising by the communists is suppressed, giving Vargas the proof he needs of a Bolshevik threat. In response the government institutes martial law, giving near dictatorial powers to the president.

1937 Declaration of *Estado Novo*—Brazil becomes a full-fledged dictatorship. The new constitution gives Vargas extraordinary powers, dismantles local political machines, and introduces a new corporate state structure. Although the new regime resembles European fascist regimes in Portugal and Italy, Vargas outlaws the fascist Integralist movement, along with all other political parties.

A fascist Integralist putsch against the presidential palace is suppressed with relative ease; still, Vargas and his twenty-three-year-old daughter are forced to return fire and wait until dawn for government reinforcements to arrive.

1942 Brazil declares war on the Axis in August, after initially maintaining neutrality in World War II (and waiting for the United States to pay for Brazilian support). Brazil offers raw materials and coastal bases in return for U.S. military equipment, technical aid, and financial assistance. Brazil becomes the only Latin American nation to commit land forces fighting under its own flag.

1943 Vargas announces that the presidential election will be postponed until after the war due to the wartime emergency and associated uncertainties.

1945   Ouster of Getúlio Vargas in a bloodless military coup; elections are held under a caretaker government, and a new constitution devolves power to states, as strong central government is associated with the dictatorship under Vargas. General Eúrico Gaspar Dutra wins the presidency. Some 6 million Brazilians vote, three times the number of voters in 1930.

Inauguration of Volta Redonda, the first national steel mill, a key example of Brazil's use of state-owned corporations to promote rapid industrialization.

1951   Ex-dictator Getúlio Vargas is elected president, albeit with considerable opposition. This time Vargas establishes himself as a populist. Once in power, Vargas actively promotes industrialization, invoking nationalism and patriotism to support state intervention in the economy.

1954   Following a military ultimatum to resign or be overthrown, Vargas commits suicide while in office, leaving an inflammatory suicide note. Vargas's suicide transforms the hostile political environment, making life considerably more difficult for his opponents and disrupting their plans to take over the government.

1956–1961   After caretaker regimes, Juscelino Kubitschek is elected president in 1955. Kubitschek opts to push rapid economic growth and industrialization with his ambitious *Programa de Metas* (Program of Goals). The objective is to bring the state and the private sector together to promote rapid growth and industrialization. Inflation and balance-of-payments difficulties are unintended results.

1957   One great example of Kubitschek's plan is the building of Brasília, a new capital designed to open up the country's interior. Construction starts on the new city, located 700 miles from São Paulo and more than 600 miles from Rio de Janeiro. The nation's capital is moved to Brasília in 1960.

1958   Brazil wins its first World Cup soccer championship.

1960   Jânio Quadros is elected president, but plunges the country into political crisis when he resigns after a short period in power. Quadros is succeeded by his left-wing vice president, João Goulart, who lasts less than three years in the presidency.

1962   Brazil wins its second World Cup soccer championship.

1964	Armed forces oust civilian leadership in bloodless coup; the military dictatorship brings both repression and a focus on rapid, state-led economic development. The first military leader is General Castello Branco, the army chief of staff.
1967	Castello Branco transfers the presidency to General Costa e Silva, an army minister and the second military president to be elected by Congress.
1968	The Additional Act (No. 5) closes Congress and tightens the military dictatorship; all crimes against "national security" are subject to military justice. Censorship is also introduced, with particular focus on television, radio, and print media.
	The beginning of a six-year period of strong economic growth in Brazil often referred to as the "economic miracle." The boom years are characterized by very high annual rates of growth, which average 10.9 percent.
	Outbreak of guerrilla actions against government—armed opposition to the Brazilian government is essentially wiped out by 1974, although official repression continues.
1970	Brazil wins its third World Cup soccer championship.
1974	General Ernesto Geisel is elected president, introducing reforms that allow limited political activity and elections. The military regime begins an internal struggle between soft- and hard-line factions over a potential return to civilian rule. The interaction between soft-liners and increasingly vocal civilian opposition acts to erode authoritarianism.
1979	Geisel is replaced by the fifth general-president, João Batista Figueiredo, who is hand-picked by his predecessor; Figueiredo continues the process of relaxing authoritarian power, including an amnesty law for all political crimes.
1981	After the two OPEC oil shocks of 1973 and 1979 leave Brazil economically vulnerable, a global credit squeeze led by the U.S. Federal Reserve Bank hits the industrial world in 1981. Brazil, like the rest of Latin America, suffers from dramatically increased interest payments on its massive foreign debt, just as global demand and prices for Brazilian output begin to plummet.

1982	Brazil halts payments on its main foreign debt, which is among the largest in the world, inaugurating Brazil's debt crisis and the beginning of the so-called lost decade.
1985	Civilian government is restored, and Tancredo Neves becomes the first civilian president to be elected in twenty-one years (still, he is elected by an electoral college set up by the military rather than by open elections). Neves falls ill before his inauguration, and his vice president, José Sarney, becomes president amidst economic chaos.
1986	Sarney introduces the Cruzado Plan, which freezes wages and prices in an effort to control inflation; inflation explodes when the freeze is lifted. A Constituent Assembly is elected in November to draft a new constitution, a task that takes well over a year to complete. The result is the Constitution of 1988, considered by many to be a victory for the forces of populism.
1990–1992	Fernando Collor de Mello is elected president in 1989 and introduces radical economic reform upon assuming office in 1990 (including a much hated freeze on Brazilian savings accounts). The president is forced to resign under the threat of impeachment following a corruption scandal. He is replaced by vice president Itamar Franco, whose best-known move as president is to appoint Fernando Henrique Cardoso to his cabinet in 1993.
1994	Hyperinflation reaches 2,500 percent during the hapless Franco's presidency; Cardoso is appointed finance minister and introduces the Real Plan. As the new currency is introduced, Brazil is on its way to winning its fourth championship in soccer's World Cup. Fernando Henrique Cardoso rides the Real Plan's popularity to win the presidential election in November.
1997	Brazil's constitution is changed to allow President Cardoso (and succeeding presidents) to run for reelection. Cardoso goes on to win the 1998 elections for a second term in office.
1998	A new constitution is introduced, which dramatically reduces presidential power. President Fernando Henrique Cardoso completes his first term in office, only the second president to do so since 1930. The International Monetary Fund (IMF) provides a rescue

package to Brazil following the onset of the Asian financial crisis. Despite the strong financial support, speculation increases that the growing global financial crisis will spread to Brazil.

Facing waves of capital flight and unsustainably high interest rates, Brazil devalues its currency but largely withstands the full impact of the Asian financial crisis, which begins in late 1997. Ex-President Itamar Franco's threat, now as governor of Minas Gerais, to default on state debt to the federal government, is the last straw leading to the end of the currency's "peg" to the dollar.

2002   Brazil celebrates its victory in the World Cup soccer championship, the country's fifth such triumph. Financial markets panic over the likely victory of left-leaning Luiz Inácio Lula da Silva in the upcoming October presidential elections. Lula ultimately wins the elections and surprises the markets by his relatively market-friendly policies.

2005   Corruption scandals rock President Lula's Workers' Party; high-level resignations follow, and Lula is forced to apologize to the nation. Lula survives the scandals, but many wonder whether his chances for reelection are diminished.

2006   Despite ongoing and additional corruption scandals, the popular Lula is able to win a second term to the Brazilian presidency in October's second-round voting, beating his challenger, Geraldo Alckmin, by a wide margin.

Observers suggest that the elections have brought out in a dramatic way the divides that permeate Brazil, such as the gap between the rich and the poor and the separation between the North and the South. Lula's long-term success will depend not only on providing benefits to the poor but also on improving the economic growth outlook as demanded by the country's middle and upper classes.

A violent "war" breaks out between prison gangs and authorities in São Paulo, leaving more than eighty people dead. The violence is believed to be the result of gang retaliation for the transfer of some of its members.

Significant People in Brazilian History

"Aleijadinho" (Francisco Lisboa, Antonio; 1730 or 1738–1814). A mulatto sculptor and architect noted for the churches he designed in Ouro Prêto, Sabará, and São Paulo do Rei. He also created full-size sculptures of the prophets in Congonhas do Campo, at the Sanctuary of Bom Jesus of Matosinhos. Aleijadinho is considered one of the greats of Brazilian art history, successfully overcoming both his racial status and debilitating leprosy (his nickname refers to the latter, meaning the "Little Cripple").

Alvarengo, Manuel Inácio da Silva (1749–1814). A mulatto writer and poet from the Arcadian school, whose poems were meant to be sung. His writing portrayed Brazil as a bucolic setting, filled with nymphs and shepherdesses. After 1777 he took up residence in Lisbon.

Amado, Jorge (1912–2001). Amado, a writer from the modernist school, is the best-known of Brazil's modern writers. He came from Ilhéus, south of the Bahian capital Salvador on the Bahian coast, and was the son of a cacao planter. Amado published his first novel, *O País do Carnaval,* at the age of eighteen; a second novel at the age of nineteen increased his popularity. While socially and politically active as a young man (which at times required exile from Brazil), Amado as an older writer focused on popular regional fiction and works filled with colorful characters and humorous plots. Among Amado's most internationally famous works are *Dona Flor and Her Two Husbands* and *Gabriela, Clove and Cinnamon.*

Andrada e Silva, José Bonifacio de (1763–1838). A states-man and a naturalist, Bonifacio returned from Portugal to Brazil in 1819, serving in important government posts for Pedro I and as a member of the Constituent Assembly. His democratic principles, visible in his work on the constitution rejected by Dom Pedro I, resulted in his dismissal from office and exile from Brazil. He was the first to discover petalite, which contains lithium, in the late 1700s on a trip to Sweden.

Barbosa de Oliveira, Ruy (1849–1923). Barbosa was a famous Brazilian politician, diplomat, and lawyer. He was a Bahian deputy to the Constituent Assembly that drafted Brazil's 1891 constitution; many consider Barbosa largely responsible for this republican constitution.

Buarque, "Chico" (Francisco Buarque de Hollanda; b. 1944). A writer, singer, composer, and dramatist, Buarque is best-known for his songs that appealed to sophisticated audi-ences as well as ordinary Brazilians. Songs such as "A Banda" and "Roda Viva" quickly gained him fame. Buarque was known for evading government censorship during military rule by using double entendre; still he spent the years from 1968 to 1970 in exile in Italy (but the censors were never able to ban him outright). Many attribute Buarque's success to his ability to combine traditional *samba* and *bossa nova* with his own playfully original style.

Cabral, Pedro Álvarez (c. 1467–c. 1520). The commander of a new expedition to follow Vasco de Gama's voyage that opened the sea route to India. A distinguished nobleman, Álvarez's fleet ran into trouble almost as soon as it left Portu-gal, as the lead ship swung off course out into the Atlantic, sailing due west. Cabral and crew reached the coast of Brazil, in today's state of Bahia, on April 23, 1500. Some historians have suggested that Cabral's "discovery" of Brazil was in fact not an accident, but rather a planned move to claim new territory. Whether accidental or deliberate, the discovery of Brazil would change history.

Câmara, Bishop Dom Hélder Pessoa (1909–1990). Widely considered one of the most important Catholic figures of the twentieth century, Dom Hélder Câmara was the archbishop of Olinda and Recife and an important advocate of the poor. He is well-known for his statement, "When I give food to the poor, they call me a saint. When I ask why the poor have no food, they call me a Communist." Given his focus on the poor, his theology is widely considered a key influence in liberation theology.

Cardoso, Fernando Henrique (b. 1931). Cardoso was the president of Brazil for two consecutive terms, from January 1, 1995, to January 1, 2003. Before entering politics, Cardoso was a highly respected and influential sociologist and coauthor of the important book *Dependency and Development in Latin America,* written with Enzo Faletto. Cardoso's rise to political popularity was largely the result of his introduction of the Real Plan during the presidency of Itamar Franco, which ended Brazil's hyperinflation. Cardoso's emphasis on macroeconomic stability and reform brought him considerable domestic criticism as a neoliberal, although he was highly respected internationally.

Chagas, Carlos Justiniano Ribeiro (1879–1934). Part of a wave of scientists who focused on Brazil's diseases and social problems, Chagas was a medical researcher who helped conquer malaria in a number of regions in the country. Chagas is best-known for his contribution in 1909 to conquering a deadly disease that bears his name, which blinds and kills victims in the country's interior (Chagas disease is also called American trypanosomiasis). Chagas identified the carrier, a beetle that lives in the walls and ceilings of mud huts; he then spent a great deal of time helping to educate public officials about how to fight both the carrier and the disease. Chagas helped lead the movement in Brazil to fight the numerous diseases caused by unmet sanitary and medical needs, which in turn led to major public health campaigns in the 1910s and 1920s.

Chalaça (Francisco Gomes da Silva; 1791–1852). The personal secretary to Emperor Pedro I, he came to Brazil with the Portuguese court in 1808 and stayed when independence was declared. He was a member of Pedro's so-called secret cabinet.

Chateaubriand, Assis (Francisco de Assis Chateaubriand Bandeira de Mello; 1892–1968). Chateaubriand came from the northeastern state of Paraíba, and after studying law went on to become one of Brazil's most distinguished journalists and newspaper publishers. Chateaubriand also ventured into radio, magazines, and television, in addition to serving in Congress and later as an ambassador to Great Britain.

Cícero, Padre (Cícero Romão Batista; 1844–1934). A defrocked Catholic priest who in the early 1900s attracted thousands of rural people to his backlands town of Juazeiro in Ceará to live lives of piety and devotion; to this day backlands families maintain shrines containing statues of the priest in his monk's habit.

Collor de Mello, Fernando (b. 1949). From a political family in the northeastern state of Alagoas, Collor de Mello entered politics at the local level, first as a mayor of the state capital of Maceió and then as governor of the state (1987). In 1989 Collor beat Luiz Inácio Lula da Silva in a two-round presidential race to become Brazil's first democratically elected president since the onset of military rule. As president he instituted the famous Collor Plan in an attempt to fight rampant inflation; the plan included a highly unpopular freeze on bank accounts. Collor's presidency came to a premature end in 1992 due to a corruption scandal. He resigned on December 29, 1992, the day the Senate delivered its verdict on impeachment charges. Found guilty, he lost his right to hold political office for eight years. In a turn of political fortunes, he most recently won a 2006 election to become a senator and took office in January 2007.

Conselheiro, Antonio (Antônio Vicente Mendes Maciel; 1830–1897). "Anthony the Counselor" was a lay clergyman, pilgrim, and leader of the religious community at Canudos, also known as Bello Monte, often characterized as a place of religious fanatics. The Counselor and Canudos filled the void for a church that could not staff its parishes in the interior. After local and state authorities failed to subdue the community, the federal army was brought in, as the community was increasingly seen as a threat to the relatively new republican government. But even federal troops failed three times before they could declare victory over the backlanders, and this only with the help of modern German cannons. Not a single male defender of Canudos lived, while surviving women and children were shipped elsewhere. The Counselor likely died of dysentery on September 22, 1897, following a period of praying and intense fasting. The struggle at Canudos is recounted in Euclides Da Cunha's *Rebellion in the Backlands* (*Os Sertões*). The Counselor and the events at Canudos are also portrayed in Mario Vargas Llosa's *The War of the End of the World.*

Crespo, Antonio Gonçalves (1846–1883). A mulatto poet who lived for most of his life in Portugal, Crespo wrote nostalgic poems about his life in Brazil. Many point out the writer's ambiguous stance on ethnicity, since he both praised blacks and then at times linked them to various vices and defects.

Cruz e Silva, João (1861–1898). A poet born to slaves in the southern province of Santa Catarina, he was tutored by a Brazilian army officer and apprenticed to a printer; Cruz e Silva was also a well-known abolitionist. His writings are considered an important contribution to Brazilian Symbolism.

Da Cunha, Euclides (1866–1909). A former army officer who was sent to Canudos to cover the unfolding conflict for the newspaper *O Estado de S. Paulo,* the city's leading daily. Da Cunha was immortalized by his 1902 book chronicling the events, *Rebellion in the Backlands (Os Sertões)*. Generally Da Cunha's work is seen as highlighting the tremendous divide between the relatively well-to-do populations of the coast and the neglected masses of the interior. The book had a major impact on the country's relatively small reading public.

Damião de Bozzano, Frei (1898–1997). An Italian-born Capuchin monk who spent sixty-six years in Brazil's impoverished Northeast, for the most part in the arid interior. The monk was famous for his apocalyptic sermons and preached against dancing, popular music, and the like. He attracted a large following and is credited with numerous miracles and faith healings.

Fernandez, Florestan (1920–1995). Raised in poverty, Fernandez became one of Brazil's leading sociologists, teaching at the University of São Paulo. A Marxist, the author was critical of Brazilian capitalism as well as the country's race relations. Importantly, Fernandez was one of the founders of the Workers' Party (PT). Florestan's most famous protégé was Fernando Henrique Cardoso.

Franco, Itamar Augusto Cautiero (b. 1930). Franco is a Brazilian politician who served as Brazil's president from October 2, 1992, until January 1, 1995, when Fernando Henrique Cardoso was elected to office. Franco was the running mate of presidential candidate Fernando Collor de Mello, who won the election but was then forced to resign when threatened with impeachment. Franco took over after Collor's resignation, at a time of severe economic instability (inflation reached almost 6,000 percent in 1993). Franco appointed Cardoso to his cabinet. Cardoso then launched the Real Plan and swept the presidential election in 1994. Franco's announcement of a moratorium on state debt payments to the federal government while serving as governor of the state of Minas Gerais is often attributed to animosity between Franco and Cardoso and is seen by many as the last straw leading to Brazil's devaluation in 1999.

Freyre, Gilberto (1900–1987). An anthropologist and writer who became the most influential interpreter of the Brazilian character and society of the twentieth century. Freyre argued among other things that the Portuguese were less prejudiced than other Europeans against Africans, one key factor helping to create a "racial democracy" in Brazil. Freyre's masterpiece is *The Masters and the Slaves,* which describes the plantation world of the colonial era and its influence on modern Brazil. Freyre's work marked a sharp reorientation in the thinking about race in Brazil, in which African, and to a lesser extent indigenous, elements came to be seen as positive influences.

Furtado, Celso (1920–2004). A brilliant and well-known economist from Brazil's Northeast, whose seminal work was entitled *The Economic Growth of Brazil* (the Brazilian edition of the book was first published in 1959). Furtado worked for a number of Brazil's governments, had considerable influence in economic policymaking, and was the nation's best-known left-leaning economist.

Gil, Gilberto (Gilberto Passos Gil Moreira; b. 1942). Gil is a songwriter, guitarist, and singer, as well as Brazil's current minister of culture. The musician is perhaps best-known for his contributions to "tropicalismo," a form of protest against the military regime (which earned him arrest and exile during the period). Along with fellow singer Caetano Veloso, Gil is one of Brazil's best-known musicians.

Gilberto, João (João Gilberto Prado Pereira de Oliveira; b. 1931). A Brazilian musician who is typically considered one of the main creators of Brazil's unique style of music called *bossa nova,* along with Tom Jobim.

Goulart, João Belchior Marques (1918–1976). Goulart was a controversial figure in Brazilian politics, acting as the last leftist president of the country until the election of Lula in 2002. Known by the nickname "Jango," Goulart was a protégé of Vargas and elected vice president in 1956 and again in 1960 as the running mate of Jânio Quadros. The latter resigned in 1961, leaving Goulart president amidst political crisis. Accused of extreme leftist policies (including by the U.S. government), Goulart was overthrown in the 1964 revolution, which ushered in two decades of military rule.

Jesus, Carolina Maria de (1914–1977). An illegitimate black woman born to poverty in a small town in the state of Minas Gerais, she went on to become the author of the best-selling book in Brazilian publishing history when, in 1960, her diary, *Quarto de Despejo,* was published. Despite her accomplishment she spent her last years of life in isolation and poverty.

João VI (1769–1826). The prince regent when the Portuguese court arrived in Brazil in 1808, João was named Dom João VI when his mother died in 1816. Fearing for the loss of his throne he returned to Portugal in 1821, leaving his son Pedro behind to administer Brazil as the prince regent.

Jobim, Tom (Antônio Carlos Brasileiro de Almeida Jobim; 1927–1994). Jobim was a highly talented musician, working as a composer, arranger, guitarist, pianist, and singer; he is also generally considered one of the two cofounders of *bossa nova* (along with João Gilberto). Among his best-known work was his collaboration with Vinícius de Moraes on the score for *Black Orpheus* (1959). Many experts consider Jobim to be one of the most important composers of the twentieth century.

Kubitschek de Oliveira, Juscelino (1902–1976). Kubitschek was a prominent Brazilian politician who rose to become president of the republic from 1956 to 1961. Famous for his slogan "Fifty years of progress in five," Kubitschek was successful in promoting rapid economic growth and industrialization. Unfortunately, inflation was one unintended consequence, in good measure a function of "inflation financing." Perhaps his most famous project was the construction of Brasília, the new capital of Brazil. He also pushed for major improvements in the transportation infrastructure and founded Brazil's automotive industry. Kubitschek was succeeded by Jânio Quadros in 1961; he went into self-imposed exile when the military took power in 1964, returned to Brazil in 1967, and died in a car wreck in 1976.

"Lula" (Luiz Inácio Lula da Silva; b. 1945). The current president of Brazil, Lula rose to prominence as a leader of São Paulo autoworker's strikes in the late 1970s and as an opponent to military rule. Lula became a leading figure of the PT (Partido dos Trabalhadores) and became their candidate in a number of presidential elections. After losing to Collor and to Cardoso twice, Lula was finally elected president in 2002, taking office in January 2003. Despite a number of corruption scandals plaguing his administration, Lula successfully managed to win reelection in 2006.

Miranda, Carmen (1909–1955). Miranda was born in Portugal but raised in Brazil, and became a singer and an actress. As a cartoonlike white *baiana,* Miranda dressed in platform heels and banana-laden tutti-frutti headdresses, eventually becoming one of Hollywood's highest-paid stars during the 1940s. She was forced to play nearly identical roles in her movies, causing Brazilians to boo her. She died depressed at the relatively young age of forty-six.

Moraes, Vinícius de (Marcus Vinícius da Cruz Melo Morais; 1913–1980). Sometimes called "the little poet," de Moraes was a highly influential figure in contemporary Brazilian music; he was also a playwright, composer, and diplomat. He wrote the lyrics for a number of classic Brazilian songs, often working in tandem with Tom Jobim. He wrote the highly acclaimed play *Orfeu da Conceição*, which was later turned into the Academy Award–winning film *Black Orpheus* (*Orfeu Negro*).

Nabuco, Joaquim (Joaquim Aurélio Barreto Nabuco de Araújo; 1849–1910). A well-known Brazilian abolitionist, Nabuco organized a national drive to emancipate slaves in the 1880s. Nabuco, from Pernambuco, became Brazil's best-known abolitionist with his 1884 publication *Abolitionism.*

Neves, Tancredo de Almeida (1910–1985). A well-known Brazilian banker and politician who served in the administration of Getúlio Vargas and played an important role during the crisis years of Quadros and Goulart. Neves is best-known historically as the person elected to the presidency in 1985 by the majority of Congress to be the first civilian president after the long military dictatorship. One day before he was to take office Neves became ill; he died on April 21, 1985, and was succeeded by José Sarney.

Nóbrega, Manuel da (1517–1570). One of Brazil's most well-known Jesuits, who exerted strong influence in early colonial Brazil through control of education and the creation of Indian missions, among other things, da Nóbrega was an outspoken defender of the colony's indigenous populations. He tried to generate respect for their native cultures (aside from practices such as polygamy and cannibalism).

Pedro I (1798–1834). Left to administer Brazil as prince regent when his father, Dom João VI, returned to Portugal, Pedro proclaimed Brazil's independence and was then named Emperor Pedro I in 1822 (in essence following the advice his father gave him regarding any potential conflict between colony and mother country). Facing pressure both from Brazilians and Portuguese, he returned to his homeland in 1831, leaving his five-year-old son Pedro II as the heir to the Brazilian throne.

Pedro II (1825–1891). Born in Rio, Pedro II was Brazil's only native-born monarch, as well as the second and last Brazilian emperor. Brazil was ruled by regents during his childhood; Pedro II then assumed the throne at age fourteen in 1840 and ruled for forty-nine years, during which time he was widely respected. Recognizing the inevitable end of the monarchy, Pedro II abdicated in 1889 and headed with his family to exile in Portugal.

Pombal, Marquês de (Sebastião José de Carvalho e Melo; 1699–1782). He was the de facto prime minister of Portugal from 1750 to 1777 who attempted to use enlightened despotism to restore Portugal to economic health. Pombal was a mercantilist who tried to improve Brazil's function of producing primary goods for export to the home country, thereby improving the trade balance; in the process Brazil continued to miss out on the industrial revolution.

Prestes, Luis Carlos (1898–1990). Prestes helped organize the failed *tenente* rebellion of 1922, a revolt against the agrarian oligarchies dominating the Old Republic. He then led the column of former tenentes across the length of Brazil's interior and into the jungles of Bolivia, a movement that was dubbed the Prestes Column. The soldiers demanded universal suffrage, union freedom, nationalism, and socialism. While the long march was largely a failure, the tenente revolt marked the end of Old Republic *Café com Leite* politics. Prestes later turned to Marxism, although the communist movement faced official repression (Prestes spent considerable time in Russia).

Quadros, Jânio da Silva (1917–1992). Quadros was a Brazilian politician who served briefly as president in 1961, after a rapid rise based on populist rhetoric and extravagant behavior. His resignation from the presidency (which most assume was a ploy intended to win himself greater powers), and the subsequent turmoil of the Goulart presidency led to a serious political crisis in Brazil. The political turmoil of the early 1960s was ended only by a coup d'etat and military rule in 1964.

Rebouças, André (1838–1898). Rebouças was one of the most important mulattoes of the imperial era in Brazil. Rebouças was an engineer and made his fortune overseeing the construction of docks in Rio de Janeiro and other Atlantic ports. Importantly, he went beyond calling for abolition, suggesting as well the need for land reform in Brazil. Rebouças committed suicide in Portugal.

Ribeiro, Darcy (1923–1997). Ribeiro's career included stints as an anthropologist, cabinet minister, educator, and official for the federal Indian Protection Agency during the 1940s. He stood out in his efforts to convince the government of the need to protect Brazil's indigenous populations in the Amazon and northern frontier regions. He was exiled in 1964, but returned when he was diagnosed with lung cancer. He survived another twenty-three years, continuing his work with indigenous Brazilians.

Rondón, Cândido Mariano da Silva (1865–1927). The founder and first director of the Indian Protection Service in 1911, which was organized as an agency of the Brazilian army; the agency was dedicated to bringing basic services, like health care and education, to the Indians without destroying their culture. The state of Rondônia is named after this important figure, who was accompanied on one of his well-known frontier explorations by Theodore Roosevelt.

Sarney, José Ribamar Ferreira de Araújo Costa (b. 1930). Sarney is an important Brazilian politician who served as president from March 15, 1985, to March 15, 1990. A prominent figure during the transition to democracy, Sarney was the candidate for vice president with Tancredo Neves. Neves won the election, but became ill and died before assuming office; Sarney assumed office as acting president and then became formal president upon Neves's death. The Sarney years were characterized by significant economic instability and included the failed economic plan called the Cruzado Plan.

Segall, Lazar (1891–1957). Segal was born in Lithuania, studied in Europe, and then became one of the most famous portraitists of Brazilian life in the twentieth century. He arrived in Brazil in 1912, but returned to war-torn Europe and became known there as an artist. He then came to stay in Brazil in 1912, although he split his time between Brazil and Paris. He was considered a member of the modernist school of art.

"Tiradentes" (Joaquim José da Silva Xavier; 1746–1792). Nicknamed Tooth-puller for his amateur dentistry, Tiradentes was executed on April 21, 1792, for his role in the *Inconfidencia* (conspiracy) in Minas Gerais in 1788–1789, in which a group of prominent citizens plotted to assassinate the governor and proclaim an independent government. While better-born conspirators were spared execution, Tiradentes was hanged, decapitated, and then quartered, with various body parts displayed in Ouro Prêto. The plot has long been considered the precursor to Brazilian independence; Tiradentes had become a national hero by the end of the nineteenth century.

Vargas, Getúlio Dornelles (1882–1954). A major figure in Brazilian history, Vargas was Brazil's president from 1930 to 1945, and again from 1951 until his suicide in 1954. Born in the State of Rio Grande do Sul, Vargas started his political career in state politics; as governor of his home state he then became a leader against the corrupt politics of the central government. Vargas became provisional president after the bloodless coup d'etat in 1930 ended oligarchic rule. Vargas eventually instituted the Estado Novo dictatorship in 1937, which was reminiscent of the fascist regimes of Europe. However, the pragmatic Vargas sided with the Allies in World War II and somewhat liberalized his authoritarian regime—probably contributing to its downfall in a 1945 coup. Vargas returned to politics as the elected president in 1951. His term would be a turbulent one, and ended with his suicide in 1954.

Veloso, Caetano (b. 1942). Veloso is one of the most popular and influential musicians in modern Brazil. He began his career singing bossa nova, but he also experimented in tropicalismo, a sort of fusion of Brazilian pop with rock and roll and more avant garde forms of music (which was often used to protest military rule). Over the years Veloso has collaborated with many greats of Brazilian music, including Gilberto Gil and Chico Buarque. Ironically, while Veloso was detested by the military dictatorship and many of his songs were banned, he was also often unpopular among the socialist left in Brazil due to his nonnationalist stance.

Brazil-Related Organizations

BUSINESS AND ECONOMICS

Brazilian-American Chamber of Commerce, Inc.
509 Madison Avenue, Suite 304
New York, NY 10022
Phone: (212) 751–4691
Fax: (212) 751–7692
Web site: http://www.brazilcham.com/
E-mail: info@brazilcham.com

The Brazilian-American Chamber of Commerce, Inc., is an independent, not-for-profit business organization that aims to promote trade and investment flows between Brazil and the United States. In the process it also tries to promote closer ties between the business communities in both countries.

Brazil-U.S. Business Council
1615 H Street NW
Washington, DC 20062
Phone: (202) 463–5485
Fax: (202) 463–3126
Web site: http://www.brazilcouncil.org/
E-mail: host@brazilcouncil.org

The Brazil-U.S. Business Council is a private-sector organization focusing on trade and investment flows between Brazil and the United States. The group has both a U.S. section, focused on large U.S. investors in Brazil, and a Brazil section, managed by the Brazilian National Confederation of Industry. The group offers its members a wide variety of services and networking opportunities, such as executive information services, policy advocacy services, and a Brazil event series.

World Trade Organization (WTO)
Rue de Lausanne 154, CH–1211
Geneva 21, Switzerland
Phone: (41–22) 739–51–11
Fax: (41–22) 731–42–06
Web site: http://www.wto.org
E-mail: enquiries@wto.org

The WTO is an important international organization that deals with the rules of international trade. It supports free trade in general and specifically promotes free trade among its member nations. Brazil has been a member of the WTO since January 1, 1995.

CULTURE, EDUCATION, AND EXCHANGE

American Field Services—U.S.A. (AFS-USA)
71 West 23rd Street, 17th Floor
New York, NY 10010
Phone: (212) 807–8686
Fax: (212) 807–1001
Web site: http://www.afs.org/usa
E-mail: info.centers@afs.org

AFS is an international, nonprofit, voluntary organization that provides international and intercultural learning opportunities. The organization's goal is to help people develop knowledge, skills, and understanding to help create a more peaceful and just world. AFS sponsors an impressive international exchange program with thousands of students participating annually. Each year American students are able to participate by living, studying, and volunteering in a multitude of countries overseas, including Brazil.

The Americas Society
680 Park Avenue
New York, NY 10021

Phone: (212) 249–8950
Web site: http://www.americas-society.org/
E-mail: inforequest@a-coa.org

The Americas Society, started in 1965 by a group of businessmen led by David Rockefeller, is a not-for-profit institution that promotes the understanding of the political, economic, and cultural issues facing the nations of the Americas today. An understanding of the peoples and societies of the region is essential to the Americas Society agenda, which includes promoting democracy, the rule of law, and free trade.

Brazilian-American Business Group (BABG)
Web site: http://www.mccombs.utexas.edu/students/babg/
E-mail: babg@mccombs.utexas.edu

BABG is a group at the University of Texas at Austin that promotes an exchange of ideas and the development of business relationships through a variety of professional, academic, and social activities in Brazil and the United States. While the group actively seeks to promote the McCombs School of Business at the University of Texas–Austin, its efforts focus on efforts such as expanded recruiting efforts, alumni and business networking, and placement of future leaders in the United States and Latin America. This organization offers a wide range of exchange opportunities, as well as resources to U.S. and Brazilian organizations.

Fulbright Program for U.S. Students—Sponsored by U.S.
　State Department
Institute of International Education/Headquarters
809 United Nations Plaza
New York, NY 10017–3580
Phone: (212) 984–5330
Web site: http://www.iie.org
General Inquiries: Walter Jackson, Program Manager, wjackson@iie.org

South America, Mexico, and Canada: Jody Dudderar, Program Manager, jdudderar@iie.org

The Fulbright program is the largest U.S. international exchange program, offering students, scholars, and professionals opportunities to undertake international graduate study, advanced research, university teaching, and teaching in elementary and secondary schools worldwide. In 2004 alone the program awarded 6,000 grants to U.S. students, teachers, scholars, and professionals to study, teach, lecture, and conduct research in more than 150 foreign countries, including Brazil. The Fulbright Program's main source of funding is an annual appropriation from the U.S. Congress to the Department of State.

BRAZIL'S GOVERNMENT REPRESENTATIVES IN THE UNITED STATES

Brazilian Embassy in Washington, D.C.
3006 Massachusetts Avenue, NW
Washington, DC 20008–3634
Phone: (202) 238–2700
Fax: (202) 238–2827
Web site: http://www.brasilemb.org/
E-mail: consular@brasilemb.org

This is an important resource for anyone interested in Brazil, from those needing a visa to visit Brazil to those wanting information on topics like trade and investment to those needing more basic consular services. This is the best place to start the process of getting a visa to visit Brazil—there are a variety of classes of visas, and interested parties will need to peruse this site carefully to identify their needs. Click on visas in the main site to see the rules and the different classes of visas; then click on consular offices to find the various regional consulates, their jurisdictions, and important contact information. It is always important to follow the directions for obtaining a visa precisely—failure to do so can often result in delays or even the denial of a visa request.

Embassy of the United States in Brazil
SES—Av. das Nações,
Quadra 801, Lote 03
70403–900—Brasília, DF
Phone: (55–61) 3312–7000
Fax: (55–61) 3225–9136
Web site: http://www.embaixadaamericana.org.br/
E-mail: contact@embaixadaamericana.org.br

Like U.S. embassies around the world, the U.S. Embassy in Brazil represents the U.S. government in Brazil, provides services to Americans traveling and doing business in Brazil, as well as processes visa applications for Brazilians wishing to visit the United States. Information and services provided by the embassy include tax and voting information, passport handling, and birth registration. The general Web site is an important resource and includes, in addition to considerable general information, the contact information for the three consulates the United States maintains in Brazil: Recife, Rio de Janeiro, and São Paulo.

NEWS

There is no shortage of sources to get news on Brazil; anyone who is interested simply needs access to a computer—an incredible wealth of sources is a few clicks away. One place to start is the Brazilian Embassy's Web site listed above, which is a tremendous source of information. For example, by clicking "The Economy" and then selecting "Brazilian Economy" links, one is presented with multiple links from the Brazilian government, such as the Ministry of Finance and the Central Bank of Brazil. For anyone looking for the latest statistics, from inflation estimates to population figures, this is a good place to start. Another great source is the University of Texas's Brazil-LANIC Web site listed as the first source in the annotated bibliography. This is a wonderful source for all sorts of information on Brazil, including countless sources of news.

Brazilink.org is another good resource for students and researchers looking to access current news or keep up to date with the central issues relating to Brazil. The site is http://www.brazilink.org/. Some news and analysis is available at no charge, while access to other information requires a subscription.

Brazil News is another comprehensive source available on topix.net. As the site suggests, it is a great place to get local news for the whole world. The Web site for Brazil is http://www.topix.net/world/brazil. In addition to *Brazil News*, interested readers can also access *Brazil Forums*, which contains an archive of months' worth of important news stories

Brazil Post is an additional source of news for interested readers. The site gives access to all the latest news and contains scores of links allowing access to all sorts of information, from financial and economic news to the latest sports scores. The Web site is http://www.brazilpost.com/. Like most of these sources, all that is needed is a little imagination and persistence—with this the interested reader can find nearly anything he or she is looking for.

Finally, *The World Factbook: Brazil,* provided by the U.S. Central Intelligence Agency, is a great place to find important economic and political facts about Brazil, along with a variety of maps. This can be found at https://www.cia.gov/cia/publications/factbook/geos/br.html.

TOURISM

Fodor's
Web site: http://www.fodors.com
The Fodor's Web site provides "one stop shopping" for anyone interested in visiting Brazil. The site is easy to use, providing everything from mini-guides to major cities to travel tips, restaurant and hotel recommendations, and maps. This is a great place to start planning a trip to Brazil. However,

a simple search of the Google search engine, typing in "Brazil travel," will yield a large number of additional sources.

Lonely Planet
Web site: http://www.lonelyplanet.com
Like Fodor's, Lonely Planet is a great place to start planning a visit to Brazil. The site is easy to navigate—from the main site one simply has to type in "Brazil" to get started. From this point one can begin looking at flights, hotel recommendations, possible sites to visit, and so forth. One can also find overviews on history, religion, and culture, as well as a resource section with additional Web links. Finally, there are helpful hints from other travelers that might come in handy for first-time visitors to Brazil.

Annotated Bibliography of Recommended Works on Brazil

The sources discussed below are organized according to the chapters of the book, with a few important general works mentioned first. The works are meant to be general sources that can help students greatly in understanding modern Brazil. All sources are in English. There are a multitude of great sources on Brazil; the following should serve simply as a starting point. While countless articles have been published on the country in magazines and periodicals, I have focused here on books. Not only have these books been of tremendous help in putting together this manuscript but they are for the most part recognized as "industry standards" among Brazil experts. Any reader wishing to find more detailed or specialized sources should start with both the Reference section at the end of each chapter and with the bibliographies listed within these sources.

GENERAL WORKS

One great place to start with all of the subjects in this book is with the University of Texas's Web site dedicated to Latin American studies (LANIC), which has separate sites for most of the region's countries. For Brazil the site is www1.lanic. utexas.edu/la/brazil//. The site contains a multitude of information on subjects as diverse as the African Diaspora in Brazil to education, history, arts, and contemporary culture. This site can serve as an excellent companion to the scholarly sources listed below.

Levine, Robert M., and John J. Crocitti, eds. *The Brazil Reader: History, Culture, and Politics.* Durham, NC: Duke University Press, 1999. This volume is another great place for interested readers to start building a broad-based knowledge of Brazil. The book contains more than a hundred entries from a variety of authors, and as the title suggests these entries cover a huge range of topics about Brazilian life, history, and culture. The volume spans Brazilian history, from colonization to the present day, and includes diverse sources such as letters, photographs, fiction, and scholarly writings.

Page, Joseph A. *The Brazilians.* Cambridge, MA: Da Capo Press, 1995. Page's book is wide-ranging in its focus, examining everything from history, economics, and culture to film, literature, and psychology. The author, while not a native Brazilian, draws on deep personal experience in Brazil to help readers understand the modern country and its inhabitants. The book is long, numbering more than 500 pages, but it is a highly recommended entry point.

Skidmore, Thomas E. *Brazil: Five Centuries of Change.* New York: Oxford University Press, 1999. This is perhaps the best source to begin with for a deeper understanding of historical and modern Brazil. While the work is nominally a history of Brazil from the time of its discovery to the modern era, it is also a valuable introduction to the key social, economic, and political issues of Brazil's history.

GEOGRAPHY AND HISTORY OF BRAZIL

Alden, Dauril, ed. *Colonial Roots of Modern Brazil.* Berkeley: University of California Press, 1973. There are a number of books on the colonial era in Brazil. While I would recommend the articles in the Cambridge volumes (see the next entry) as a starting point, this book is interesting for those looking to dig a bit deeper into colonial history.

Bethell, Lesley, ed. *The Cambridge History of Latin America, Vols. I–VIII, X.* Cambridge, U.K.: Cambridge University Press, 1984–1995. The Cambridge volumes begin with colonial times, including an examination of the existing indigenous cultures in Brazil, and move up through the modern era, including important pieces on independence, the empire, and the Old Republic. A final volume largely devoted to modern Brazil has yet to be published. Still, this is a great source of important articles on Brazilian history. There are also more general articles on the region, which help readers build a conceptual framework.

Burns, E. Bradford. *A History of Brazil,* 3rd ed. New York: Columbia University Press, 1993. This is one of the classic short histories of Brazil, and a source for any student wishing to delve into the subject. Like many of the general works, the book also contains interesting maps and a discussion of Brazil's unique geography.

Fausto, Boris. *A Concise History of Latin America.* New York: Cambridge University Press, 1999. This is a very good, complete history of Brazil that begins with Portugal's world explorations and examines the highlights of Brazilian history up through the transition to democracy.

Schneider, Ronald M. *"Order and Progress": A Political History of Brazil.* Boulder, CO: Westview Press, 1991. While this volume may fit more appropriately in the section on politics and government, it is a very good political history of the entire Brazilian republic. This is a good companion volume to more general historical pieces.

Skidmore, Thomas E., and Peter H. Smith. *Modern Latin America,* 5th ed. New York: Oxford University Press, 2001. As the title suggests, this book covers all of Latin America. However, there are two good reasons to turn to this volume in order to dig deeper into Brazil. First, it contains an excellent, short, introductory chapter on Brazilian history. Second, it contains two chapters on general Latin American history, from its colonial foundations all the way to the debt crisis and the transition to democracy. This chapter provides an excellent framework within which to understand Brazil's own unique historical trajectory.

Viotti da Costa, Emília. *The Brazilian Empire: Myths and Histories*. Chicago: Dorsey Press, 1985. This is probably the single best place to probe deeper into the complexities of the Brazilian empire. The book consists of a series of essays that span the six decades of the Brazilian empire. While the empire itself is examined in detail, the book also provides a great look at two key transition periods: Brazil's independence from Portugal and the establishment of the republic.

ECONOMY OF BRAZIL

Baer, Werner. *The Brazilian Economy,* 3rd ed. Westport, CT: Praeger, 1989. This is one of the best sources to begin analyzing the Brazilian economy. It analyzes not only the current issues of the Brazilian economy but also its historical development. The book provides good analysis of the central economic dilemmas of Brazil's history, for example the logic leading to public sector enterprises.

Bresser-Pereira, Luiz Carlos. *Economic Crisis and State Reform in Brazil: Toward a New Interpretation of Latin America*. Boulder, CO: Lynne Rienner, 1996. This is an important volume contributing to both an understanding of economic crisis in Brazil and the political forces involved in the economic reform process.

Cardoso, Eliana, and Ann Helwege. *Latin America's Economy: Diversity, Trends, and Conflicts*. Cambridge, MA: MIT Press, 1995. This book covers all of Latin America, rather than simply Brazil. It is, however, an excellent place to understand the economic challenges that face both Brazil and the region in general, from inflation and debt crises to poverty, inequality, and land reform. Brazil features prominently in the book as the authors use the region's countries to illustrate their points. Any student wishing to delve deeper into Brazil's economy should use this book as a general companion volume to works dealing specifically with Brazil.

Evans, Peter. *Dependent Development: The Alliance of Multinational, State, and Local Capital in Brazil.* Princeton, NJ: Princeton University Press, 1979. While dependency theory has become less popular in explaining Latin American underdevelopment, Evans's book is nonetheless a classic and an important contribution to an understanding of the interplay between politics and economics in the development process. This is a good source to understand the role of Brazil's public sector in economic development.

Font, Mauricio A. *Transforming Brazil: A Reform Era in Perspective.* New York: Rowman and Littlefield, 2003. This is an excellent presentation of the complexities surrounding the years of economic reform in Brazil, especially the key reforms of the Cardoso era. While the piece deals with economic reform, it also provides important political insights into the process.

Furtado, Celso. *The Economic Growth of Brazil: A Survey from Colonial to Modern Times.* Berkeley: University of California Press, 1963. While this book is somewhat dated, it is nonetheless one of the most important works of economic history for students of Brazil. An understanding of Furtado's analysis is essential to the ongoing debate concerning the country's economic development. This is a great source for those wishing to examine subjects from Brazil's economic history, for example the role of sugar in the colonial economy.

Merrick, Thomas W., and Douglas H. Graham. *Population and Economic Development in Brazil.* Baltimore, MD: Johns Hopkins University Press, 1979. While this is yet another volume examining Brazil's history of economic development, the authors add important concepts and data regarding the role of demographics in the process.

POLITICS AND GOVERNMENT

Roett, Riordan. *Brazil: Politics in a Patrimonial Society.* Westport, CT: Praeger, 1999. Roett's book is an excellent one, providing in one source a complete assessment of Brazilian politics, including important chapters on the Brazilian economy, foreign policy, and social agenda.

Roett, Riordan, and Susan Kaufman Purcell, eds. *Brazil under Cardoso.* Boulder, CO: Lynne Reinner, 1997. This volume provides a number of different perspectives on this important era of Brazilian politics, which was one of important economic reforms.

Schneider, Ronald M. *Brazil: Culture and Politics in a New Industrial Powerhouse.* Boulder, CO: Westview Press, 1996. While this book is primarily one on Brazilian politics, it contains interesting chapters on geography, society and social problems, and culture and Brazilian ways. As such it is a great single source for students of Brazil and thus highly recommended.

Skidmore, Thomas. *The Politics of Military Rule in Brazil, 1964–85.* New York: Oxford University Press, 1988. While there are many books dealing with the period of authoritarian military rule in Brazil, Skidmore's volume provides comprehensive coverage of this complex topic. General knowledge of the history and politics of this era can be obtained in any of the basic history texts; however, those wishing to explore the era in more detail should begin with this book.

Stepan, Alfred, ed. *Democratizing Brazil: Problems of Transition and Consolidation.* Oxford, U.K.: Oxford University Press, 1989. While Skidmore's volume provides comprehensive detail on the politics of military rule, Stepan's volume adds important insight into the complicated process of the transition back to civilian rule. This edited volume adds important historical voices, such as that of Fernando Henrique Cardoso, on the relationships between economics and politics during this complicated era.

Wynia, Gary W. *The Politics of Latin American Development,* 3rd ed. New York: Cambridge University Press, 1990. Like Skidmore and Smith's *Modern Latin America,* Wynia's book deals with all of Latin America. Similarly, the book provides both a good, short, introductory analysis of Brazilian politics as well as a more general chapter on how to approach Latin American politics—the latter provides an excellent framework for analysis.

SOCIETY AND CULTURE

Before listing additional sources to consult regarding Brazilian society and culture, it is important to reiterate the importance of two previously mentioned volumes. First, Ronald Schneider's book, *Brazil: Culture and Politics in a New Industrial Powerhouse,* mentioned in the section on politics, adds very interesting commentary both about Brazilian society and its unique culture. Together, the politics section and Schneider's book are indispensable sources for students wishing to explore these topics.

In addition, Joseph Page's *The Brazilians,* mentioned in the section on general works, is a fantastic source for those interested in this subject. The author explores a variety of topics in this field, from Brazil's "soccer madness" to the Orixás of Candomblé to the nation's obsession with telenovelas. Page also explores the people of Brazil by examining in detail the Portuguese, indigenous peoples, African slaves, and immigrants.

For those truly wishing to delve into the culture of Brazil, this book should be read in its entirety. This is not an academic text, nor is the author Brazilian; however it is a great place for non-Brazilians to start exploring this complex topic.

Fontaine, Pierre-Michel, ed. *Race, Class and Power in Brazil.* Los Angeles: University of California Press, 1985. This edited volume is an interesting source to begin exploring the fundamental problems facing Brazilian society relating to race and class. Like other subjects, introductory analysis can be gotten in the more general texts on Brazil; however, for those wishing more detailed knowledge this is a good place to start.

Freyre, Gilberto. *New World in the Tropics: The Culture of Modern Brazil.* New York: Vintage Books, 1963. While many of Freyre's arguments (especially about race in Brazil) have been disputed by more recent scholarship, this is nonetheless a classic piece on Brazilian culture and society, and one cannot begin an exploration into the topic without becoming familiar with Freyre's contributions.

Hess, David J., and Roberto deMatta, eds. *The Brazilian Puzzle.* New York: Columbia University Press, 1995. As we have discussed, Brazilian society and culture present a number of important puzzles, and debate about such issues continues to be strong. This volume provides a picture of everyday life in Brazil, from a variety of authors and often from a comparative perspective. The subjects include everything from race and gender to politics, music, and sports. The authors show that traditional values, such as personalism and respect for hierarchy, continue to play an important role in modern Brazil.

Hulet, Claude L. *Brazilian Literature.* Washington, DC: Georgetown University Press, 1974. This is an accessible volume and a helpful introduction to Brazilian literature.

Mainwaring, Scott. *The Catholic Church and Politics in Brazil, 1916–1985.* Stanford, CA: Stanford University Press, 1986. Once again, most of the introductory history texts provide good information on the role of the Catholic Church in Brazil, and the Cambridge volumes contain specific articles on the church throughout history. However, for those wanting more detail, and specifically analysis on the role of the church in politics, this volume is helpful.

Patai, Daphne. *Brazilian Women Speak.* New Brunswick, NJ: Rutgers University Press, 1988. The role of women in Brazilian society is a complex one, and one in which scholarship is relatively new. This is a good source to begin examining this complex subject; it is also a great source to find additional references.

Wagley, Charles. *An Introduction to Brazil.* New York: Columbia University Press, 1971. While this text is somewhat dated, it is nonetheless a good starting point for delving into the issue of Brazilian culture.

Glossary of Selected Terms

Abertura   The political opening that unfolded during the final years of the military dictatorship, generally considered to have taken place from 1978 until the transition to democracy in 1985. The process included a general political amnesty, additional freedoms of the press, restoration of habeas corpus, and eventually direct elections for municipal, state, and national offices.

Agrarian reform   This is a term typically applied to a set of policies aimed at alleviating rural poverty and income inequality through some sort of change in land ownership. It is based on the notion that these problems are directly related to Latin America's, and Brazil's, highly unequal distribution of land tenure.

Alvorado Palace   The name of the presidential residence in Brasília.

ARENA   Alliance for National Renewal, the promilitary government party during the military dictatorship.

BNDES   National Economic and Social Development Bank.

Bacharal   A holder of a B.A. degree; in the nineteenth century, the term referred to a law school graduate.

Bandeirantes   The colonial-era group of individuals that prospected for precious metals and hunted for Indians; often considered to be Brazil's rough equivalent to the pioneers in U.S. history.

Brazilian Miracle   The high-growth years of the Brazilian economy between 1968 and 1974, in which economic growth rates averaged 11 percent. It is often pointed out that this high growth was accompanied by a marked worsening of income inequality.

Brazilwood (*pau-Brasil*) A type of wood common in early colonial Brazil, from which the country derived its name. The wood was used to extract a dye, which was widely used in Europe's burgeoning textile industry.

Bumba Meu Boi A folkloric celebration taking place in the rural Northeast.

Bureaucratic authoritarianism Often referred to as BA, the term has come to be synonymous with the repressive military regimes seen in Latin America in the 1960s and 1970s, notably in countries like Brazil, Argentina, and Chile. In such regimes, bureaucrats from areas like the military, civil service, and private sector were commonly selected for public office. The working classes and popular sectors were tightly controlled and typically excluded from politics; solutions to political problems were deemed to be administrative or technical in nature. One critical focus of such regimes was economic growth, which was pushed through ties to the international economy and multinational corporations.

CNBB National Conference of Brazilian Bishops.

CSN National Steel Company.

CVRD Vale do Rio Doce Company, the world's largest producer of iron ore.

Caboclo A person of mixed African, Indian, and European ancestry.

Cabra A person of mixed Indian and European background.

Café com Leite "Coffee with milk" refers to the informal policy of rotating control of government between São Paulo and Minas Gerais, the former a coffee-producing region and the latter a dairy region.

Candomblé An Afro-Brazilian religion, considered by many to be a "spiritist" religion.

Capoeira A highly choreographed Afro-Brazilian martial art developed during the slave era.

Captaincies The hereditary land grants given in early colonial Brazil to rich nobles in the hope that they would exploit the resources of the colony for the benefit of themselves and the Crown. Fourteen captaincies were granted between 1534 and 1536; only two were successful: São Vicente and Pernambuco.

Carioca   An informal term referring to an inhabitant of Rio de Janeiro (or someone who is from that city).

Coronel   A rural strongman who is usually a political boss.

Crente   An evangelical Protestant.

Creole   A person born in the New World.

Cruzeiro, Cruzado   Units of Brazilian currency; ultimately replaced by today's real.

Debt crisis   The crisis that hit Brazil and Latin America in the early 1980s, which followed a dramatic run-up in overseas borrowing and accumulating foreign debt in the 1970s. When the United States's credit-tightening policies led to both higher debt service payments and global recession (and therefore lower demand and prices for Brazil's exports), a crisis became inevitable. Many countries, including Brazil, went into default on their international obligations.

Despachante   An expediter, or someone to cut through "red tape" or get special treatment for a client.

Donatarios   This term refers to the private individuals heading the captaincies-general in early colonial Brazil. The fourteen hereditary captaincies represented Brazil's first rudimentary form of government and were later transformed into the country's provinces.

Empire   Brazil's government from 1822 to 1889, which was headed by a constitutional monarch. This followed the relocation of the Portuguese court to Brazil, which in turn followed Napoleon's invasion of Portugal. Brazil is the only country in Latin America to have had a monarchy. Many historians consider the empire, and the political cohesion it represented, a key reason that Brazil did not splinter into a number of republics the way Spanish America did.

Engenho   Sugar plantation with a mill that was powered by oxen or water.

Estado Novo Brazil's authoritarian regime, headed by Getúlio Vargas, which lasted from 1937 to 1945. This period was characterized not only by Vargas's dictatorial powers but also by a dramatic expansion in state control over all aspects of Brazilian life, including in particular growing control over the economy. The *Estado Novo* came to an abrupt end in 1945.

Exú A Candomblé spirit.

Farinha Flour made from dried and roasted manioc.

Favela An urban shantytown, prevalent throughout Brazil but emblematic of Rio; called a *mocambo* in the Northeast.

Fazenda A ranch or rural agricultural property.

Fazendeiro The proprietor of a *fazenda*.

Feitorias A series of fortified trading posts set up by Portuguese explorers along the coast of Africa in the early days of exploration. This mechanism was used in Brazil for a short time after discovery, until a more intensive pattern of settlement and exploitation was implemented.

Filhotismo Nepotism.

Fluminense An inhabitant of the state (or province) of Rio de Janeiro.

Forro A colonial-era term for a free black.

GDP Gross domestic product, or the total value of a country's production of final goods and services, not counting those directly transformed into other goods and services. GDP per capita divides this figure by the total population, allowing comparison with other economies.

Gaúcho The term for an inhabitant of the state of Rio Grande do Sul; also cowboy.

Golden Age The term refers to the so-called golden age of export growth taking place roughly between 1880 and 1910, which corresponded to a generalized expansion of economic activity in Brazil. This period was interrupted by the two world wars and the intervening Great Depression.

IMF International Monetary Fund.

ISI Import-substitution industrialization—a development strategy common in postwar Latin America, which closed economies to imports in an attempt to bolster domestic production, especially of industrial goods.

Inconfidência Mineira The unsuccessful plot in Minas Gerais to separate from Portuguese control.

Industrialization Occurs when industry becomes the leading sector of the economy—the real driver of growth—and reflects dramatic structural change in an economy. It is typically preceded by a period of industrial growth, in which an economy still depends primarily on the expansion of agricultural exports.

Inflation The persistent and substantial increase in the general level of prices in an economy—this has been a common phenomenon in Latin America in general and in Brazil specifically. The debate about the origins of inflation in Brazil has been between monetarists and structuralists. The former blame inflation largely on the lack of control over government spending; the latter suggest that inflation's origins are more structural.

Inflation financing This term refers to the common practice of covering public sector deficits by simply printing more money. The inevitable result is a surge in inflation. Historically this has been a problem in Brazil.

Informal sector This is the segment of the economy that operates outside of the official, taxed economy—transactions in the informal economy typically take place in cash. Informal workers pursue a multitude of occupations, from selling goods on the streets to working in households as maids, gardeners, and nannies.

Integralist Member of the Brazilian fascist movement of the 1930s.

Ipiranga The site of Brazil's declaration of independence in 1822; Pedro was then crowned Emperor Pedro I.

Itaipú Refers to the Itaipú hydroelectric power plant. The dam at Itaipu is the largest in the world. The project was one of a number of huge projects implemented by Brazil's military rulers to accelerate the country's economic development.

Jagunço A term denoting a backlands thug or gangster.

Liberalization Refers to attempts by countries to reduce the role of the state in the economy and open up to foreign trade—this can include programs like privatization of public enterprises, easing of trade restrictions, deregulation, and support for foreign investment.

Linha Dura Meaning hard line, refers to the faction within the military during the dictatorship of the 1960s and 1970s.

Lost decade The term used to describe the environment of the 1980s for much of Latin America as it suffered the impact of the debt crisis. Most countries used some combination of recession and devaluation to service debt, which was often accompanied by plummeting investment and rising inflation (frequently the result of inflation financing). In general the lost decade saw a decline in living standards, an increase in inflation, reduced investment, and stagnant growth.

MDB Brazilian Democratic Movement.

MST The Landless Workers' Movement.

Mandioca The cassava root.

Mercosul Called Mercosur in Spanish, this term refers to the trade union linking Brazil, Argentina, Uruguay, and Paraguay.

Mestizo A person of mixed Indian and European ancestry.

Mineiro An inhabitant of (or someone originating from) Minas Gerais.

Mocambo The term for favela in Brazil's Northeast.

Monocultural exports A reference to Brazil's historical reliance on one or two commodities for the bulk of economic activity and export earnings; such reliance led to boom-and-bust cycles reflecting the global fortunes of individual commodities. Examples include sugar, gold, and coffee.

Brazil's economy became significantly more diversified in the twentieth century, in good part as it industrialized.

Moradores   Landless rural renters.

Mulatto   A person of mixed African and European ancestry (mulatta for a woman).

Município   Municipality or county.

New Republic   The term refers to the return of democratic government following the fall of the Estado Novo in 1945. The New Republic proved no more durable than the Old Republic, witnessing four elections before the military stepped in to rule Brazil for twenty years starting in 1964. The period was marked by a rise in populist policies.

Novela   Highly popular primetime television soap operas.

PCB   Brazilian Communist Party.

PCdoB   Communist Party of Brazil.

PDC   Christian Democratic Party.

PDS   Democratic Social Party.

PDT   Democratic Workers' Party.

PFL   Liberal Front Party.

PL   Liberator Party and Liberal Party.

PMDB   Party of the Brazilian Democratic Movement.

PPB   Brazilian Progressive Party.

PPS   Popular Socialist Party.

PSB   Brazilian Socialist Party.

PSD   Social Democratic Party.

PSDB   Brazilian Social Democracy Party.

PSP   Social Progressive Party.

PT   Workers' Party.

PTB   Brazilian Labor Party.

Panelinha   An informal network of friends and relatives.

Pantanal   The largest ecological sanctuary in the world, covering 140,000 square kilometers in the central region of Brazil.

Pardo   A person of African ancestry.

Paulista   A person originating from, or residing in, São Paulo.

Paulistano   Refers to an inhabitant of the state of São Paulo.

Periphery   A term used in economic analysis, typically to distinguish between countries of the industrialized "core" and those of the nonindustrialized, or industrializing, "periphery." Often an argument is made that the fortunes of peripheral economies depend on events and conditions in the core.

Petrodollars   Refers in general to a period in the 1970s characterized by easy credit, in part a reflection of the vast sums of money that oil exporters recycled into the global financial system via multinational banks. At the time, countries like Brazil vastly increased their foreign debt to speed up development plans. This would prove shortsighted when global economic conditions deteriorated in the early 1980s.

Poder Moderador   The "moderating power" of the emperor, which allowed him such actions as vetoing legislation, dissolving parliament, and appointing lifetime members of the Senate.

Política dos governadores   Politics of the governors was an informal agreement between leaders of Brazil's key states of São Paulo and Minas Gerais and the leaders of smaller states during the Old Republic. In effect, the larger states would dominate national affairs, rotating the presidency, in exchange for leaving the smaller states to manage their own internal affairs. The agreement broke down in 1930, leading to the rise of Getúlio Vargas.

Privatization   A key component of liberal economic reforms, the term refers to the selling of state-owned enterprises to private-sector investors. Proponents argue that the process brings resources to the state, reduces budget deficits, and improves economic efficiency. Critics suggest the process is riddled with corruption and amounts to a giveaway of the national patrimony, among other problems.

Quilombo   A settlement of fugitive slaves; Palmares was the most famous of such settlements.

Real, Reias The colonial-era unit of Brazilian currency; the name was revived in the 1990s with the Real Plan, which was designed by Fernando Henrique Cardoso to reduce Brazil's runaway inflation.

Republic, The The name for the period between 1889 and 1930 that was characterized by federalism and the political domination of a number of strong states; sometimes referred to as the "Old Republic" or "First Republic."

SNI Brazil's National Intelligence Service.

Senhor Mister.

Senhor de Engenho The proprietor of a sugar plantation.

Sertão The arid backlands of Brazil's interior.

Sindicato A trade union.

Stabilization This refers to an attempt to control inflation and typically involves economic pain, as wages fall, credit is tightened, and the economy moves into recession. Brazil's debate about inflation has seen both orthodox and heterodox plans to reduce inflation. The latter attempts to minimize economic pain by using political consensus to control wages and prices.

Subúrbio Outlying working-class districts in Brazil's large urban areas.

Tenentes Military rebels in 1922 and 1924 who eventually rose to power after the 1930 revolution.

Tropicalismo A popular musical movement of the 1960s and 1970s that protested against the military regime.

UDN National Democratic Union.

Umbanda A spiritist cult or religion that has similarities to Candomblé.

Valorization Brazil's attempts to use its market power to control the price of coffee; this refers largely to efforts to control supply, often by destroying stocks, on world markets to support the price of coffee.

War of the Triple Alliance Also called the Paraguayan War by Brazilians, the conflict lasted from 1865 to 1870, pitting Brazil, Argentina, and Uruguay against Paraguay. While Brazil ultimately triumphed, the war came at a tremendous cost to the country and was highly significant to subsequent political events that culminated in the end of slavery and the fall of the empire.

Zona de Mata   A term for the coastline of Brazil's Northeast that refers to its previous forested state, which was lost as land was cleared for plantations.

Zumbi   The leader of the fugitive slave settlement at Palmares.

Index

About the Author

Todd L. Edwards is an independent writer, consultant, and investment strategist based in Fort Collins, Colorado. He received his Ph.D. in Latin American Studies from Tulane University in 1995, with concentrations in development economics, political science, and public policy. His dissertation research focused on political economy and institutional reform, using Mexico's stock market reform as a case study. He then pursued a career on Wall Street, working for firms such as the U.S. investment bank Salomon Brothers and Spain's Banco Bilbao Vizcaya Argentaria (BBVA). On Wall Street, Mr. Edwards specialized as an investment strategist for Latin America. In this role he combined political, economic, and financial analysis to assist major global investors (primarily American and European) operating in the region. Mr. Edwards was also the director of Latin American equity research for BBVA, running a team of research analysts based in New York as well as in the major financial capitals of Latin America, such as Buenos Aires, Mexico City, and São Paulo.